SALT, SOIL & SECOND CHANCES

The Life & Times of John Frawley

Pegasus Publishing

SALT, SOIL & SECOND CHANCES
The Life & Times of John Frawley

by Dr. Tracy Rockwell (1955)

Volume 5 of
Australian Ancestry Series:
True Stories of Convicts, Settlers and Pioneers

First Published in Australia in 2025
by Pegasus Publishing
PO Box 980, Edgecliff, NSW, 2027

Orders: pegasuspublishing@iinet.net.au
www.pegasuspublishing.square.site

Copyright © Pegasus Publishing
An Ashnong Pty Ltd Company

All rights reserved. No part of this publication may be reproduced, stored in a retrieval system, or transmitted in any form or by any means, electronic, mechanical, photocopying, recording or otherwise, without the prior written permission of the copyright owner.

A CIP catalogue record for this book is available from the National Library of Australia.

ISBN: 978-1-925909-21-0

Printed and sold on Demand through:
Pegasus Publishing   -   www.pegasus-publishing.square.site
Ingram Lightning Source   -   www.ingramspark.com

Volumes In The - 'Australian Ancestry Series':

Vol. 1 - Salt, Soil & Second Chances: The Life & Times of John Frawley

Front Cover: 'The Settler's Hut', painted by Albert Henry Fullwood.
Back Cover: Early photgraph of the village of Pambula, on the NSW south coast, c.1870.

SALT, SOIL & SECOND CHANCES

The Life & Times of
John Frawley

Volume 1 of
Australian Ancestry Series:
True Stories of Convicts, Settlers & Pioneers

by
Dr Tracy Rockwell

Pegasus Publishing

Contents

Preface	7
Map of South East New South Wales	8
Exploration Timeline of South East New South Wales	9
Prologue	11
Chapter 1 - Discovering the South Coast of NSW	17
Chapter 2 - Explorers of the Shoalhaven & Illawarra	35
Chapter 3 - The Frawley Ancestors	47
Chapter 4 - Land Grants & Squatters	61
Chapter 5 - An Unwilling Pioneer [c.1816-1839]	77
Chapter 6 - Berry's Coolangatta Homestead	89
Chapter 7 - The McGarry Ancestors	105
Chapter 8 - Mary Ann McGarry, The Convict [c.1815-1839]	118
Chapter 9 - John Frawley & Mary Ann McGarry [1840-1844]	129
Chapter 10 - Twofold Bay & Maneroo	140
Chapter 11 - Warragaburra Homestead	155
Chapter 12 - Pioneers of 'Pamboola' [1845-1860]	168
Chapter 13 - The Frawleys of Bungaree	181
Chapter 14 - Property & Prosecutions	193
Chapter 15 - Frawleys Under Fire [1861-1874]	203
Chapter 16 - Final Days in The North [1875-1901]	214
Chapter 17 - Descendants of John Frawley & Mary Ann McGarry	226
Epilogue	247
Index	251
The Author	261

Preface

Welcome to the story of John Frawley (c.1816–1901) and his wife, Mary Ann McGarry (c.1815–1889), two Irish convicts whose lives were shaped by hardship, endurance, and quiet courage. Torn from their homeland by poverty and punishment, they were cast across the world to a raw, uncertain land. In time, these unwilling exiles became pioneers of Pambula, on the far south coast of New South Wales, carving out a life from bushland and adversity in a colony still struggling to define itself.

This first volume in the Australian Ancestry Series seeks to bring to life not just names and dates, but human stories of convicts and settlers, of endurance and transformation. The aim is threefold: to uncover and honour the truth of our ancestors' lives; to present history faithfully, without embellishment or sentimentality; and to preserve those fragile remnants of memory, the pedigrees, anecdotes, and verses that might otherwise fade into silence.

What began as a modest inquiry to learn how and why these ancestors came to Australia, soon became a far-reaching exploration. Each discovery opened another door, revealing kin from distant counties and countries, forgotten voyages, and unexpected connections that reached back across oceans and generations. The research took me through archives and landscapes alike from Ireland's windswept hills to the quiet graveyards and coastal settlements of New South Wales. To stand where they once stood was to sense their presence still... ghosts of endurance, lingering just at the edge of time, slowly ebbing away but never gone.

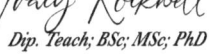

Dip. Teach; BSc; MSc; PhD

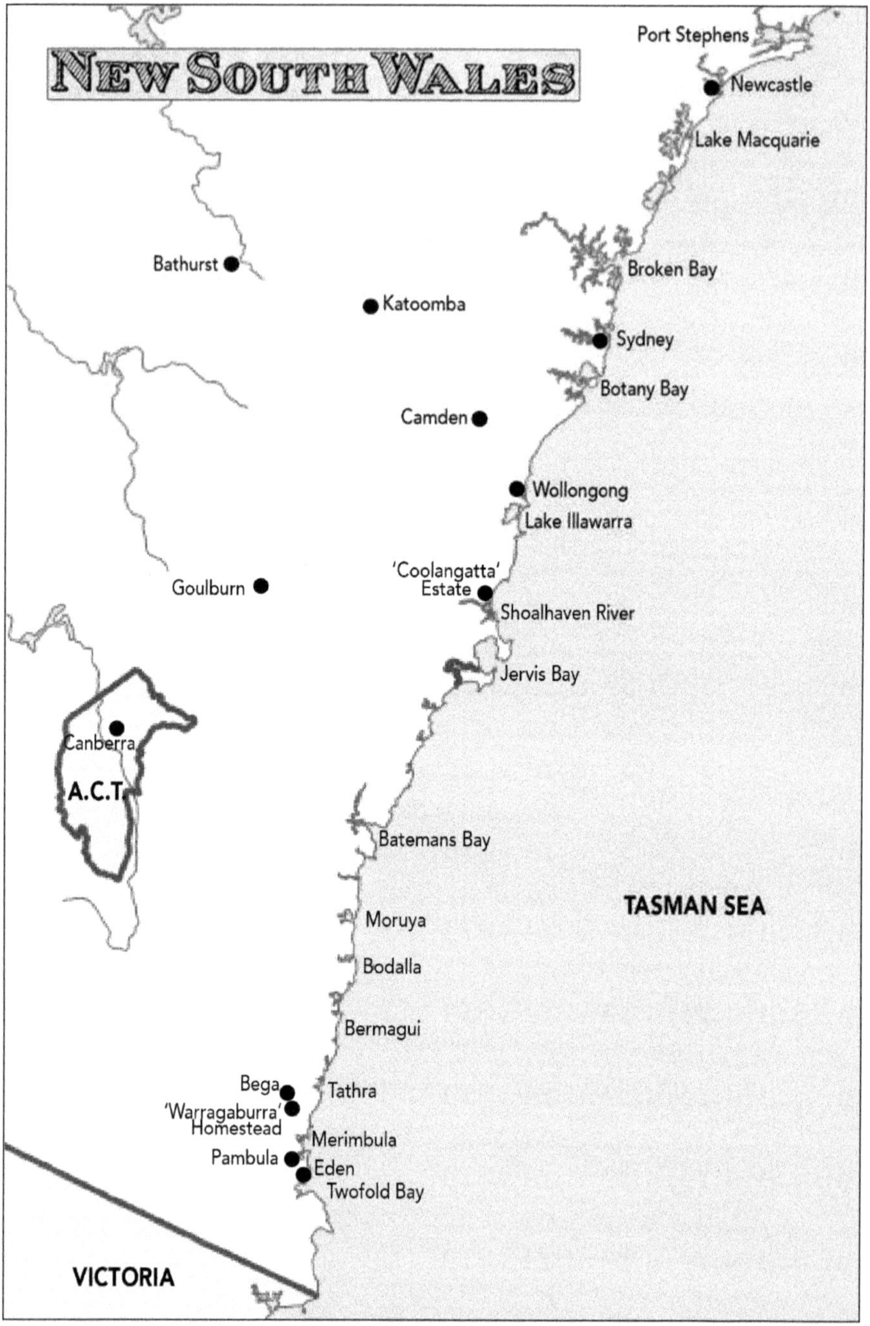

Map of the South Coast of NSW, showing Pambula as well as Coolangatta & Warragaburra Homesteads.

Timeline of Exploration on the South Coast of New South Wales

WHEN	WHOM	WHERE
1770-Apr	Lt. James Cook	"HMS Endeavour" sailed north from Point Hicks to Botany Bay recording features and sightings along the way.
1788-Jan	Gov. Arthur Philip & The First Fleet	"First Fleet" sailed north from Van Diemans Land to Botany Bay & Port Jackson recording features and sightings along the way.
1791-Nov	Lt. Richard Bowen & Capt. Weatherhead	Lt. Richard Bowen in the "Atlantic" & Capt. Matthew Weatherhead in the "Matilda" both entered Jervis Bay and recorded depth soundings.
1795-Oct	Dr. George Bass & Lt. Matthew Flinders	Sailed south from Port Jackson in the tiny sailboat "Tom Thumb" and explored the Georges River as far as Bankstown.
1796-Mar	Dr. George Bass & Lt. Matthew Flinders	Sailed south again to explore Port Hacking & the Illawarra in the "Tom Thumb."
1797-May	Survivors of the "Sydney Cove"	After being wrecked on Preservation Island in the Furneaux Group, 17 survivors of the "Sydney Cove" trekked over 500 miles north along the south east coast, with only three being rescued and brought to Sydney.
1797-Dec	Dr. George Bass	Sailed south in a larger open whaleboat he called "Tom Thumb II" to explore Kiama, Shoal Haven, Jervis Bay, Ulladulla, Durras, Tuross River, Twofold Bay, and then explored the Victorian coast as far as Western Port Bay.
1798-Oct	Dr. George Bass & Lt. Matthew Flinders	The "Norfolk" circumnavigates Van Diemans Land and verifies the existence of Bass Straight, and stressed the lack of harbours other than Jervis Bay and Twofold Bay.
1800-Dec	Lt. James Grant	The "Lady Nelson" sailed through and proved that Bass Straight separated Van Diemens Land from the mainland, which was confirmed by the "Harbinger" and the "Margaret" just a few weeks later.
1801-Mar	Lt. James Grant, Barrallier & Cayley	Aboard the "Lady Nelson" they explored Jervis Bay, then sailed to Western Port Bay and returned to Sydney.
1805-Feb	Lt. Bartholemew Kent & James Meehan	Sailing in the colonial cutter "Anne" to explore the Shoal Haven region, but had to anchor in Jervis Bay and walk overland. They explored as far north as todays town of 'Berry' and west to 'Burrier' reporting on the landscape.
1811-Nov	Gov. Lachlan Macquarie	Took a return voyage aboard the "Lady Nelson" to Van Diemans Land, staying at Jervis Bay for two days and was so impressed that he commissioned a survey of the region.
1812-Jan	Cedar Getters	Cedar was covertly transported out of the Illawarra by the "Speedwell" and at least nine other ships, with sealers and whalers also beginning to operate along the coast at this time.
1812-Mar	George W. Evans	Sailing aboard the "Lady Nelson", George Evans landed at Jervis Bay and explored a land route through Shoal Haven and the Illawarra to Appin from the 3rd to 17th April.
1813-Apr	Capt. Collins	Sailing in the "Matilda", he began an exploration from Jervis Bay, and possibly reached the southern bank of the Shoalhaven River, but after being deserted by their natives at a distance of 12 or 14 miles from the vessel, they were reduced to the necessity of abandoning the project.
1815-Mar	Messrs Batty & Howell	Accompanied by Aboriginals, they trekked from Shoal Haven to Five Islands (Kembla), and Watermoolly [sic. Wattamolla] to Sydney.
1815-	Charles Throsby	Throsby found an overland trail from Appin to Five Islands and weeks later moved his stock in a repeat of the journey, which was followed by a number of other stockholders.
1817-	Dr William Elyard, R.N.	The erection of the Red Point Barracks at Five Islands (Kembla), under Dr William Elyard, R.N. (superintendant).
1818-Apr	Throsby, Meehan, Hume, Grimes, Wild, Bundell & Broughton	Departing the Moss Vale area, they crossed the Wingecarribee River, and passed though Marulan, Bungonia Creek, but the party split with Meehan's party discovering the Goulburn Plains. Throsby's expedition guided by Aboriginals explored Bundanoon Creek, Meryla Pass, Yarrunga Creek and Kangaroo Valley, reaching the Shoalhaven River at Burrier, and Jervis Bay at Huskisson Hill before returning to Exeter.
1819-Oct	Oxley, Meehan, Hume & Broughton	Sailing on the "Emmeline", they set out from Jervis Bay, with Oxley turning about. Meehan and Hume continued north-west, tracing Throsby's route to Burrier, and keeping to the east they came to Fitzroy Falls and the precipitous cliffs, which they climbed to arrive at present day Bong Bong.
1821-Nov	Lt. Robert Johnston	Explored the River Clyde in the "Snapper" taking soundings for a distance of 35 miles, and was enthusiastic about the possibility of settlement.
1822-Jan	Lt. Robert Johnston & Alexander Berry	Sailing aboard the "Snapper" they entered the Crookhaven River and dragged their whaleboat across a narrow neck of land, describing the Shoalhaven River to Burrier. Retracing their steps they also sailed to Jervis Bay and then to Batemans Bay where they once again sailed up the River Clyde. As a consequence of this expedition Berry decided the Shoalhaven River afforded him the best prospects of settlement.
1822-Feb	William Kearns	A party consisting of Messrs. Kearns, Marsh, Packard and Aboriginal guides travelled overland from the southern end of Lake George to near Batemans Bay (Pigeon House Mountain), to investigate the possibilities of a road to the coast and survey the land.
1822-May	Alexander Berry	Establishes a settlement at 'Coolangatta' mountain on the Shoalhaven River.
1824-Oct	Hamilton Hume & William Hovell	Undertook a land journey of exploration over four months from Appin to Port Phillip Bay in eastern Australia, and returned by January of 1825.
1827-	H.S. Badgery & Henry Burnell	Settlers and cattlemen began moving down from Goulburn and Braidwood to Moruya & the banks of the River Clyde on what became Bateman's Bay..
1828-	Whalers & Sealers	At Twofold Bay, whalers set up a tri-works and began whaling.

Compiled by Dr Tracy Rockwell.

PROLOGUE

In the early decades of the nineteenth century, the city of Limerick crouched beside the River Shannon like a wounded sentinel of Ireland's past. Its medieval walls still bore the scars of the 1798 Rebellion, when the dream of Irish liberty was crushed beneath British artillery. The cannons had fallen silent, yet the silence that followed was heavier still, a silence filled with hunger, poverty, and the slow grind of oppression. The Union Jack fluttered from King John's Castle and soldiers patrolled its narrow streets. Beneath them, an Irish people endured, proud, weary, and defiant in small, unseen ways.

Around 1816, among the tenements and quays of this bruised city, a boy named John Frawley was born. His parents, like so many displaced country folk, had been driven from the land into the city's underbelly. His father may have worked as a clerk, his mother taking in washing to keep food on the table. Their home would have been cramped, the air thick with the smell of turf smoke and the river's tidal mud. To be young in Limerick then was to grow up fast, to learn that bread was dear, authority cruel, and opportunity fleeting.

Across the same city, perhaps only a few lanes away, a girl named Mary Ann McGarry entered the world about a year earlier, around 1815. She, too, was born into the grey aftermath of rebellion, into a world where the church bells tolled for faith, but the streets belonged to poverty. The McGarry family's prospects were meagre: domestic service for the daughters, hard labour for the sons, and the ever-present spectre of want. Mary Ann learned to work early, to keep her head down, and to find pride in survival itself.

By the 1820s, Limerick's fortunes had declined. The once-bustling butter markets and linen mills struggled, while the poor multiplied. While the landlords tightened rents, the Catholic population, still excluded from full rights, crowded into squalid courts and backstreets. Disease and hunger visited every winter. To steal a loaf, a shawl, or a length of cloth could mean imprisonment, or worse. For the British courts, theft by the poor was not mere crime, it was insubordination, and the gaols overflowed with the dispossessed.

It was in this harsh crucible that John Frawley's fate was sealed. In March 1833, at barely seventeen, he was convicted in Limerick for the theft of clothes, a petty offence born of desperation, but treated as a felony. The sentence was harsh, transportation for seven years to the penal colony of New South Wales. Within weeks he was shackled, marched to Cork, and placed aboard the convict ship "Java".

The "Java" was a barque of 411 tons, commanded by Captain John Todd with Surgeon Robert Dixon in charge of the prisoners' welfare, if welfare it could be called. Two hundred Irish convicts were packed below decks, chained and sleeping in hammocks, their days measured by the creak of timbers and the lash of waves. Disease and despair travelled with them. John Frawley fell ill with pneumonia midway through the voyage but recovered, one of the lucky few.

After 117 days at sea, the "Java" dropped anchor in Port Jackson on 18th November 1833. Five convicts had died while others were landed sick. Frawley, gaunt and sunburnt, stepped onto a continent unlike any he could have imagined. The air smelled of eucalyptus and salt. Red soil clung to his boots. Ahead lay years of servitude, but also, unknowingly, it was the beginning of his redemption.

From Sydney he was assigned to labour on Alexander Berry's Coolangatta Estate on the South Coast, a sprawling enterprise near the Shoalhaven River. There, amid cane grass and cedar forests, he learned the rhythm of colonial life: the dawn muster, relentless work, the occasional kindness, the daily endurance. Convict life was ruled by discipline, yet it offered one fragile promise, that good conduct could earn a Ticket of Leave, and with it, a chance at freedom.

Back in Ireland, another life was unraveling. Mary Ann McGarry, a servant in one of Limerick's modest homes, was accused of receiving stolen goods, perhaps a gown or pair of stockings. For such small crimes, women were branded "habitual offenders." In truth, many were victims of circumstance: single, impoverished, and cornered by hunger. Tried and convicted, Mary Ann received the same sentence as John Frawley, seven years' transportation.

In November 1837, she was marched aboard the convict ship "Diamond", which sailed from Cork with 160 women. The voyage lasted nearly four months. The women were mostly confined below deck, their world reduced to darkness, damp air, and the endless rocking of the sea. Some prayed, others cursed or sang to drown the fear. Yet in that cramped underworld, bonds of resilience formed, friendships that would endure long after they reached Australia.

When the "Diamond" dropped anchor in Sydney Cove five months later, Mary Ann was mustered, inspected, and assigned as a domestic servant. Her labour was her life's currency, obedience her safeguard. The colony's severe gender imbalance meant that emancipated women, once free, were sought after as wives and housekeepers, a strange, harsh blessing in a world built on exile.

By the early 1840s, John Frawley was free and Mary Ann was

mid way through her sentence. The expanding districts of Illawarra and Shoalhaven offered work to emancipists who knew hard labour and could be trusted. Here, among farms and sawmills carved from the bush, it was at Berry's Coolangatta Estate, that their paths likely crossed. Two Irish Catholics, both branded as convicts, both bearing the quiet pride of survivors.

But love among emancipists was rarely romantic in the storybook sense, it was a partnership of endurance, a joining of two souls determined never again to be owned. Their union, whether formalised by the church or sealed only by circumstance, became the foundation of a new family line. From this point the book's chapters unfold: their early years under Berry's dominion, the echoes of their Irish ancestry, and Mary Ann's own ordeal as a transported woman. Together they forged a foothold in a foreign land, and gradually their story carried them southward to the rugged frontier of Twofold Bay and Pambula.

The 1840s brought new opportunities as settlers pushed beyond the Shoalhaven into the wide, untamed country of the far south Maneroo District. Roads were rough tracks, rivers were crossed by driftwood and prayer, and the nearest neighbours might be miles away. Yet John and Mary Ann Frawley made the journey, ex-convicts turned pioneers. At 'Warragaburra' Station and later Pamboola, they built a home, raised children, and tilled the stubborn soil. Their courage mirrored that of countless emancipists who transformed punishment into permanence.

By mid-century, their names appeared not in convict lists but in parish registers, land ledgers, and family bibles. They were no longer prisoners of empire but settlers of a new society, living witnesses to the strange alchemy by which exile could become belonging.

From the emerald county of Limerick to the sapphire coast of Pambula, their lives spanned the transformation of two worlds, one lost, one found. Mary Ann Frawley would reach the age of seventy-four, and witness Ireland's Great Famine from afar, the gold rushes, the rise of railways, and the birth of a generation free from the stigma she had carried across the sea. John Frawley lived a dozen more years, dying in 1901, the year of Australian Federation.

Their descendants would scatter across the east coast of New South Wales, and to Toowoomba, bearing a surname once whispered in courtrooms now spoken with pride. The chapters that follow trace this journey in full: from exploration and settlement to endurance and legacy, from discovery and conviction, through Coolangatta's ordered fields and Pambula's rugged paddocks, to the final reckoning of a family whose roots were forged in chains yet flourished in freedom.

John and Mary Ann never returned to Ireland. Yet through them, a small fragment of Limerick's story found new soil on Australia's far shore. Their tale is not merely one of crime and punishment, but of transformation, a testament to the resilience that shaped a nation. Theirs was the courage of the unwanted, the endurance of the displaced, and the quiet triumph of those who, though torn from their homeland, built another from their own hands.

From the misty Shannon to the sunlit Shoalhaven, and onward to the windswept plains of Pambula, their footsteps mark the path from bondage to belonging, the opening line in a saga of discovery, endurance, and renewal that unfolds in the chapters ahead.

1

DISCOVERING THE SOUTH COAST OF NSW

The story of John Frawley is one of resilience, transformation, and legacy. Born in Limerick in 1816, he was just 17 years old when his life was irrevocably altered, sentenced to transportation to Australia for the minor crime of stealing clothes. Uprooted from his homeland, stripped of his future, and cast into the unknown, he became one of the 40,000 Irish convicts who were forcibly exiled from their homeland from between 1791 and 1867. Yet, rather than being merely a victim of history, John Frawley became a pioneering figure in colonial Australia, shaping the very land to which he was sent in chains.

This book chronicles the life and lineage of John Frawley (c.1816–1901), tracing his ancestry, his personal journey, and his enduring impact. Through meticulous genealogical research, we have been able to reconstruct his family's past, bringing to life the key individuals whose choices, struggles, and triumphs shaped his destiny.

But this is more than just a family history, it is a sweeping narrative that places John Frawley within the grand forces of his time. From the Napoleonic Wars to World War I, from the Industrial and Irish Revolutions to the Victorian era, his story is deeply intertwined with some of the most pivotal moments in modern history. Long before John Frawley's fateful transportation, the British had already begun their colonization of Australia, establishing the settlement of Sydney in 1788. By a twist of fate, Frawley would go on to forge a new life as a pioneer on the continent's rugged southeastern frontier, and to understand his remarkable journey, we must first explore the land he was forced to call home.

The exploration, mapping, and gradual opening up of New South Wales to European settlement played a crucial role in shaping the world into which he arrived. The challenges, opportunities, and transformations of this frontier landscape would not only define his survival, but also his legacy.

However, before exploring John Frawley's personal odyssey, a story of endurance, adaptation, and survival; this book will first examine the key events that shaped a timeline of explorations and discoveries along Australia's South East Coast (*see Appendix A*). From the first European encounters to the rise of civilization in the decades before Frawley's arrival, this historical context helps illuminate how a young Irishman, exiled to an unfamiliar land, became not just a footnote in history but a pivotal part of Australia's story.

The Voyage of "HMS Endeavour"

Lt. James Cook (1728-1779)

The discovery of the east coast of Australia began with the arrival of that talented and able seaman Lieutenant James Cook, navigator, cartographer and later captain in the Royal Navy, and Fellow of the Royal Society. Cook became famous for his three outstanding voyages of discovery between 1768 and 1779 into the Pacific Ocean, to Tahiti and Hawaii, but most particularly his circumnavigation of New Zealand and discovery of the east coast of Australia.

On the 25th May 1768, the British Admiralty commissioned Cook to command a voyage to the Pacific Ocean.[1] The purpose of the expedition wasn't to colonise new lands or subjugate 'inferior' races, but primarily to advance scientific knowledge by observing and recording the 1769 transit of Venus across the Sun, which when combined with observations from other places around the world, would help to determine the distance of the Earth from the Sun.[2] At age 39, Cook was promoted to lieutenant to grant him sufficient status to take command of the voyage.[3,4] For its part, the Royal Society agreed that Cook would receive a one hundred guinea gratuity in addition to his Naval pay.[5]

Aboard "HMS Endeavour", the expedition departed from Plymouth, England on the 26th August 1768.[6] After an eight month voyage Cook and his crew arrived at Tahiti on the 13th April 1769, where the observations of the transit were made.[7] However, the result of the observations was not as conclusive or accurate as had been hoped. Once his work there was completed, Cook opened his sealed orders, which were additional instructions from the Admiralty for the second part of his voyage, with dictates to search the south Pacific for signs of the postulated rich southern continent of Terra Australis.[8]

Cook then sailed to New Zealand where, with only some minor errors, he completely circumnavigated and mapped the two islands. With the aid of Tupaia, a Tahitian priest who had joined the expedition, Cook became the first European to communicate with the Maori.[9] Cook then voyaged west, reaching the southeastern coast of what they correctly assumed was New Holland, and in doing so his expedition became the first recorded Europeans to encounter the eastern coastline of Australia.

Cooks landfall was recorded in the ship's log as being sighted at 6 a.m. on Thursday 19 April 1770, but because the south-east coast of Australia is now regarded as being 10 hours ahead relative to Britain, that date is now called Friday, 20th April.[10] He named the point of contact as Cape Hicks, in honour of his second in command Lieutenant William Hicks (1788-1874), who had first sighted the mainland that morning.

Over the next seven days Cook sailed north, noting in his journal many prominent features of Australia's south east coast including Ram Head and Cape Howe, which he named after Richard Howe (1726-1799), 1st Earl Howe, a distinguished naval commander best known for his victory of the 'Glorious First of June' over the French, in 1794. Being 20km out to sea Cook missed Twofold Bay, but noted Mount Dromedary, Pigeon House Mountain and three or four small islands he called Bateman Bay, after Nathaniel Bateman (c.1723-1797), captain of the "Northumberland."[11]

If the sea was calmer Cook may have landed at Murramarang, but it was there that they glimpsed their first aboriginals, who they described in the following journal entry:

> "As we stood along shore we saw four or five of the Indians sitting near the fire; they appeared to be naked and very black, which was all we could discern at that distance."
>
> *Richard Pickersgill, Master's Mate*

Having failed to land on the 23rd April, Cook stood away from the shore passing present day Ulladulla at a distance of 20-25km, but he named Cape St George, noting also the existence of Jervis Bay although he did not name it. At that time a fresh gale blew up from the southwest and Cook could not take a closer look without beating up, which would have taken more time than he was willing to spare.

With the gale behind them the next day, Cook made good progress and attempted another landing near present day Bulli, putting off in the yawl accompanied by Joseph Banks (1743-1820), Dr Daniel Solander (1733-1782) and Tupaia, his interpreter, at a place where four or five natives gathered near the shore. Unfortunately the natives disappeared as the boat came near and no landing could be made because of the surf. That evening there was no wind and the "Endeavour" drifted within two km of the shore inside a line of breakers, which caused some concern. Fortunately a light breeze came off the land, which carried them out of danger. At daylight next day on April 29th, they sighted a large bay and entered it that afternoon, which he later named Botany Bay.

Cook landed at Kurnell, on the southern bank of Botany Bay, at what is now Silver Beach, and his arrival marked the beginning of Britain's interest in Australia and in the eventual colonisation of the new found 'southern continent'.[12] Initially the name 'Stingrays Harbour' was used by Cook and other journal keepers on his expedition, for the plentiful number of stingrays they caught,[13] a name which was also recorded on the Admiralty charts.[14] Cook's log for the 6th May 1770 records...

"The great quantity of these sort of fish found in this place occasioned my giving it the name of Stingrays Harbour". However, in the journal prepared later from his log, Cook wrote instead: (sic) "The great quantity of plants Mr. Banks and Dr. Solander found in this place occasioned my giving it the name of Botanist Botany Bay".[15,16]

Two Aboriginal men came down to the boat and Cook's party attempted to communicate their desire for water and threw gifts of beads and nails ashore. But the two Aboriginals made attempts to oppose the landing and Cook ordered the firing of a warning shot. One responded by throwing a rock, and Cook fired on them with small shot, wounding one of them in the leg. The crew then landed, and the Aboriginals threw two spears before Cook fired another round of small shot, when they retreated. The landing party found several children in nearby huts, and left some beads and other gifts with them. The landing party collected 40 to 50 spears and other artefacts.[17,18,19]

Cook and his crew remained at Botany Bay for a week, collecting water, timber, fodder, botanical specimens and explored the surrounding area. The indigenous inhabitants observed the Europeans closely, but generally retreated whenever they approached. Cook's party made several attempts to establish relations with the native people, but they showed no interest in the food and gifts the Europeans offered, and occasionally threw spears as an apparent warning.[20,21]

While Cook's chart of the southeast coast shows few major errors, it is interesting that nowhere in his original papers did he refer to the land as New South Wales. The first mention of that name appears in the account of Cooks voyage written-up by Dr John Hawksworth LLD (1715-1773), the officially appointed editor. At that time the map of the known world already showed a New Britain, New England, New Scotland, New Ireland and even a New North Wales, so Hawksworth apparently chose New South Wales as the best of what was left.

Transportation Beyond The Seas

Banishment or forced exile from a society has been used as a punishment since at least the 5th century BC in ancient Greece. The practice of banishment reached its height in the British Empire during the 18th and 19th centuries.[22] Penal transportation not only deterred crime, but removed the offender from society, mostly permanently, and was seen as being more merciful than capital punishment. This method was used for criminals, debtors, military and political prisoners. Penal transportation was also used as a method of colonization as from the earliest days of English colonial schemes, new settlements beyond the seas were seen as a way of alleviating domestic social problems committed by criminals and the poor, and at the same time it increased the colonial labour force, for the overall benefit of the new colony and the realm.[23]

Following the introduction of the Transportation Act into the House of Commons (1717), by the Whig government in 1717, transportation was legitimised as a punishment.[24] During an era of great inflexibility persons convicted of the most inconsequential of misdemeanors and crimes, saw offenders being commonly sentenced to 'transportation beyond the seas.' But where were these convicts sent and what purpose was fulfilled by transporting them to other destinations around the world? The story that follows explores why the colony of New South Wales was chosen as a prison, how that immense continent was explored and gradually became their new home.

After Cook departed from Botany Bay in 1770, it took 18 long years for the British to return. But why did they bother? What was it that motivated them to return to a place so foreign, destitute, and so very far away?

All the available evidence points to Botany Bay on the east coast of New South Wales as being selected for settlement for two main reasons. First and most important, was the need to establish a base in the Pacific as a strategic imperitive to counter French expansion;[25] and second, the American Revolution brought an abrupt end to the transportation of convicts to North America.[26]

John Montagu (1718-1792), the 4th Earl of Sandwich, together with the President of the Royal Society Sir Joseph Banks, the eminent scientist who had accompanied Lt. James Cook on his 1770 voyage, were among the first to advocate the establishment of a British colony at Botany Bay.[27,28] Under the guidance of Banks, American loyalist James Matra (1746-1806) accepted an offer to assist with "A Proposal for Establishing a Settlement in New South Wales", which was published on the 24th August 1783. Matra developed a set of reasons for a colony composed of American Loyalists, and Chinese and South Sea Islanders, but not convicts.[29] The final decision to establish a colony in New South Wales was made by Thomas Townshend (1733-1800), otherwise known as 1st Viscount Sydney, who was then the Secretary of State for the British Home Office.[30]

The First Fleet (1788)

Under the leadership of Capt. Arthur Phillip (1738-1814), who was also appointed the honour of being the very first governor of the fledgling colony, the 'First Fleet' left from Portsmouth, England on 13 May 1787.[31] En route they stopped at Rio de Janeiro in June, and again at Table Bay off the Cape of Good Hope to take on supplies in October, before Phillip transferred to the "HMAT Supply" on the 25th November 1787. Together with "Alexander", "Friendship" and "Scarborough", the fastest ships in the fleet, which were carrying most of the male convicts, "Supply" hastened ahead to prepare for the arrival of the rest. Phillip intended to select a suitable location, find good water, clear the ground and perhaps even have some huts and other structures erected before the others arrived. This was a planned move, discussed with the Home Office and the Admiralty prior to the Fleet's departure.[32] However, this "flying squadron" reached Botany Bay only hours before the rest of the Fleet, so no preparatory work was possible.[33] "Supply" reached Botany Bay on the 18th January 1788; the three fastest transports in the advance group arrived on the 19th January; and the slower ships, including "Sirius", arrived on the 20th January.[34] Although Phillip's initial instructions were to establish the colony at Botany Bay, he was authorised to establish the colony elsewhere if necessary.[35]

It was quickly realised that Botany Bay did not live up to the glowing account that Cook had provided.[36] The bay was open and unprotected, the water was too shallow to allow the ships to anchor close to the shore, fresh water was scarce, and the soil was poor.[37] First contact was made with the local indigenous people, the Eora, who seemed curious but suspicious of the newcomers. The area was studded with enormously strong trees. When the convicts tried to cut these down, their tools broke and the tree trunks had to be blasted out of the ground with gunpowder. The primitive huts built for the officers and officials quickly collapsed in rainstorms. The marines developed a habit of getting drunk and not guarding the convicts properly, whilst their commander Major Robert Ross (c.1740-1794), drove Phillip to despair with his arrogant and lazy attitude. Crucially, Phillip worried that his fledgling colony was exposed to attack from those described as 'Aborigines' or from foreign powers.

On the morning of the 21st January, Phillip and a party which included Capt. John Hunter (1737-1821), departed from Botany Bay in three small boats to explore other bays to the north. Phillip quickly discovered that a natural harbour, about 12 kilometres to the north, would be an excellent site for a colony with sheltered anchorages, fresh water and fertile soil. Cook had seen and named the opening Port Jackson, but had not entered it. Phillip's initial impressions of the harbour were recorded in a letter he sent to England lauding "the finest harbour in the world, in which a thousand sail of the line may ride in the most perfect security." The party returned to Botany Bay on the 23rd January.[38]

On the morning of the 24th January, the party was startled when two French ships, the "Astrolabe" and the "Boussole", were seen just outside Botany Bay. This was a scientific expedition led by Jean-François de La Pérouse (1741-c.1788). The French had expected to find a thriving colony where they could repair ships and restock supplies, not a newly arrived fleet of convicts considerably more poorly provisioned than themselves.[39] There was some cordial contact between the French and British officers, but Phillip and La Pérouse never actually met. The French ships remained until the 10th March before setting sail on their return voyage to France. However, they were never seen again and were later discovered to have been shipwrecked off the coast of Vanikoro in the present-day Solomon Islands.[40]

On the 26th January 1788, the fleet weighed anchor and sailed north for Port Jackson.[41] The site selected for the anchorage had deep water close to the shore, was sheltered, and had a small stream flowing into it. Phillip named it Sydney Cove, after Lord Sydney, the British Home Secretary.[42] This date is celebrated as Australia Day, marking the beginning of British and European settlement,[43] while the British flag was planted and formal possession was annexed. This was done by Phillip and some officers and marines from "Supply", with the remainder of her crew and the convicts observing from on board ship. The remaining ships of the fleet did not arrive at Sydney Cove until later that day.[44] Writer and art critic Robert Hughes popularized the idea in his 1986 book "The Fatal Shore" that an orgy occurred upon the unloading of the convicts, though more modern historians regard this as untrue, since the first reference to any such indiscretions is as recent as 1963.[45,46]

In the beginning the geographical features of Sydney and adjoining country, on which now stands the City of Sydney, consisted of a picturesque panorama of water, with hills clothed with dense scrub. Sydney Cove was at the head of the harbour, into which flowed a pure stream of fresh water they called 'the Tank Stream'. Eleven vessels, carrying not more during than 3800 tons aggregate, dropped anchor at this site in January 1788. The secretary to the governor, David Collins Esq. (1756-1810), one of the earliest chroniclers, reported:[47]

> "The confusion that ensued during the landing will not be wondered at, when it is considered that every man stepped from a boat literally into a wood. Parties of people were everywhere heard and seen variously employed, some in clearing the ground for different encampments, others pitching tents or bringing up some stores as were more immediately wanted; and the spot which had so recently been the abode of silence and tranquility was now changed to that of noise, clamour, and confusion."
>
> David Collins Esq., Judge Advocate

Collins went on to provide some interesting figures at the start of the colony:

> "On 1st May, 1788. the number of live stock in Australia was 1 stallion, 3 mares, 3 colts, 2 bulls, 5 cows, 29 sheep, 19 goats, 49 hogs, 29 small pigs, 5 rabbits. 18 turkeys, 29 geese, 35 ducks, 142 fowls, 87 chickens." In the 'Illustrated London Library', an important publication of those days reported: "In April, 1788, two bulls and four cows wandered away from the 'pickpocket' herdsmen in the new settlement of New South Wales into the bush and were lost. They were undoubtedly the first discoverers of the several gorges leading down from the coast ranges to the sea."

Early Explorations of the South Coast

Although Governor Phillip and his successor, Major Francis Grose (1758-1814) were too concerned with events in the near vicinity of Port Jackson to spare effort in exploring the southeast coast, some information did trickle in, so that as early as August 1794, David Collins apparently thought there was nothing unusual in a Mr. Melville going on a fishing (sealing?) trip to Jervis and Bateman Bays. The latter had been named by Cook, while Jervis Bay was discovered and named in August of 1791 by Lt. Richard Bowen (1761-1797).

Lt. Bowen & Capt. Weatherhead (1791)

Governor Phillip finished his term and embarked for England on

11th December, 1792, and settled at Bath on a pension granted by the British Government of £500 per year, which was where he died in 1814. Next to make signifant discoveries was Lt. Richard Bowen of the "Atlantic", a convict transport of the Third Fleet, who made an eye-draft of Jervis Bay and named Bowen Island to the south of the entrance in 1791. He found deep water and a good anchorage and named the bay in honour of Admiral Sir Richard John Jervis (1735-1823), later Lord St Vincent, under whom he had served.

Later that same year Captain Weatherhead of the "Matilda" entered Jervis Bay for minor repairs and made a second eye-draft, reporting "an exceedingly good anchorage with room for the largest ships to work in or out with great safety." For three years after Governor Phillip's departure the settlement was practically a military despotism, but it is likely that unknown sealers and whalers visited the South Coast from that date forward. The government first devolved upon Major Francis Grose, and secondly on Capt. William Paterson (1755-1810), both senior officers of the New South Wales Corps, as Lt-Governor, where incompetency and militarism were blazed on the face of their every act.[48]

The official notification of the appointment of Capt. John Hunter, R.N., as Governor of New South Wales appeared in the "London Gazette" on the 5th February, 1794, and the commission passed the Great Seal on the following day.[49]

George Bass & Voyages of "Tom Thumb" (1796)

Dr. George Bass (1771-1803) attended Boston Grammar School and later trained in medicine at the hospital in Boston, Lincolnshire. At the age of 18, he was accepted as a member of the Company of Surgeons in London, and in 1794 he joined the Royal Navy as a surgeon. He arrived in Sydney aboard "HMS Reliance" on 7th September 1795.[50] Also on that voyage was his surgeon's assistant William Martin, Matthew Flinders (1774-1814), Capt. John Hunter, and Bennelong (c.1764-1813), who was returning to Sydney after five years in Britain. Bass had brought with him on the "Reliance" a small boat with an 8-foot (2.4m) keel and 5-foot (1.5m) beam, which he called the "Tom Thumb" on account of its size. The first "Tom Thumb" voyage occurred between the 26th October and 5th November 1795, which included Bass, Flinders and Bass's servant William Martin, as they explored the Georges River further upstream than had been done previously by the colonists. Their reports on their return led to the settlement of Banks' Town.[51]

On the 24th March 1796 the same party embarked on a second voyage in a slightly larger boat with the same crew, which they called the "Tom Thumb II."[52,53] During this trip they explored Port Hacking and sailed down the coast to Lake Illawarra, and named Tom Thumb Lagoon. Amongst other discoveries this voyage demonstrated to the colonists that indigenous Australians from different parts of the country spoke very different languages.[54] Later that year Bass discovered good land near Prospect Hill, and found lost cattle brought out with the First Fleet, but failed in an attempt to cross the Blue Mountains. It was on this journey that Matthew Flinders and George Bass feared for their safety when they encountered the fearsome native Dilba.

The "Sydney Cove" Survivors (1797)

Little official notice was reported about the South Coast until in 1797, three survivors from the wreck of the "Sydney Cove" were rescued by a fishing boat to the south of Botany Bay. Under Captain Guy Hamilton, the "Sydney Cove" with a crew of nearly 50, left Calcutta with merchandise for Port Jackson on the 10th November 1796, intending to follow the usual route south of Van Diemen's Land (Tasmania). They ran into continuous bad weather and developed a serious leak, becoming so waterlogged that they had to beach the ship on an isle in the Furneaux group in mid February 1797, at a place still called Preservation Island. They were fortunate that all made it safely ashore with provisions and arms as well as the ship's longboat. The next fortnight was engaged in preparing for a voyage to Port Jackson to seek help.

On 28 February 1797, leaving about 30 survivors with the wreckage, a party of 17 men set off in the ship's longboat to reach help at Sydney, which was some 400 nautical miles away. The party was led by first mate Hugh Thompson, and included William Clark (the supercargo), three European seamen, and twelve Indian lascars (sailors). But ill fortune struck again when the longboat was wrecked on the mainland at the northern end of Ninety Mile Beach in Victoria. Their only hope of survival was to walk along the coast all the way to Sydney, a distance of over 800 kilometres.

They had few provisions and no ammunition, and fatigue and hunger lessened their number as they marched. Along the way they encountered various aboriginal people, some friendly, some not. The last of the party to die on the march was killed by a man named Dilba and his people near Hat Hill, from a clan that had a reputation around Port Jackson for being ferocious.

By May of 1797, the three survivors of the march, William Clark, sailor John Bennet and one lascar had made it as far as the cove at Wattamolla and on the 15th May 1797, with their strength nearly at an end, they were able to signal a fishing boat, which took them on to Sydney.[55] On the march, Clark had noted coal in the cliffs at what is now called Coalcliff between Sydney and Wollongong, which was the second instance of coal being discovered in Australia.[56]

Bass & Flinders (1797)

On the 3rd December 1797, this time without Flinders, inthe same open whaleboat with a crew of just six, Bass sailed to Cape Howe, the farthest point of south-eastern Australia. From here he went westwards along what is now the coast of the Gippsland region of Victoria, to Western Port, almost as far as the entrance to Port Phillip, on the north shore of which is the site of present-day Melbourne. His belief that a strait separated the mainland from Van Diemen's Land, was backed up by his astute observation of the rapid tide and the long south-western swell at Wilson's Promontory.

On this voyage Bass visited the Kiama area and made many notes on its botanical complexity and the amazing natural phenomenon they called 'the Blowhole', noting the volcanic geology around the waterspout, which contributed much to its understanding. The journey was highly regarded at the time as one of the great feats of seafaring. The whaleboat was left on the shores of Sydney Harbour and was regarded, for many years as something of an icon by the locals. French naturalist Francois Peron recorded that "some snuff-boxes made from the wood of its keel form relics of which the possessors are as proud as they are careful".

The whaleboat voyage, along with Flinders' separate voyage to the Furneaux Islands on the "Francis" convinced the pair that Tasmania was an island, and they set out to prove their theory. On the 7th October 1798, they attempted a circumnavigation of Van Diemen's Land, in the sloop "Norfolk". In the course of this voyage Bass visited the estuary of the Derwent River, found and named by Captain John Hayes in 1793,[57] where the future city of Hobart would be founded on the strength of his 1803 report. When the two returned to Sydney, Flinders recommended to Governor John Hunter that the passage between Van Diemen's Land and the mainland be called 'Bass Strait'.

> "This was no more than a just tribute to my worthy friend and companion," Flinders wrote, "for the extreme dangers and fatigues he had undergone, in first entering it in a whaleboat, and to the correct judgement he had formed, from various indications, of the existence of a wide opening between Van Diemen's Land and New South Wales."
>
> *Mathew Flinders*

The summer of 1798-99 was remarkable for one of the colony's first protracted droughts on record. For ten months scarcely a shower of rain fell. The drought finally ended with a disastrous flood in the Hawkesbury River, of which local weather conditions gave no warning. The banks were "overflowing with vast rapidity." The Government store and all the provisions it contained were swept away. The river was more than fifty feet above its common level, and the torrent was so powerful that it carried all before it. Settler's houses and furniture, livestock and provisions were alike swept away, and "the whole country looked like an immense ocean." About this time, Captain Hunter, who had taken up the governorship from August 7th, 1795, had a survey made of the coast south of Botany Bay, and the Shoalhaven River was also explored and named.[58]

Lt. James Grant (1800)

The original "Lady Nelson" was built at Deptford, in England in 1799, for service to the Transport Office on the River Thames. She was designed with a sliding keel (centre board), a device invented by Captain John Schank of the Royal Navy. On completion she was selected for exploration services in the colony of New South Wales and sailed for Port Jackson on the 18th March 1800, under the command of Lt. James Grant (1772-1833). As a man, Grant was upright and sincere with a mind of his own, as well as being a gallant and skilful officer.[59]

A brig of 60 tons, the "Lady Nelson" carried a crew comprising the commander, two mates and 12 seamen. As she left the River Thames sailors on nearby ships ridiculed her because of her size and shape, calling her, as she sailed past, 'His Majesty's Tinderbox'. At Portsmouth on the 9th February 1800, she was fitted out with four brass carriage guns, three to four pounders, in addition to the two guns already on board. Because of the heavy load she was carrying, the "Lady Nelson" sat very low in the water, having only two feet nine inches of freeboard amidships. The ship finally left Portsmouth on 17th March 1800 as part of an East Indian convoy.

After leaving the convoy on 23rd March, the ship sailed on alone and arrived at St. Jago, Cape Verde Islands on the 13th April 1800, where two of the crew made off with one of the ship's boats. They were, however, soon captured by the Portuguese and brought back to the ship "both riding the one ass." Dissension and unrest amongst the crew had been stirred up by the second mate, and Grant sent him back to England, with two young Portuguese men being signed on as replacement crew.

As she sailed into Table Bay, South Africa on the 8th July 1800, the crew of "Lady Nelson" saw a convoy of ships that had left England at the same time. These ships had suffered heavy damage from rough weather and yet the "Lady Nelson" had survived the journey without mishap. It was here that Grant received dispatches from William Bentinck, 3rd Duke of Portland (1738-1809), advising him of the discovery of a straight between New South Wales and Van Diemen's Land, and that he was to sail through it on his way to Port Jackson, instead of sailing around Van Diemen's Land.

On leaving the Cape on 7th October 1800, the ship took on board a Dr. Brandt, ship's surgeon who had been wrecked at Delagoe Bay some years earlier. Grant also secured a ship's carpenter for the journey, but had to refuse many offers from young seamen who wished to join the "Lady Nelson" on her journey of discovery. One of these was John Johnston (aka Jorgen Jorgenson, 1780-1841) and his is a fascinating tale of adventure,[60] which was later tied to the colony of New South Wales. However, Grant had to refuse a disappointed Johnston, and was obliged instead to take a fellow Dane and convict, who had to be transported to Port Jackson.

At daybreak on 3rd December 1800 in latitude 38° south, the crew first sighted the land of New Holland, near present day Mount Gambier. A few days later she sailed through the straight, becoming the first ship to sail from west to east through what was later named 'Bass Strait', charting the then unknown coastline. The "Lady Nelson" entered the heads at Port Jackson at six in the evening on the 16th December, after a passage of seventy-one days from Cape Town.[61] Grant spent little more than twelve months in Australian waters, but he played quite an important role as an explorer, being the first commander to traverse Bass Strait from west to east and to explore the Hunter River.

While skilled and determined explorers were expanding the boundaries of knowledge and British influence along the South Coast of New South Wales, events back in the British Isles were reshaping the empire in a very different way. Efforts to reduce British control, particularly in Ireland, culminated in the Act of Union of 1801, which merged the 'Kingdom of Ireland' with the 'Kingdom of Great Britain' to form the 'United Kingdom of Great Britain and Ireland.' This unification was largely a response to the 1798 Irish Rebellion, an event that undoubtedly impacted the ancestors of John and Mary Frawley.

Although John Frawley's story had yet to unfold, his family's history became deeply intertwined with the Shoalhaven, Illawarra, and Maneroo regions on the South Coast of New South Wales. To fully understand their journey, it is essential to first explore how this part of Australia was discovered and developed during the colony's first 50 years.

References

1. Kippis, Andrew (1788). Narrative of the voyages round the world, performed by Captain James Cook; with an account of his life during the previous and intervening periods. Chapter 2. Archived from the original on 3 October 2018. Retrieved 3 October 2018.
2. Collingridge, Vanessa (2003). Captain Cook: The Life, Death and Legacy of History's Greatest Explorer. Ebury Press. ISBN 978-0-09-188898-5., p. 95.
3. Rigby, Nigel & van der Merwe, Pieter (2002). Captain Cook in the Pacific. National Maritime Museum, London. ISBN 978-0-948065-43-9., p. 30.
4. Beazley, Charles Raymond (1911). "Cook, James". In Chisholm, Hugh (ed.). Encyclopædia Britannica. Vol. 7 (11th ed.). Cambridge University Press. p. 71.
5. Beaglehole, J. C., ed. (1968). The Journals of Captain James Cook on His Voyages of Discovery. Vol. I: The Voyage of the Endeavour 1768–1771. Cambridge University Press. OCLC 223185477., p. cix.
6. "The Sydney Morning Herald". National Library of Australia. 2 May 1931. p. 12. Retrieved 4 September 2012.
7. "BBC – History – Captain James Cook". Archived from the original on 16 October 2014. Retrieved 31 July 2017.
8. "Secret Instructions to Captain Cook, 30 June 1768" (PDF). National Archives of Australia. Archived (PDF) from the original on 27 April 2020. Retrieved 3 September 2011.
9. Salmond, Anne (1991). Two worlds : first meetings between Maori and Europeans, 1642–1772. Auckland, N.Z.: Viking. ISBN 0-670-83298-7. OCLC 26546558.
10. Arthur R. Hinks, "Nautical time and civil date", The Geographical Journal, 86 (1935) 153–157.
11. Pleaden, Ronald F. (1990). 'Coastal Explorers,' Milton/Ulladulla & District Historical Society, p.4.
12. Cook, James; Hawkesworth, John (1773). "Entrance of Endeavour River in New South Wales. Botany Bay in New South Wales" (Map). David Rumsey Historical Map Collection. State Library of Queensland. Retrieved 7 September 2012.
13. Wales, Geographical Name Board of New South. "Extract – Geographical Names Board of NSW". gnb.nsw.gov.au. Archived from the original on 7 November 2016. Retrieved 7 November 2016.
14. Beaglehole J. C., ed. (1968), op. cit., p. ccix.
15. Beaglehole J. C. (1968), op. cit., p. ccix.
16. The strikethrough is in the Cook's original, reflecting a change of mind sometime after leaving the Bay in 1770.
17. Cook's Journal: Daily Entries, 29 April 1770". southseas.nla.gov.au. South Seas. Retrieved 25 October 2019 [https://webarchive.nla.gov.au/awa/20110403094436/http://southseas.nla.gov.au/journals/cook/17700429.html].
18. Blainey, Geoffrey (2020). Captain Cook's Epic Voyage: the strange quest for a missing continent, Viking (Australia). pp. 141-43.
19. Smith, Keith Vincent (2009). "Confronting Cook". Electronic British Library Journal (2009) [https://bl.iro.bl.uk/concern/articles/9740df81-e9c9-4776-b2fe-5c5b862bacdb?locale=en].
20. FitzSimons, Peter (2019). 'James Cook : the story behind the man who mapped the world'. Sydney, NSW. ISBN 978-0-7336-4127-5. OCLC 1109734011.
21. Blainey (2020). op. cit., pp. 146-57.
22. Maxwell-Stewart, Hamish & Watkins, Emma (n.d.). "Transportation". Digital Panopticon. Digital Panopticon Project. Archived from the original on 8 January 2019. Retrieved 7 February 2019.
23. Ibid.

24. Beattie, J.M. (1986), Crime and the Courts in England 1660–1800, Oxford: Oxford University Press, p. 503.[ISBN 0-19-820058-7].

25. Cameron-Ash, Margaret (2021). Beating France to Botany Bay: The race to found Australia. Balmain: Quadrant Books. ISBN 9780648996125.

26. "Why were convicts transported to Australia". Sydney Living Museums. Archived from the original on 2 December 2013. Retrieved 16 December 2013.

24. Frost, Alan; Moutinho, Isabel (1995). The precarious life of James Mario Matra : voyager with Cook, American loyalist, servant of empire. The Miegunyah Press. ISBN 9780522846676., p. 110.

28. Gascoigne, John (1998). Science in the service of empire : Joseph Banks, the British state and the uses of science in the age of revolution. Cambridge, UK. p. 187. ISBN 0-521-55069-6. OCLC 39524807. Archived from the original on 18 July 2021. Retrieved 18 July 2021.

29. Carter, Harold B. (1988). "Banks, Cook and the Century Natural History Tradition". In Delamothe, Tony; Bridge, Carl (eds.). Interpreting Australia: British Perceptions of Australia since 1788. London: Sir Robert Menzies Centre for Australian Studies. pp. 4–23. Archived from the original on 29 May 2014. Retrieved 18 July 2021.

30. George Burnett Barton (1889). "History of New South Wales From the Records, Volume I – Governor Phillip – Chapter 1.4". Project Gutenberg of Australia. Charles Potter, Government Printer. Retrieved 25 April 2019.

31. Project Gutenberg Australia. "The First Fleet". Retrieved 24 November 2013, [https://gutenberg.net.au/first-fleet.html].

32. Frost, Alan (2012). 'The First Fleet: the real story'. Collingwood: Black Inc. ISBN 9781863955614., p. 174.

33. Frost, Alan (2012). op. cit., p.175.

34. "Timeline-1788". The World Upside Down: Australia 1788–1830. National Library of Australia. 2000. Retrieved 27 May 2006.

35. "Governor Phillip's Instructions 25 April 1787 (UK)". Museum of Australian Democracy. Retrieved 24 November 2013 [https://www.foundingdocs.gov.au/item-sdid-68.html].

36. Frost, Alan (2012). op. cit., p.177.

37. Parker, Derek (2009). 'Arthur Phillip: Australia's First Governor.' Warriewood: Woodslane P. ISBN 9781921203992., p.113.

38. Parker, Derek (2009). op. cit., pp.115–116.

39. Parker, Derek (2009). op. cit., p.118.

40. John Dunmore, "Introduction", The Journal of Jean-François de Galaup de La Pérouse, Vol. I, Hakluyt Society, 1994, pp. ccxix–ccxxii.

41. Project Gutenberg Australia. "The First Fleet", op. cit.

42. Parker, Derek (2009). op. cit., pp.115–116.

43. "About Our National Day". National Australia Day Council. Retrieved 25 November 2013.

44. Hill, David (2008). 1788: The brutal truth of the First Fleet: the biggest single migration the world had ever seen. North Sydney: Heinemann. ISBN 9781741667974.

45. Hughes, Robert (1986). 'The Fatal Shore'. Alfred A. Knopf. p. 88-89. ISBN 9780099448549.

46. Eamon Evans (November 2015). Great Australian Urban Legends. Affirm Press. p. 116-17. ISBN 9781925475241.

47. McCaffrey, Frank (1922). 'The History Of Illawarra And Its Pioneers,' John Sands Ltd, Sydney, p.10.

48. Pleaden, Ronald F. (1990). op. cit., p.11.

49. McCaffrey, Frank (1922). op. cit., p.11.

50. Scott, Ernest (1914). The Life of Captain Matthew Flinders, RN. Sydney: Angus & Robertson. p. 100.

51. Scott, Ernest (1914). op.cit., p. 86.

52. Flinders, Matthew. 'Narrative of expeditions along the coast of New South Wales, for the further discovery of its harbours from the year 1795 to 1799'. Archived from the original on 11 July 2011.

53. The Journal of Daniel Paine 1794–1797, p.39.

54. Museums Victoria, Collections, George Bass, Surgeon & Navigator (circa 1771-1803), [https://collections.museumsvictoria.com.au/articles/10413].

55. Wikipedia - Sydney Cove (1796 ship). [https://en.wikipedia.org/wiki/Sydney_Cove_(1796_ship).

56. "Timeline 1 (1791–1862)". www.illawarracoal.com. Retrieved 12 November 2015.

57. Roe, Margriet (1966). "Hayes, Sir John (1768–1831)". Australian Dictionary of Biography. Melbourne University Press. ISSN 1833-7538. Retrieved 17 October 2013 – via National Centre of Biography, Australian National University.

58. McCaffrey, Frank (1922). op. cit., p.11-12.

59. "Lady Nelson", Tasmania [https://www.ladynelson.org.au/history/short-history]).

60. Wikipedia - "Jorgen Jorgensen" {https://en.wikipedia.org/wiki/Jørgen_Jørgensen].

61. Wikipedia - "HMS Lady Nelson" (1798) [https://en.wikipedia.org/wiki/HMS_Lady_Nelson_(1798)}.

2

EXPLORERS OF THE SHOALHAVEN & ILLAWARRA

The story of John Frawley and his family is closely tied to the Shoalhaven, Illawarra, and Maneroo regions on the South Coast of New South Wales. To fully appreciate their journey, it's important to understand how this part of Australia was discovered and developed during the colony's first 50 years.

In the early years of white settlement, exploration south of Sydney was limited and primarily conducted by sea. Land-based expeditions were rare, as the colony's early Governors prioritized defense, self-sufficiency, and expansion westward and southwestward, and especially concentrated on efforts to cross the Blue Mountains. The South Coast, considered largely barren at the time, remained a lower priority for exploration. However, the early 19th century marked the first significant attempts to explore and chart the regions directly south of Sydney.

Governor Philip Gidley King

Captain Philip Gidley King, R.N. (1758-1808), was invested with civil and military powers in New South Wales when he took up the duties as governor on the 28th September 1800, which he continued to hold until the 12th August 1806. But he was a weak man in many respects, as his power over certain members of the military authorities was such that they did much as they liked. King was nervous and frightened of troubles coming on him from within and from foreign parts. It was during his watch that a return of government held stock was conducted on 12th May 1804, "which included the holdings of five cattle stations of Parramatta, Toongabbie, Castle Hill, Seven Hills and Sydney that then comprised 17 bulls, 678 cows, 735 male calves, 672 female calves, 129 bullocks."[1]

Clash of Cultures

As the colony developed, so too did the number of vessels to Sydney increase, and some of these had reason to take shelter along the coast, which often involved unintended, but violent clashes with the Aborigines. These encounters often resulted in a collision of cultures between the technologically superior whites, and the innocent blacks, who like the kangaroos and koalas had been held captive and isolated in Australia since the land bridge to Asia had closed some 40,000 years previously.

One of the first of such clashes occurred in July of 1804, when the sloop "Contest" arrived in Sydney from Jervis Bay, with a report that the crew and a detachment of soldiers had been involved in a skirmish with the local Aborigines, with one native being killed.[2]

The next year brought news of the crew of the cutter "Nancy", which was wrecked to the south of Jervis Bay on the 18th April 1805. Eleven survivors reached that bay on the 20th April and guided by an Aborigine, they trekked overland to Sydney, whence they arrived on the 1st of May.[3]

In October of that year, after six persons had left from Sydney in a whaleboat making for Kings Island, a report was received of the spearing of a Mr Murrell by natives at Twofold Bay, with the killing of two natives there. The account given was as follows:[4]

> "That everywhere along the coast the natives wore a menacing appearance, and manifested a wish to attack them. Upon making Twofold Bay, they percived a small group round a fire, who greeted them in a very friendly tone, but a flight of spears was soonafter thrown... with one of the weapons, most dangerously barbed, lodging in Mr Murrell's side. They made for the boat, leaving their inhuman assailants to express their joy of the barberous event by reechoed peals of mirth, and were soon out of reach. Unable to proceed for their destination they reversed their course, but could only reach Botany Bay, on account of contrary wind."

This was followed a month later by a report by Mr Rushworth, master of the "Fly", who received several spear wounds at Jervis Bay, and of Thomas Evans, who was killed.[5]

Then in January 1806, the sloop "George" was wrecked at Twofold Bay. After the vessel was beached a large party of Aborigines set the nearby grass on fire and threw spears, but were dispersed when Captain Birbeck and his men opened fire, killing several of them. A section of the crew later sailed to Sydney, whilst the remainder walked overland from Jervis Bay.[6] In April, further disagreeable accounts were received by the "Venus", another private colonial vessel, of the inimical disposition of the natives at Twofold Bay. The sealers were employed there in the hope of getting off the "George" or her iron-work, but they were obliged to act with the greatest caution for fear of assassination. The gang of 11 were soon attacked en-masse by a large group of natives, causing them to open fire and kill nine of their assailants, whereupon all the rest made off. "To intimidate them it was thought advisable to suspend those that fell on the limbs of trees, but before daylight the next morning they were taken down, and carried off."[7]

By May a report was received of the fate of some of the survivors of the "George" wrecked at Twofold Bay in January, who had travelled overland from Jervis Bay and were involved in a skirmish with the natives.[8]

> "About the 20th May, one of their party 'Yankey Cambell' went missing and had presumably fallen victim to native barbarity, with the white men later being attacked by a large group of Aboriginals

on the beach, which was answered by musketry. The engagement continued with the intended victims of native animosity being rushed like a torrent, who fled to their boat of only 7 feet keel, which was only reached with extreme difficulty. Beyond the reach of their missiles, they watched as the stock were massacred and everything destroyed by their assailants, yet were thankful for their deliverance. They abandoned their boat at Jervis Bay and subsisted entirely on shellfish along the coast walk, but were assisted by two Sydney natives, which enabled them to complete their tedious and distressing travel in eight days."

Sydney Gazette & NSW Advertiser, 18 May 1806

Another unfortunate incident was reported in 1808 when three of the crew of the colonial vessel "Fly", were murdered by Aborigines at Batemans Bay. The "Fly" had sailed for Kangaroo Island, but being overtaken by bad weather and contrary winds was obliged to take shelter at Batemans Bay, and to send on shore for water. The three unfortunate persons whose fate it was to fall under the barbarity of the natives, were sent on shore with a cask, but were confronted by a large group of natives. The three men quickly returned to their boat, but had no sooner put off from the shore than a flight of spears was thrown, which continued until all three fell from their oars. The natives immediately took and manned the boat, with a number of canoes preparing to attack the vessel, which only narrowly escaped their fury by cutting the cable and standing out to sea. The names of the murdered men were Charles Freeman, Thomas Bly and Robert Goodlet...[9] and relations with the Aborigines afterwards descended into a state of 'kill or be killed.'

Exploring the Shoalhaven

In the meantime, Governor King had despatched Capt. William Kent (1760-1812), with a number of labourers and ample provisions, to explore the coast as far south as the Shoalhaven. Captain Kent, of "HMS Buffalo", in company with James Meehan (1774-1826) returned on Sunday, 3rd March 1805, from a five week examination of the coast about Shoals Haven. After walking 18 miles they were fortunate to find a small boat lost in a gale of wind exactly at the place they wanted to make use of it, to trace the river 18 miles up when it became impassable. Unfortunately, they reported the entrance to the river was closed by a bar on which there is a constant surf.[10]

Following a stint at the Cape of Good Hope, George William Evans (1780-1852) was persuaded by Capt. Kent to go to New South Wales, and he arrived at Port Jackson in "HMS Buffalo" on 16 October 1802, where in August 1803 he was appointed acting surveyor-general. He commenced exploring and by September 1804 had discovered the Warragamba River, and penetrated upstream to the present site of Warragamba Dam.

Further troubles came upon the head of Governor King with droughts, cattle disease and floods. It is recorded that in the month of March, 1806, one of the heaviest floods occurred that up to that time had ever visited the Hawkesbury. It rained every day for a month, causing loss of life and property. The loss of property was estimated at £35,000, with several persons being drowned, and those who escaped with their lives had to face starvation.

After 1800, ideas of settlement along the south east coast were temporarily shelved partly because of the unfavourable report furnished by George Bass and also at that time, the Hawkesbury and Hunter River districts provided enough land for expansion. Nevertheless, the government always had South Coast colonisation on its mind and by the end of 1804, Governor King was once again discussing the possibilities with London, writing to the Secretary of State, Lord Portland:

> "The next object of research will be the Shoalshaven, between this place and Port Jarvis."
>
> *Governor King, 6th January 1805*

Kent & Meehan at Shoalhaven

Almost immediately the acting Surveyor General, George Evans was instructed to carry out an investigation of the Shoalhaven with the following notice being published:

> "Acting Lieut. B. Kent of His Majesty's ship "Buffalo" and Mr. Evans, Surveyor, in the "Anne", Colonial cutter going to examine the entrance and course of the Shoal's Haven, 52 miles to the Southward of this place, are also detained by foul winds."
>
> *Sydney Gazette, 27th January 1805*

The notice was misleading as it is now known that Evans did not go, but instead sent his assistant James Meehan in his place. Meehan was at that time a convict on conditional pardon, and likely due to his lowly status, his name was ignored. The object of the expedition was the Shoalhaven River, not the Shoals Haven.

Lt. Kent and Meehan boarded the "Anne" on the 28th January 1805, but were unable to progress further than Botany Bay until the 4th February due to adverse winds. When they did arrive off the Shoalhaven River they were unable to enter due to the sandbar across the mouth and the heavy surf thrown up by the wind, whereupon the ship's boat was lost in the heavy seas. Kent continued south and entered Jervis Bay, where they spent several days putting the ship to rights after the rough passage, so it was not until the 11th February that Kent, Meehan and their small party of sailors landed near present day Callala Beach, and embarked on their expedition to the Shoalhaven River.

They travelled a track north, reaching the southern bank of the Crookhaven near Billy's Islands, where the river opened into a lagoon, with Meehan describing the country in derogatory terms as "sandy scrub, swampy, and bad ground". Walking north, by extraordinary good fortune they found the boat that had been lost at sea the previous week, which was still in a usable condition. The boat had been "hauled up by the natives and covered with bark exactly at the place where they wanted to make use of it." This enabled them to row out of the Crookhaven, along the coast and into the Shoalhaven River, thus renewing their original goal.[11]

During the next three weeks they explored the river system, assessing the possibilities of future farming and described the north bank of the Shoalhaven as "apparently good soil, chiefly brush-covered, to the foot of the Coolangatta Mountain." The party penetrated as far west as the present day settlement of Burrier before turning back. They also followed what was later named Broughton Creek, nearly as far as the present day town of Berry. Kent and Meehan surveyed about 40km of the Shoalhaven River and 20km of Broughton Creek before returning to Jervis Bay and thence to Sydney. Kent's report appears to have been favourable, as Governor King relayed it to Charles Pratt, 1st Earl Camden in London:

> "The officer and surveyor who I sent to examine the country about Shoals Haven report much good land on the banks of the two small bar rivers, which will hereafter prove of great benefit to the extension of these settlements."
>
> *Governor King, 30th April 1805*

However, the matter rested there until some six years later when the incoming governor became interested in the area.[12] While sealers and whalers had been intermittently operating in these waters at least as far south as Jervis Bay, it was not until the arrival of Governor Lachlan Macquarie that possibilities of settlement were reconsidered. Macquarie visited Van Diemen's Land aboard the "Lady Nelson" in 1811 and had to take shelter in Jervis Bay on the outward journey due to bad weather. He spent two days there, walking with Mrs Macquarie on the mainland and being impressed by the 'stout well-made good looking natives.' The new governor was so impressed by the chances of settlement, that on his return to Sydney, he instructed the Deputy Surveyor George Evans to make a further examination.[13]

The 'Rum Rebellion' was brewing and King's real troubles were with the military authorities. These people went so far as to comment that…"the administration of Governor King was barren of good fruit." This was no doubt owing to his great antagonism to the military 'ring' whose influence, owing to his previous concessions, he found himself powerless to break. It was said that "the influence of the officers of the New South Wales Corps shortened King's period of service in the colony."[14]

Whalers evidently became well acquainted with the seaboard of New South Wales during the years from 1800 to 1806. It was also known that many hundreds of acres of land was good open forest country, and that much land along the seaboard was free from timber and covered with native grass that was only kept in check by hordes of marsupials. The official returns for 1806 were given as follows… "Quantity of land occupied by Government or granted to private individuals - 125,476 acres; quantity of land cleared - 16,624 acres. Average production of land in wheat - 7118 acres; in barley, maize, etc. - 5279 acres; of wheat per acre - 18 bushels. Number of horned cattle - 3264; of sheep - 16,501; of pigs - 14,300; of horses - 458; and of goats - 2900."[15]

While we have a great deal of information in certain directions, stores of records and more than we know how to use, little that is precise and serviceable about those brave pioneers of the bush or open forest country, the bushmen who penetrated the dense scrubs in search of cedar, and the cattlemen who took up the open country adjacent to those dense scrubs to raise bullocks to haul the timber to market.

These hardy men penetrated the deepest gullies and ravines in search of cedar. The finest trees were at all times where vegetation was the most luxuriant, and where the scrubby undergrowths were always the thickest. Their position in such places was that of isolation not at all times of a voluntary nature. Many of these sawyers were half-fed, ill-clothed mortals, who had escaped from the iron gangs, stockades or penal settlements, dreading capture. Having experienced 'torture,' they were the prey of the more cunning members of the society, who used them for selfish ends. The heavy scrubs in many of the gullies and gorges were considered dank, damp, and unhealthy, consequently many of the early sawyers died off early owing to the want of sunlight. They left their records behind, and passed to the 'Great Beyond.'

Before his departure on 28th September 1806, Governor King gave the incoming governor, Captain William Bligh, R.N. (1754-1817), a grant of 1000 acres of land. In return, on taking command Bligh gave Mrs. King a grant of 1000 acres as a token of mutual friendship. At this time, the population of the colony was estimated at 9000, of which number 8472 were in New South Wales and 528 at Hobart Town.[16]

Governor William Bligh, 1806-1808

In 1788 when on a visit to Tahiti in command of the ship "HMS Bounty", by order of the British Government to transport the breadfruit tree of the South Sea Islands to the West Indies, the sailors were allegedly harassed to such an extent by Bligh, that they mutinied, seized the ship, and set Bligh and his officers adrift in a launch. Bligh displayed such good seamanship that he covered 4,000 miles in the launch, and reached Timor safely. This drastic action was the means of making Captain Bligh an Admiral and a governor, as a few years later he was then considered a fit officer to rule the convict colony of New South Wales.

He was returned to England and was despatched again with two ships, the "Providence" and the "Assistant", and in due course landed in Van Dieman's Land, and spent 12 days there planting fruit-trees, acorns and vegetables. He was sometimes called "Bread Fruit Bligh," but he found trees did not flourish in Van Diemen's Land. His assistant botanist Mr. Brown however, landed at Adventure Bay, and planted the first apple tree on Tasmanian soil. Bligh's next visit to Tasmania was in 1808, immediately after the Rum Rebellion in Sydney. Between 1806 and 1808, Mr Brown made botanizing visits to beautiful Illawarra, and hence we have Mount Brown and Brown's Mountain.[17]

Exploring the Illawarra

The Illawarra consists of a grassy coastal plain, narrow in the north and wider in the south, bounded by the Tasman Sea on the east and the mountainous, almost impassable Illawarra escarpment, forming the eastern edge of the Southern Highlands plateau, to the west. In the middle of the region is Lake Illawarra, a shallow lake formed when sediment built up at the entrance to a bay. The district extends from the southern hills of the Royal National Park in the north to the Shoalhaven River in the south, and today contains the thriving city of Wollongong, the fourth largest urban area in New South Wales.

The Illawarra region was originally inhabited by the Dharawal indigenous Australians *(see Appendix B)*. While the first Europeans to visit the area were the navigators George Bass and Matthew Flinders, who landed at Lake Illawarra in 1796, a few people had unofficially visited the Wollongong area in the early 1800s.[18] Possibly as early as 1807, noted bushman Joe Wild was assisting bird collectors to enter the area.[19] And although others may have come before, the first settlers of the region were likely to have been the cedar cutters, who cut and shipped cedar from Illawarra as early as 1810.[20]

> "cedar was carried from the inner shores of Lake Illawarra, in small craft, during convenient periods to Sydney in 1810, and bullock teams were used to haul cedar logs and planks to the edges of the Lake, for years before any real settlement took place."

In the course of a few years the white settlers learned to follow the tracks of the blacks into the several valleys and gorges of the Illawarra and the Shoalhaven River districts, at a time when things were very unsettled under the regime of Governor Bligh.

During a drought in 1815 all the country around Liverpool was burnt up, consequently Charles Throsby and a few others who had good cattle asked Governor King's leave to send cattle to Illawarra. Captain Nicholls, a relation of the old Major, brought them down in a boat and put them ashore at Five Islands, with two ex-convicts being placed in charge. The foregoing remarks are quite in keeping with statements that have been made by the descendants of the old time sawyers...

> "The chief point touched in the early history of Illawarra, goes to prove that our history is not a myth as it would appear to those who lived outside of the district. Most writers are compelled to study Illawarra from the outside, as the early Governors merely mentioned its existence, as viewed from the sea. It was not the case with the real settlers who took the risks and breathed the air of solitude. Such men saw instinctively what the authorities failed to understand."

The early pioneers of Illawarra did much to wear down the rage of governors, and saved and preserved hundreds of valuable cattle from the ravages of disease, droughts and floods. The region was circumscribed by natural barriers, hence its difficulties of ingress caused it to be nature's granary and a natural stockyard for a given number of cattle in all seasons.[21]

"We are all aware that no human skill known to the old pioneer of Illawarra could turn the barren rocky passes over the coast range into easy ways of ingress and egress for cattle, nor could they, with the material at their command, construct safe harbours. They had to take things as they found them. Yet, it is evident by such skill and forethought as they possessed, they employed their limited resources to the best advantage, and thereby turned even the privations of their day into such blessings, that in a short time they became a great power for good."

As the 19th century dawned, the embers of the 1798 Irish Rebellion still smoldered. Though the uprising had been crushed, its spirit lived on, with many Irishmen continuing to face arrest, conviction, and forced transportation to New South Wales. From the distant colony, these events may have seemed like echoes from another world, yet their impact shaped the Irish diaspora in ways both seen and unseen. While the rugged South Coast of New South Wales was gradually being explored, across the ocean, John Frawley's ancestors were navigating a very different struggle, one that would set the course for generations to come. Their story begins next...

References

1. McCaffrey, Frank (1922) 'The History Of Illawarra And Its Pioneers,' Johns Sands Ltd, Sydney, p.13.
2. Sydney Gazette & NSW Advertiser, 22nd July 1804.
3. Sydney Gazette & NSW Advertiser, 5th May 1805.
4. Sydney Gazette & NSW Advertiser, 27th October 1805.
5. Sydney Gazette & NSW Advertiser, 8th December 1805.
6. Sydney Gazette & NSW Advertiser, 16th February 1806.
7. Sydney Gazette & NSW Advertiser, 6th April 1806.
8. Sydney Gazette & NSW Advertiser, 18 May 1806.
9. Sydney Gazette & NSW Advertiser, 15th May 1808.
10. McCaffrey, Frank (1922). op.cit., p.13.
11. Pleaden, Ronald F. (1990). 'Coastal Explorers,' Milton/Ulladulla & District Historical Society, p.23-26.
12. Ibid.
13. Ibid, p.27.
14. Ibid.
15. Ibid.
16. Ibid.
17. McCaffrey, Frank (1922). op.cit., p.16.
18. Jervis, James, (1942). 'Illawarra: A Century of History' JRAHS, XXVIII, p.273.
19. Ibid.
20. Hagan, Jim & Andrew Wells, (ed, 1997). 'A History of Wollongong', University of Wollongong, Wollongong, p.24.
21. McCaffrey, Frank (1922). op.cit., p.21.

Salt, Soil & Second Chances

The Ancestors & Descendants of John & Mary Ann Frawley of NSW & Queensland

▲ = Served in Australian Military Forces

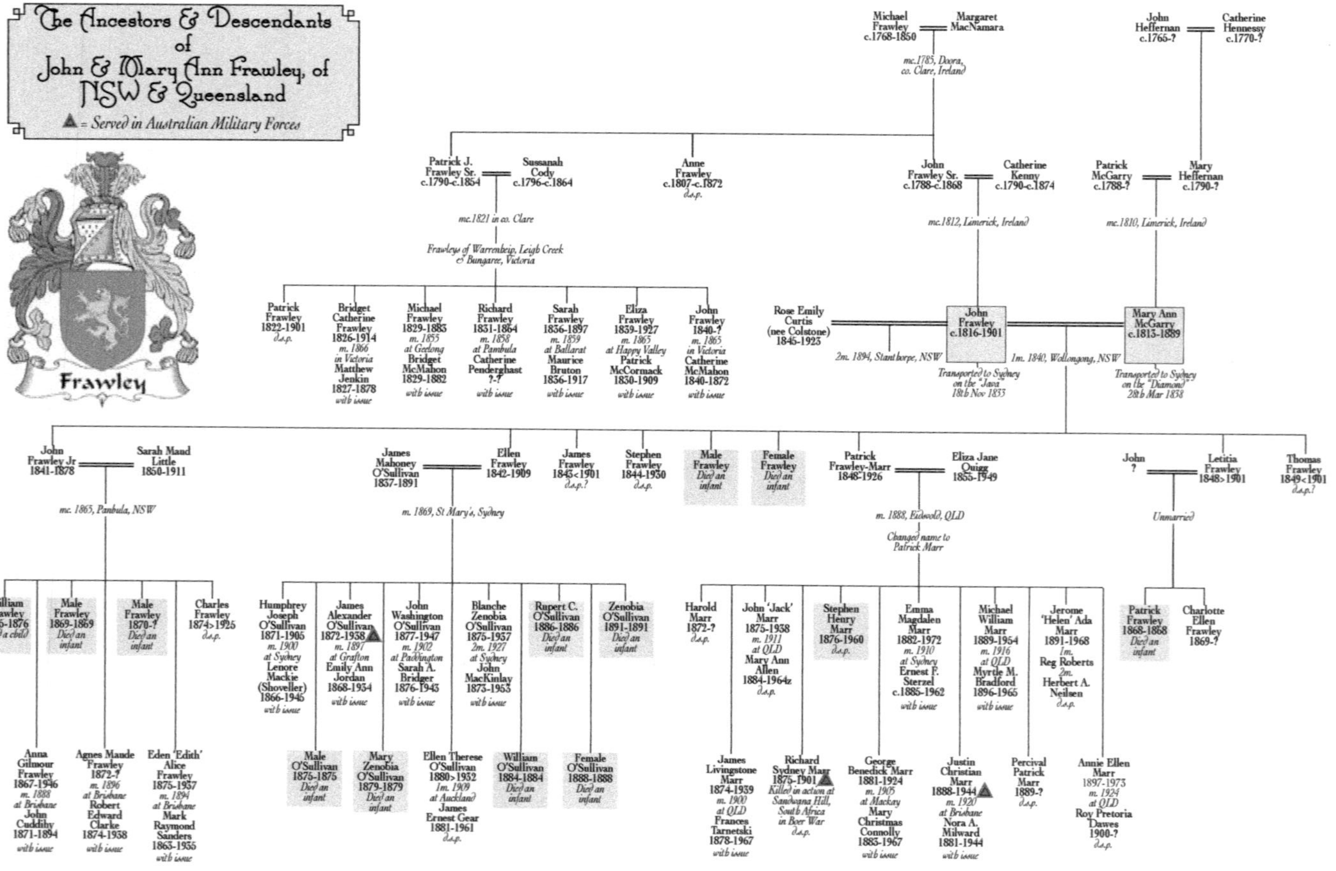

3

THE FRAWLEY ANCESTORS

Although John Frawley was not born until 1816, his story begins long before then. This chapter traces the origins of the Frawley name and delves into the earliest known ancestors of the family, who appear to have lived at Doora, near Ennis in Co. Clare, in western Ireland. Understanding their history provides essential context for John Frawley's own life and legacy.

In addition to exploring the Frawley lineage, this chapter examines the broader historical landscape of Ireland, particularly in Limerick, between 1800 and 1816. This was a turbulent period marked by significant events that shaped the country's social, political, and economic fabric. The Act of Union (1801) formally united Ireland with Great Britain, dissolving the Irish Parliament and intensifying tensions between Irish nationalists and the British Government. The early 19th century also saw widespread hardship due to economic struggles, agrarian unrest, and the ongoing impact of the Penal Laws, which disproportionately affected Catholic families like the Frawleys.

Limerick, a city with deep political and economic significance, was particularly affected by these changes. The Napoleonic Wars (1803–1815) fueled both economic opportunities and challenges, as trade fluctuated and many Irishmen were recruited into the British Army. At the same time, secret societies such as the 'Whiteboys' and the 'Rockites' emerged in response to oppressive landlord policies and rural poverty, leading to unrest in the region.

By weaving together family history with the broader historical backdrop, this chapter provides a foundation for understanding the world John Frawley was born into and the legacy he inherited.

Irish Australians have emerged as a distinct ethnic group, tracing their ancestry to Ireland. Since the late 18th century, they have played a significant role in shaping Australia's history. The first arrivals included both convicts, many of whom were prisoners of war from the 1798 Irish Rebellion, and free settlers seeking new opportunities. The great Irish Famine and the economic hardships that followed drove many more to Australia, where they made substantial contributions across various fields.

By the late 19th century, Irish Australians comprised up to a third of the country's population. According to the 2011 Australian Census, 2,087,800 people identified as having Irish ancestry, either alone or in combination with another heritage. This made Irish ancestry the third most commonly reported, after English and Australian, representing 10.4% of the total population. Additionally, the Australian Embassy in Dublin estimates that up to 30% of Australians have some degree of Irish heritage.

Limerick & Its History

The history of Limerick stretches back to its establishment by the Vikings as a walled city on King's Island, on the River Shannon in the year 812AD. Luimneach originally referred to the general area along the banks of the Shannon Estuary as 'Loch Luimnigh'. The original pre-Viking and Viking era settlement on Kings Island was known in the annals as 'Inis Sibhtonn' and 'Inis an Ghaill Duibh'. The earliest provable settlement dates from 812 however, history suggests the presence of earlier settlements in the area surrounding King's Island.[1]

Antiquity's map-maker, Ptolemy, produced in 150 the earliest map of Ireland, showing a place called "Regia" at the same site as King's Island. History also records an important battle involving Cormac mac Airt in 221 and a visit by St. Patrick in 434 to baptise an Eóganachta king, 'Carthann the Fair'. Saint Munchin, the first bishop of Limerick died in 652, indicating the city was by then a place of some note. In 812 the Vikings sailed up the Shannon and pillaged the city, burned the monastery of Mungret, but were forced to flee when the Irish retaliated and killed many of their number.[2]

The Normans redesigned the city in the 12th century and added much of its notable architecture, such as King John's Castle and St Mary's Cathedral. In early medieval times Limerick was at the centre of the Kingdom of Thomond, which corresponds to the present day Mid West region however, the Kingdom also included North Kerry and parts of South Offaly. One of the kingdom's most notable kings was Brian Boru, ancestor of the O'Brien's of the Dalcassian Clan. The word Thomond is synonymous with the region and is retained in place names such as Thomondgate, Thomond Bridge and Thomond Park.[3]

Limerick in the 16th and 17th centuries was often called the most beautiful city in Ireland. The English-born judge Luke Gernon, a resident of Limerick, wrote in 1620 that at his first sight of the city he had been amazed at its magnificence with "lofty buildings of marble, like the colleges in Oxford."[4]

During the civil wars of the 17th century the city played a pivotal role, besieged by Oliver Cromwell (1599-1658), in 1651 and twice by the Williamites in the 1690's. The 'Treaty of Limerick' ended the Williamite War in Ireland, which was fought between supporters of the Catholic King James II (Jacobites) and the Protestant King William of

Orange (Williamites). The treaty offered toleration to Catholicism and full legal rights to Catholics that swore an oath of loyalty to William III and Mary II, which was of national significance as it ensured closer British and Protestant dominance over Ireland. However, the articles of the Treaty protecting Catholic rights were not passed by the Protestant Irish Parliament, which rather updated the Penal Laws against Catholics with major implications for Irish history. Reputedly the Treaty was signed on the Treaty Stone, an irregular block of limestone which once served as a mounting block for horses, and Limerick is sometimes known as the Treaty City. This turbulent period earned the city its motto: "Urbs antiqua fuit studisque asperrima belli", meaning an ancient city well studied in the arts of war.[5]

The peace that followed the turmoil of the late 17th century allowed the city to prosper mostly through trade in the 18th century. During this time Limerick established itself as one of Ireland's major commercial ports exporting agricultural produce from the 'Golden Vale', one of Ireland's most fertile areas, to Britain and America. This increase in trade and wealth, particularly amongst the city's merchant classes saw a rapid expansion of the city as Georgian Limerick began to take shape. This prosperity gave the city its present-day look including the extensive terraced streets of fine Georgian townhouses, which remain in the city centre today. The Waterford and Limerick Railway linked the city to the Dublin–Cork Railway line in 1848 and to Waterford in 1853. The opening of a number of secondary railways in the subsequent decades developed Limerick as a regional centre of communications. However, the economic downturn from the European conflicts of the French Revolution and Napoleonic eras, and following the Act of Union (1801), as well as the impact of the Great Irish Famine of 1848 caused much of the 19th century to be a troubled period.[6]

The Frawley Ancestors

A historical connection has been suggested between Irish Australians and Aboriginal Australians, particularly those of mixed descent, based on their shared experience of British oppression. Whether arriving as convicts, settlers, or political exiles, Irish migrants laid deep roots in Australia, roots that would eventually lead to the 1816 birth of John Frawley, the 'boyo' from Limerick. What better way to begin this genealogy than by exploring the origins of the Frawley surname?

The Surname of Frawley

The Frawleys were the paternal ancestors of John Frawley. In Ireland, the Frawley surname comes from the Irish gaelic name O'Fearghail, which means 'man of valour' with its origin appearing in Leinster, Ireland. However, it tends to be generally a medieval English surname and is locational from various places called Fawley in the counties of Buckinghamshire, Hampshire, Herefordshire and Berkshire.[7] The surname Frawley derives from the old English pre-7th century word 'filithe', meaning a hay field, with 'leah', a clearing in a forest, whilst 'Fawley' in Buckinghamshire has for its first element the old English word 'fealg', meaning fallow land, although why a place would apparently be permanent fallow land doesn't seem logical. Fawley in Berkshire has the word 'felam' as its prefix, which possibly denotes a forest frequented by fallow deer. However, there is no such place recorded as Frawley, and the records suggest that the intrusive 'r' was probably added to Fawley in the London area as an aid to pronunciation.[8]

Examples of the surname taken from surviving registers of the diocese of Greater London include: Thomas Fowley, who married Jone Fletcher at St Margarets, Westminster, on May 27th 1543; Richard Fawly, a witness at the church of St Christopher le Stocks, on August 19th 1593; William Fawley who was christened on May 29th 1692 at St. Brides church, Fleet Street; and Andrew Frawley, the son of Andrew and Catherine Frawley, who was christened at Endell Street lying in hospital, on April 18th 1771.[9]

Research has shown that Frawley ancestors have appeared under many spelling variants ie. Fawley, Fraley, Frayley, Frewley, Frailey, Frauley, Fawly, Fowley, Frawly, and Frawley, although the surname is generally uncommon. The distribution of families sharing the relatively uncommon name of Frawley at the time of the 1891 England and Wales Census was relatively small, ranging from only 48 to 113 family units. The main concentrations across England being in Lancashire, Yorkshire and London. However, the vast majority of Frawleys at this time resided in Ireland, was a concentration in and around the town of Doora and nearby Ennis, in County Clare.[10]

Famous & Notable Frawleys

William Clement Frawley (1887-1966, no known relation) found much work as a character actor with roles in comedies, dramas, musicals, Westerns and romances.[11] He was an American vaudevillian actor, best remembered for playing landlord 'Fred Mertz' in the American television sitcom "I Love Lucy", and 'Bub O'Casey' in the television comedy series "My Three Sons", as well as the political advisor to the judge character in the film "Miracle on 34th Street" (1947).[12]

James Joseph Frawley (1936-2019, no known relation) was an American director and actor. He was a member of the Actors Studio since around 1961, and was best known for directing "The Muppet Movie" (1979) and 'The Monkees' television series.[13]

While the surname Frawley likely originated in County Clare, Ireland, from the Gaelic name "O'Frailigh," meaning "descendant of Frailigh." This name could be linked to the early Irish nobility and may have arrived with Gaelic settlers during the early medieval period. The region's rich history of Viking invasions and Norman conquests also influenced the surname's presence, as these groups interacted with local populations, resulting in the assimilation of names and customs. The Frawleys may also have been part of the Gaelic Irish clans that thrived in County Clare, influenced by the region's agricultural economy and the significance of land ownership.

Additionally, the migration of Irish families to other regions during the Great Famine in the mid-19th century contributed to the dispersal of the Frawley surname globally. Unfortunately, little is known about our Frawley ancestors. The earliest confirmed mention of John Frawley's paternal ancestors is recorded on his 1894 second marriage certificate, to Rose Emily Curtis in Stanthorpe, Queensland. On that document, John Frawley identified his parents as John Frawley Sr., a clerk, and Catherine Kenny, both apparently residents of Limerick.

But due to a lack of records, no further details about John Frawley Sr. or Catherine Kenny have been found, making it difficult to trace their lineage with confidence. A possible record for a John Frawley Sr. suggests he may have died in Limerick, in 1868 at the age of 80, placing his birth around the year 1788. Unfortunately, this record does not provide information about his parents or an exact birthplace. Despite these uncertainties, the 1868 death notice remains the only registration in the International Genealogical Index (IGI) that aligns with the necessary timeframe for being the father of our ancestor John Frawley, who was born around 1816 and transported to Sydney as a convict in 1833.

Frawleys in Victoria

In a recent development in 2023, a family booking into Ribbon Gum Lodge in Katoomba, with guests bearing the uncommon name of Frawley, revealed somewhat of a breakthrough. I couldn't resist asking about their ancestry, to which they very kindly supplied a lengthy list of ancestors, and a modest booklet entitled "From Clare to Bungaree", by Ray Frawley, which provided a detailed coverage of the family of Patrick and Susan Frawley, and the emigration of their family to Victoria. This fortuitous incident established a clear family connection, which has enabled the addition of Michael Frawley (c.1768-1864) and his wife Margaret MacNamara as the paternal grandparents of our ancestor, John Frawley the convict, although at this stage, we know nothing more than their names, and the fact that they likely resided in County Clare (*see chapter 13*).

The Kenny Ancestors

Unfortunately, just as little is known about our Kenny ancestors. The earliest confirmed mention of John Frawley's maternal ancestors being the same 1894 second marriage certificate, to Rose Emily Curtis in Stanthorpe, Queensland. On that document, John Frawley identified his mother as Catherine Kenny, who was apparently residing with her husband John Frawley Sr, in Limerick. While we face the same frustrating lack of information about John Frawley's maternal ancestors, we can nevertheless dive into the origins of the Kenny surname and uncover its rich history.

The Surname of Kenny

As a surname, the eponym 'Kenny' is a diminutive of several different given names. In Ireland, the surname is an Anglicisation of the Irish Ó'Cionnaith, sometimes spelled Ó'Cionnaoith. It is also a name common from Waterford to Cork, which is derived from MacKenny. One bearer of the name was Cainnech of Aghadoe, better known in English as Saint Canice, a 6th century Irish priest and missionary after whom the city and county of Kilkenny is also named.[14] It is thought that the Ó Cionnaith sept was part of the Uí Maine kingdom, based in Connacht. Within this region, the name is associated traditionally with the counties of Galway and Roscommon.

The surname Kenny is ranked at number 76 in the list of most common surnames in Ireland. Other spellings include O'Kenny, Kenney, Kennie, Kinnie and Kinny. Kenny (or Kenney), now common in Britain as well as Ireland, can be of Scottish or Irish origin. In both cases the name is derived from the popular Gaelic personal name 'Cionaodha', thought to be made up of two elements 'cion', meaning love or affection, and 'Aodh', the name of the pre-Christian god of fire. It might therefore be translated as "cherished by Aodh" or, perhaps, "fiery love." In addition the purely Irish 'O'Coinnigh' and 'O'Coinne' have been anglicised as Kenny.[15]

The surname came into being independently in a number of places in Ireland, including Tyrone, Donegal/Leitrim and Down, where the original Irish was 'O'Coinne'. The most prominent family of this name however, arose in the area of east Galway and south Roscommon known in ancient times as 'Ui'Maine', where they were of the same stock as the Maddens, and it is in Galway and Roscommon that the name of Kenny is still most frequent today.[16]

Famous & Notable Kennys

Born in Dublin, James Kenney (1780-1849, no known relation) was one of the most successful and prolific playwrights of his day, and author of more than 50 plays. His reputation has not prospered, but Lord Byron wrote of him: "Kenney's World - ah, where is Kenney's wit? - tires the sad gallery, lulls the listless pit."[17]

Sister Elizabeth Kenny (1886-1952, no known relation), was an Australian nurse who became widely known for the treatment she developed for paralysed children. Despite widespread opposition from the medical establishment, her methods, which involved stimulation and physiotherapy instead of casts and splints, eventually gained acceptance. The Kenny Institute in Minneapolis, USA is named after her.[18]

William Kenny (1846-1921, no known relation) QC, was an Irish judge and Liberal Unionist politician. Kenny was born in Dublin, the only son of Edward Kenny, solicitor, of Kilrush, County Clare, and his wife, Catherine (née Murphy). Kenny married Mary Coffey on 13 August 1873, and produced a family of eight children.[19]

John Frawley Sr. & Catherine Kenny

John Frawley Sr. and Catherine Kenny lived in County Limerick during the late 18th and early 19th centuries, a period of immense social and political upheaval in Ireland. Born around the 1780s, they would have come of age amid the turmoil of the 1798 Irish Rebellion, when the United Irishmen, inspired by the American and French Revolutions, sought to overthrow British rule. While there is little recorded about their personal lives, they were undoubtedly shaped by the economic hardship and tensions of the time, as Limerick, an important port city, was deeply affected by trade restrictions, agrarian unrest, and growing nationalist sentiment. The Act of Union in 1801 further altered the landscape of Irish governance, binding Ireland to Britain and intensifying resentment among the rural poor, many of whom struggled under oppressive landlordism and rising rents.

Despite these challenges, John and Catherine endured, raising a family in a time when survival itself was an achievement. Their son, John Frawley (c.1816–1901), would later become entangled in the harsh realities of 19th-century Ireland, finding himself charged with stealing clothes and sentenced to transportation to Australia, a fate that befell many impoverished Irishmen. The early 19th century in Limerick saw the rise of secret societies like the Whiteboys, who resisted eviction and high tithes, suggesting that ordinary people like the Frawleys and Kennys navigated a world of quiet resistance and resilience. The Napoleonic Wars (1803–1815) brought both hardship and opportunity, as increased military demand temporarily boosted the economy but also conscripted Irishmen into service. Though we may never know the specifics of their daily lives, John and Catherine's survival through these tumultuous decades speaks to the strength and endurance of those who lived in the shadow of history's grand events, shaping the generations that followed them.

John Frawley, the Patriarch

John Frawley Sr. and Catherine Kenny likely married in the aftermath of the 1798 Irish Rebellion, a time of great upheaval when Irish patriots took a stand against English rule. Their lives unfolded in the heart of Limerick, a city steeped in history and resilience.

What we do know of John Frawley Sr. is that he worked as a clerk and that the Frawley family called Limerick home. A possible death record found in Family Search (IGI) suggests that a John Frawley of Limerick was born around 1788, but without concrete evidence, we cannot confirm if he was the father of John Frawley (c.1816–1901).

Catherine Kenny, the Matriarch

The mother of John Frawley (c.1816–1901), Catherine Kenny, remains an elusive figure. Though records have been scarce, she was likely born between 1795 and 1800, possibly in Limerick. Despite exhaustive searches, no confirmed details about her marriage or death have surfaced, leaving her story largely untold. While no further details about John Frawley Sr. or Catherine Kenny have been found, their legacy, nevetheless lives on through their descendants, who continue to piece together the fragments of their past.

The 1798 Irish Rebellion

The 1798 Irish Rebellion,[20] which occurred around the time that John Frawley Sr. and catherine Kenny were residing in Limerick, was a defining moment in Ireland's history, and while its battles were fought primarily in Ulster and Wexford, its impact rippled across the entire country, including Limerick, where John Frawley Sr. and Catherine Kenny lived. The rebellion was driven by the Society of United Irishmen, a revolutionary group founded in 1791 and inspired by the American and French Revolutions. The society first emerged in Belfast, where Presbyterians predominated, and later expanded to Dublin, attracting a mix of Catholics and Protestants. Their goals were parliamentary reform based on universal male suffrage, full Catholic emancipation, and, ultimately, an end to British rule in Ireland.

By 1795, the movement had evolved into a secret, military-style organization, fueled by an alliance between radical Presbyterians and discontented working-class groups. Agrarian unrest was widespread, and many Irish peasants, already involved in secret societies of their own, joined the United Irishmen. Hoping for foreign support, the radical Irishman Theobald Wolfe Tone (1763–1798) traveled to France in early 1796 to seek aid. That same year, a French expedition led by General Lazare Hoche (1768–1797) set sail for Ireland. However, storms scattered the fleet, and though some ships reached Bantry Bay, County Cork, but no troops were landed, dashing hopes of a successful rebellion.

The British Government responded with force. In 1796, it passed the Insurrection Act and suspended habeas corpus, granting authorities sweeping powers to suppress dissent. In 1797, General Gerard Lake (1744–1808) launched a campaign in the north, confiscating private arms and shutting down 'The Northern Star', a radical Belfast newspaper. As tensions escalated in early 1798, both the United Irishmen and the government prepared for battle.

The rebellion erupted in May 1798, though it remained concentrated in eastern Ulster and Wexford. Northern rebels suffered defeats at Antrim and Ballinahinch, while in Wexford, the uprising took on a sectarian character, with Catholic rebels attacking Protestants, further deepening religious divisions. Though the Wexford insurgents won key victories, they failed to capture strategic towns like New Ross and Arklow. By mid-June, government forces under General Lake had gathered in Wexford, crushing the rebellion at Vinegar Hill on 21st June.

Just as the uprising seemed over, a small French force landed near Killala, securing a brief victory at Castlebar before being surrounded and captured. The British response was ruthless with many Irish rebels were executed or transported to the penal colony of New South Wales.

For John Frawley Sr. and Catherine Kenny, the rebellion would have been impossible to ignore. As residents of Limerick, they lived in a city deeply affected by political turmoil. The extent of their involvement, whether in active opposition to the rebels or as mere witnesses to the unrest, remains uncertain. However, as a literate man working as a clerk, John Frawley Sr. may have had incentives to align with the British administration. Whether he quietly supported the status quo or merely sought stability in uncertain times is unknown, but what is certain is that he and Catherine Kenny married soon after, starting a family in post-rebellion Ireland. Their son, John Frawley Jr., was born in Limerick around 1816, and while his likely siblings were Patrick and Anne Frawley, it would have been unusual for John Frawley Jr., to be an only child.

The Irish Rebellion may have ended in 1798, but its effects lasted for generations. Whether as beneficiaries of British rule or cautious observers of the political landscape, the Frawleys of Limerick navigated a world forever changed by the struggle for Irish independence.

The first decade of the 19th century was a time of upheaval and hardship for John Frawley's parents as Ireland was wracked by social unrest, economic instability, and political turmoil. The aftershocks of the 1798 Rebellion lingered, with British rule tightening its grip and the effects of the Act of Union in 1801 reshaping the nation's future. For many, survival meant navigating poverty, land displacement, and the ever-present specter of transportation for even minor offenses. It was in this world of uncertainty and desperation that John Frawley's fate took a decisive turn.

Convicted and sentenced to transportation in 1833, John Frawley was cast into the vast unknown of the penal colony of New South Wales. What became of him upon his arrival, and how his story unfolded in a land so distant from his Irish roots, is central to this book. To understand the world he entered, we must first explore the early European incursions along the South Coast of New South Wales. Long before organized settlement, the rugged shores of the Shoalhaven and Illawarra districts lured sealers, cedar-cutters, and squatters, each carving out a precarious existence in the untamed frontier. It is here, in the shadow of towering cliffs and dense forests, that the next chapter of this story begins.

References

1. Wikipedia - Limerick, op. cit.
2. Ibid.
3. Ibid.
4. Gernon, Luke (1620). 'A Discourse of Ireland', edited by C.L. Falkiner 1904.
5. Wikipedia - Limerick, op. cit.
6. Ibid.
7. Wikipedia - Limerick [https://en.wikipedia.org/wiki/Limerick].
8. Surname DB - Frawley [https://www.surnamedb.com/Surname/Frawley.
9. Ibid.
10. Ancestry - Frawley [https://www.ancestry.com/name-origin?surname=frawley.
11. Wikipedia - William Frawley [https://en.wikipedia.org/wiki/William_Frawley].
12. IMDB - William Frawley [https://www.imdb.com/name/nm0292433/].
13. D23 - James Joseph Frawley - Celebrate 40 Years of The Muppet Movie with These "Muppetational" Facts [https://d23.com/the-muppet-movie-facts/].
14. Surname DB - Kenny [https://www.surnamedb.com/Surname/Kenny.
15. Ibid.
16. Ibid.
17. Wikipedia - James Kenney (dramatist), [https://en.wikipedia.org/wiki/James_Kenney_(dramatist).
18. Wikipedia - Elizabeth Kenney [https://en.wikipedia.org/wiki/Elizabeth_Kenny].
19. Wikipedia - William Kenny (Irish politician) [https://en.wikipedia.org/wiki/William_Kenny_(Irish_politician)].
20. Brittanica - The 1798 Irish Rebellion [https://www.britannica.com/event/Irish-Rebellion-Irish-history-1798].

4

LAND GRANTS & SQUATTERS

In 1833, John Frawley was torn from his homeland, sentenced to transportation, and cast adrift into the vast unknown of the New South Wales penal colony. What became of him in this distant land, so far from the green fields of Ireland, is a story of survival, reinvention, and fate. But to truly understand his journey, we must first step back into the world he entered.

Long before the first prison ships arrived, the rugged shores of the Shoalhaven and Illawarra districts beckoned the bold and the desperate. Whalers braved treacherous waters, cedar-cutters hacked their way through dense forests, and squatters laid claim to the untamed frontier, all in pursuit of fortune or survival. It was a land of opportunity and peril, where towering cliffs and ancient rainforests concealed both danger and promise. It was here that John Frawley stepped into the wild beauty and harsh realities of an unforgiving coast.

The land system from 1788, that is, from the foundation of the colony to the arrival of Governor Sir Richard Bourke (1777-1855), in 1831 is a matter of concern only to those who wish to study misfit administration. Up to the year 1824 the regulations for the disposal of land were left entirely in the hands of the governor for the time being. Land was, in the early days of the colony, bestowed on any man, bond or free, who could undertake to support himself. As the colony progressed in wealth and population, certain situations became valuable and were eagerly sought by parties of influence, but large portions were held, especially as pastures, under free licenses of occupation.

The Australian magnates emulated the white slave system by means of rum. Those who had grants of land bartered their holdings to the rum magnates. Hundreds of small land grants were allowed to pass unnoticed by the authorities into the possession of a few wealthy individuals. A keg or a bottle of rum purchased large and small holdings prior to 1831, not only in Sydney and its immediate surroundings, but north, south and west of the capital for at least a distance of one hundred miles. The Illawarra did not escape the rum traffic, sometimes a pig or a goat was substituted and many holdings could be pointed out as the result of purchase by a bottle or a keg of rum. So corrupted had the system become that the following edict was issued:

"Lands granted from the Crown are prohibited to be sold, either directly or indirectly, for the term of five years, bearing date from June 8th, 1811."

By Command of His Excellency, J. F. Campbell Secretary, 1816 [1]

Governor Lachlan Macquarie, 1810-1821

Major General Lachlan Macquarie, CB (1762-1824)[2] was a British Army officer and colonial administrator from Scotland, who served as the fifth governor of New South Wales from 1810 to 1821, and played a leading role in the social, economic, and architectural development of the colony.[3] He is considered by historians to have had a crucial influence on the transition of New South Wales from a penal colony to a free settlement and therefore to have had a major role in the shaping of Australian society in the early 19th century.[4,5]

In 1812 a committee of the British House of Commons was appointed to examine the state of the colony of New South Wales. After examining a number of witnesses, including ex-Governors King and Bligh, a report was printed from which it appeared that the population amounted to a total of 10,454 persons, distributed in the following proportions:

> "The Sydney district - 6,158; Parramatta - 1,807; Hawkesbury - 2,389; Newcastle - 100; (of these, 5,513 were men and 2,200 women); military, 1,100; of the remainder, one-fourth to one-fifth were actually bond, the rest being free or freed from servitude by pardon. In addition, 1,321 were living in Van Diemen's Land, and 177 on Norfolk Island, but orders had been sent out to compel the voluntary settlers, who had adhered to that island after the Government establishment had been removed, to withdraw."

George Evans' Land Route to Sydney (1812)

Evans and his party left Sydney on the 26th March 1812 in the "Lady Nelson", and anchored in the shelter of Bowen Island at Jervis Bay the following day. On the 28th he commenced his survey at the south entrance and traversed the Bay's coastline, using chain and compass for about 30km. Despite being bitten by a snake, he set out on the 3rd April to survey a practicable land route from the Bay to Sydney. Skirting to the west of present day Nowra, Evans and his party ascended the Good Dog Mountain to a point just north of the present Cambewarra Lookout on the 7th April. The difficult ascent took over five hours. Having decided to make his way back to the coast Evans walked along the narrow neck of Cambewarra Mountain Range from Beaumont to Bellawongarah, sleeping overnight on top of Tapitallee Mountain. Looking west from here for nearly twenty kilometres Evans was the first recorded European to view Kangaroo Valley, and in the other direction the summit presented them with magnificent views back across the coastal plain:

> "One of the finest views I have ever seen; it would be impossible for a painter to beautify it; I took a sketch although I was much tired in travelling 3 miles."
>
> George W. Evans, 7th April 1812 [6]

Evans then found the way north west was just too difficult with vertical rock walls making further progress almost impossible. So they changed course on the 9th to pass north of present day Berry, noting the presence of cedar and commenting that "this part of the country would make a beautiful settlement." The party was travelling light and only carried rations for about a fortnight, so they likely didn't intend the survey to take long and by April 11th they were running out of food. After reaching the coast the party turned north and camped overnight on April 12th at the site of the future city of Wollongong, after which they turned inland, and finally arrived at Appin on the 17th April.[7]

After an interim period of farming, Capt. William Kent returned to survey the shores of Jervis Bay in March 1812, whence he led a small party overland on foot to Appin. This journey of two weeks was conducted under most arduous circumstances and resulted in the settlement of the Illawarra District during the drought years that soon followed. His success probably induced Governor Macquarie to select him for later tasks penetrating into the interior of New South Wales.[8]

A year later, Capt. Collins in another vessel called the "Matilda" sailed from Port Jackson on the 25th March 1813 for the purpose of exploring the Shoal Haven. They arrived on Wednesday 29th and stood into Jervis Bay, which was about 24 miles to the southward of Shoals Haven. After two unsuccessful attempts, a party consisting of a naval and military officer, Mr Archer, Deputy Commissary and the commander of the "Matilda", with six of the Samarangs and three of the ship's company, set out with three natives as guides, who staid by the party just 24 hours. The party possibly reached the southern bank of the Shoalhaven River, but after being deserted by the natives at a distance of 12 or 14 miles from the vessel, they were reduced to the necessity of abandoning the project.[9]

It was by a simple means of organisation, a primitive form of co-operation that a few settlers were enabled to endure and overcome difficulties, in a spirit, and with a success, which could not otherwise be attained. All the movements of these men were neither hurriedly made nor done in a spirit of haphazardness as the Illawarra was opened up. Scouts and advance agents such as the more daring convicts, assisted by Aboriginals were employed to report on the line of march, and the place to which it should lead. There were also labourers who did much of this pioneering work, who lie here and there today, in unknown graves, whose duty it was to remove obstacles to allow the stock to pass along the narrow passes in dangerous places on the mountain range.

The halts and advances were to a great extent regulated by these men according to the amount of labour required to remove nature's obstructions. Let these considerations, therefore, be fairly weighed, as they will explain away much of the difficulties met with by the early pioneers and the perilous positions they were often in, while engaged taking their stock to Illawarra by land.[10]

In 1816, the year of John Frawley's birth in Ireland, an inspired paragraph appeared in the New South Wales "Gazette" on the 28th September, and read as follows... "The natives of the new settlement at the Five Islands are described as being very amicably disposed to us, and the general mildness of their manners to differ considerably from the other tribes known to us. Several gentlemen have removed their cattle thither, as the neighbourhood affords good pasturing; and it is anxiously hoped that the stockmen in charge of their herds will be able to maintain the friendly footing that at present exists with them." Later on the following notification appeared in the 'Sydney Gazette,' under the heading Public Notices:

> "Government House, Sydney, 16th November, 1816. Those gentlemen and free settlers who have lately obtained His Excellency the Governor's promises of grants of land, in the new district of Illawarra, or Five Islands, are hereby informed that the Surveyor-General and his deputy have received His Excellency the Governor's instructions to proceed thither in the course of the ensuing week to make a regular survey of the said district, to locate the several promised grants. And in order that the locations may be made accordingly, those persons who have obtained promises of allotments are hereby requested to avail themselves of the approaching occasion of the Surveyors on duty in Illawarra, to get their locations marked out to them. And for this purpose they are required to meet the Surveyor-General at the hut of Mr. Throsby's stock-men, in Illawarra, or the Five Islands district, at the hour of twelve noon, on Monday, 2nd day of December next, at which time he is to commence on locating the lands agreeable to the instructions which he will be officially furnished previous thereto."
>
> *By Command of His Excellency, J. F. Campbell Secretary, 1816* [11]

Exploration of the Illawarra

Shortly after the allocation of the first grants of land in Illawarra in 1817, the government formed a settlement at Red Point, Port Kembla with Dr. William Elyard Sr., R.N., he being the first government visiting officer, and superintendent of convicts stationed at Sydney. He came down in the "Snapper", and brought a sergeant, whose duty it was to count and record the strokes of the cat-o'-nine tails, and a flogger to administer the punishment. At that time the whole of the coast was policed by the military as far south as Jervis Bay.

Hence we have Barrack Point at Shellharbour and Kinghorn Point near Jervis Bay. However, the powers invested in men like Elyard were most arbitrary. It was in their power to hang delinquents on the spot, and punish others with up to 500 lashes. They moved from centre to centre with a few of the military and a flogger in order to deal with each case that came before them. But the sickening stories of the old regime could not withstand the light of day, and consequently were collected and burned.[12]

Throsby, Meehan, Hume & Others (1818)

The next exploration of the south east came from the west, after having been commissioned by Governor Macquarie to find a way overland from the Southern Tablelands to Jervis Bay. The party consisting of Charles Throsby, James Meehan, Hamilton Hume (1797-1873), and others departed from the Moss Vale area in March 1818, crossing the Wingecarribee River, they passed though Marulan and Bungonia Creek, but the expedition split with James Meehan's party discovering the Goulburn Plains. Charles Throsby's (1777-1828) party, who were guided by Aboriginals, explored Bundanoon Creek, Meryla Pass, Yarrunga Creek and came upon Kangaroo Valley. He reached the Kangaroo River at Bendeela and a day later, climbed out of the valley over the Bugong Gap and continued on to Jervis Bay, reaching the Shoalhaven River at Burrier, and Jervis Bay at Huskisson Hill before returning to Exeter.[13]

By 1818 William Emmett was in charge of the government station at Red Point, and although he was not a military man, he had the government cattle under his charge. In 1818 a general order was issued to begin on 1st January 1819, calling upon all persons, bond and free, who were engaged cutting cedar in Illawarra, to obtain permits to do so. About this time, Charles Throsby, who was born in England in 1777, was promised a grant of 1000 acres for finding a fresh track from the cow pastures to Bong Bong in 1815. His servants, Joe Wild (1750-1837) and Jack Waite received 100 acres each and another servant named Rowley got 200 acres. Joe Wild and Jack Waite understood the bush tracks in the years before the county of Camden was marked out in August of 1819. During that same year Surgeon D'Arcy Wentworth (1762-1827) was shipping cattle to his Peterborough Estate in Illawarra.[14]

It was with a view to preventing horse and cattle stealing that Capt. Richard Brooks (1765-1833), undertook the great task of stocking the Kangaroo Valley country in 1818. To do so he used the path which led from Lake Illawarra, crossing the Macquarie Rivulet to the west of Johnston's Meadows, then up the range into the Pheasant Ground to a spot known today as Hoddle's Track, and from thence along the range to the valley below. The Kangaroo Ground could also be reached from the County of Argyle, by a path leading from Bong Bong, and by another path which led from Coura to Cambewarra. Jervis Bay and Coolangatta could then be reached by paths from the Kangaroo Ground, but it was the impression of old settlers that a convenient road could not be found to carry a wheel conveyance of any description in and out of the place.[15]

In 1819 Charles O'Brien was appointed government overseer of stock at Red Point, Illawarra, and Conor Wholohan was managing David Allan's farm at Five Islands. Among the places set apart for grants of land for small settlers was Coalcliff. Cedar cutting was at that time an important industry in the Illawarra and Hamilton Hume, took advantage of the neglect of those whose grants were there to take possession, and sent gangs of sawyers there from Appin to cut cedar in 1823. So extensive was this industry that the government decided to cease controlling the affairs of the Illawarra or Five Islands district from Sydney, and arrangements were made to send a detachment of military to build barracks at Red Point. This took some time to complete in even a rough manner, but in time Capt. Peter Bishop (?-1846), of the 40th Regiment of Foot, one sergeant, one corporal and 20 privates were duly quartered there.

When the military got going in Illawarra they were victualled by the ship "Snapper" for a short period, under the command of Lt. Robert Johnston (1792-1882). She was a government cutter of 40 tons, with dimensions of 43ft. 6ins (length), 15ft. 6ins (breadth) and 6ft. 1ins (depth). Built in New South Wales and launched on the 18th May 1821. She was originally designed as a revenue cutter and/or a dispatch vessel, but was used mainly for transporting convicts to Newcastle and as a survey vessel on discovery voyages to the South Coast of New South Wales, as well as Moreton Bay and New Zealand. The "Snapper" carried Alexander Berry (1781–1873), to the Shoalhaven River in 1822, and was transferred from colonial service to private ownership in June 1823 when she was purchased by Solomon Levey (c.1794–1833).[16]

The earliest register for marriages dates from June 16th, 1820, a marriage having been performed on that date at Liverpool. The register is in excellent order in the handwriting of some individual who copied the records of all those early marriages, nearly all of which were celebrated by Father John Joseph Therry (1790-1864).[17] Therry was a Catholic priest, the son of John Therry of Cork, and his wife Eliza, née Connolly, who was educated privately at St Patrick's College, Carlow in Ireland.

Early Settlers in the Illawarra

It should not be overlooked that it was Dr. Charles Throsby Esq. (1777-1828), who was the first 'whitefella' to establish a settlement in the 'Five Islands' area in 1815, when "accompanied by a couple of men, two native blacks and a pack-horse carrying provisions, he started on his journey to move cattle into Illawarra and establish a stockyard and stockman's hut at Wollongong, creating the first official white settlement at the Illawarra."[18]

Judge Alfred McFarland (1824–1901), in his work on the Illawarra, records an account provided by Mr. Charles Throsby Smith of Wollongong, one of the region's earliest settlers. He recounts the gradual occupation and settlement of this fertile yet untamed land.

Early Settlement of Illawarra

In 1815, the county of Cumberland was suffering from a severe drought. Cattle were dying daily due to a lack of food and water. Dr. Charles Throsby, then residing at Glenfield near Liverpool, was an enterprising man. During one of his excursions, he encountered a group of Aboriginal people who told him of a land called the "Five Islands," where grass and water were abundant. Intrigued by their descriptions, he decided to see for himself.

Accompanied by two white men, two Aboriginal guides, and a packhorse loaded with provisions, Dr. Throsby set out. They spent their first night at Appin before continuing eastward. After four arduous days of carving a path through the dense bushland, they reached the mountain range's summit and caught their first glimpse of the vast ocean. The next day, they began the challenging task of cutting a track down the mountain, near what later became Bulli.

Upon arrival, they found an abundance of grass and water, more than enough to sustain livestock. Without delay, they returned to Liverpool to report their findings. Soon after, they drove a herd of cattle down into the Illawarra, making them the first cattle ever to enter the district. A stockyard was built near the site of the present-day Roman Catholic schoolhouse in Wollongong, with a hut erected nearby at what is now Smith Street.

As news of Dr. Throsby's success spread, other settlers followed. Colonel Johnston drove his cattle to what became known as Johnston's

Meadows along the Macquarie River, while Samuel Terry settled on the opposite bank. Mr. Brown from Abbotsbury brought his livestock to the shores of Illawarra Lake, known to the local Aboriginal people as "Yalla." Captain Brooks sent cattle from Denham Court to the same area, near present-day Dapto. More settlers followed, including George Cribb, who established himself near Figtree, naming the location "Charcoal Creek" after his stockman, known as "Charcoal Will."

In 1817, the father of W.W. Jenkins arrived, guided down the mountain by Throsby Smith himself. He settled near what would later become Berkeley. Smith vividly recalled the event, particularly because Charcoal Will became extremely drunk that day. By this time, some of Dr. Throsby's cattle had grown remarkably fat. A small number were driven back up the mountain to Sydney, then still a fledgling town, and slaughtered at the Government abattoir where Dawes Battery now stands. The exceptional quality of the beef quickly made "Five Islands" meat famous, and before long, the region became overstocked with horses and cattle.

In 1820, Dr. Throsby relocated his cattle to Bong Bong. Throsby Smith assisted in the move and, around the same time, decided to settle permanently in the colony. In 1823, he selected the land where he now resided, drawn to its natural harbor. In those days, settlers chose land freely before surveys were conducted. With his wife and four assigned convicts, he began clearing the land, despite occasional conflicts with local Aboriginal people. However, through kindness and mutual respect, he quickly formed friendships with them.

That same year, another drought in Cumberland County drove more settlers into Illawarra. Among them was Hamilton Hume, the "Mungo Park of Australia," who oversaw sawyers cutting cedar on the mountain between Wollongong and Bulli, the first cedar felled in the colony. The timber was cut into boards, carried up the mountain, and carted to Parramatta. These sawyers, however, were often unruly, providing shelter to bushrangers, escaped convicts, who harassed settlers. The problem became so severe that Governor Macquarie dispatched soldiers to suppress both bushrangers and hostile Aboriginal groups.

Meanwhile, the government continued expanding its presence. Surveyor-General John Oxley and Commissary Allan established a stock station at Five Islands Point, while D'Arcy Wentworth, Sydney's Police Magistrate, acquired land south of Illawarra Lake. He later sold it to M. Badgery, who used it as a stock station. The estate, known as Peterborough, passed through several hands but remains in Wentworth's family today.

To maintain order, the government deployed around 30 soldiers under Captain Bishop of the 40th Regiment to Red Point. However, due to difficult conditions, they soon relocated to Wollongong, setting up tents on the site of the current courthouse. Captain Bishop was later replaced by Mr. Butler, and soon after, barracks and a commandant's residence were built. As convicts flooded the colony, authorities also commissioned a road down Mount Keira, completed under the supervision of Mr. O'Hanly and Captain Sheaffe.

A Police Magistrate's office was soon established, first led by Captain Allman and later by others, including Captain Plunkett. In early settlement days, a court was also held monthly in Shoalhaven.

Wollongong's Development

The first church in Wollongong was St. Michael's Anglican Church, which was a small, modest chapel built in 1828 in the rented barn of Charles Throsby Smith. Archdeacon Broughton provided a catechist, who initially led the services before Rev. F. Wilkinson became their minister. He also held monthly services in Shoalhaven. Catholic services were held in Smith's barn starting in 1828, but it was not a permanent church structure. The first dedicated Roman Catholic chapel was constructed in 1836, and pastored by Father Therry, on the site of the present Catholic schoolhouse. The first permanent Church of England church was built in 1847. The first schoolhouse, built on Market Street, later became the Church of England schoolhouse. The Presbyterian Church followed, built under the Rev. J. Tait.

By this time, the settlement was beginning to take shape. Governor Bourke, Major Mitchell, Colonel Barney, and G.K. Holden visited and laid out the official plan for Wollongong. To support development, 300 convicts, accompanied by soldiers, were dispatched to construct the basin. They established a stockade on Flagstaff Hill, marking Wollongong's rapid transformation into a thriving township.

Industry followed. The first steam-powered flour mill was built near Para Creek by Peck and Palmer, with others soon appearing in Dapto and Wollongong. Dr. Grover became the first resident medical practitioner. Wilson Brothers opened the first significant store in Wollongong, while Mr. Hargraves, later famed for discovering gold, established the first country store in Dapto before leaving for California.

Land prices fluctuated. Under Governor Brisbane, land was briefly sold at five shillings per acre, and many settlers took advantage. One early farmer, Mr. Barrett, cultivated Herne Farm but perished at sea when his shipment of potatoes was lost. Later, James Shoobert acquired the Mount Keira estate and pioneered Illawarra's coal industry.

Meanwhile, roads continued to improve. Cornelius O'Brien, overseeing his uncle's cattle, discovered a new pass down the escarpment, now known as O'Brien's Road. It became the main route to the Five Islands until the Mount Keira road was constructed.

The Land & Its People

In the early years, Illawarra was densely forested, with towering trees, tangled vines, and thick undergrowth. Only a few natural clearings existed, such as the swamplands near Tom Thumb Lagoon and pockets of land around Macquarie River. The region boasted rich timber resources, including cedar, sassafras, ironbark, and stringybark, fueling a booming timber trade. However, much of it was wasted in the rush for settlement.

The Aboriginal people of Wollongong, numbering around 100, were generally peaceful. Their diet consisted of fish, kangaroos, possums, and wildfowl. The local chief, "Old Bundle," claimed Wollongong as his domain, often receiving food and supplies from settlers. Another leader, "Old Timberry," ruled the Berkeley area, though territorial boundaries were flexible. Though occasional conflicts arose, early settlers and Aboriginal groups often coexisted, sharing knowledge of the land that shaped Illawarra's future. Thus, the settlement of Illawarra was forged, through hardship, perseverance, and the meeting of two worlds.

In 1819 Charles Throsby's nephew, Charles Throsby Smith (1798-1876) was given a land grant of 300 acres at the Five Islands that was to become known as Wollongong, where he would move to after his first marriage in 1822. The recollections of Mr. Charles Throsby Smith of Wollongong, one of the earliest settlers, was published in his Honor Judge McFarland's work on the Illawarra, and this account provides a detailed summary of the gradual occupation and settlement of the Illawarra.

Land Grants in Illawarra

The earliest land grants in the Illawarra were made on the 24th January 1817 to Capt. Richard Brooks, George Johnston, Andrew Allan, Robert Jenkins and David Allan, who did not reside there, but ran cattle cared for by their employees.[19] These land grants were issued by several governors under the following conditions:

> "Each person to whom a grant was given received a number of convicts in accordance with the area of land bestowed by the Governor. These convicts were clothed and fed by the Government. Thus the landowners had absolutely free labour provided for them. This state of things was not altered much until the mid-thirties." [20]

Settlement commenced in the parish of Kembla west of the present day Wollongong running south to Dapto in 1817. When an area of 300 acres was granted to George Molle on the 11th September 1817.[21] Macquarie informed the Home Government on the 12th December 1817 of the discovery of new country at Five Islands known to the Aborigines as 'Illawarra'.[22] The first settlers in Jamberoo were two half-brothers, Messrs. John Ritchie and William Wright,[23] with other of the earliest Illawarra land grants following:[24]

- Wollongong (Berkeley) - 1,000 acres granted to Robert Jenkins; date, 24th January, 1817; quit rent, £1. Commencing 24th January, 1822. Granted by Lachlan Macquarie. Conditions: To cultivate 75 acres, and not to sell for five years.
- Wollongong (Illawarra Farm) - 1,500 acres granted to David Allan; date, 24th January, 1817; quit rent, £2.4.0 from 24th January, 1822. Granted by Lachlan Macquarie. Conditions: To cultivate 75 acres, and not to sell for five years.
- Jamberoo (Terry's Meadows) - 2,000 acres granted to Samuel Terry; date, 9th January, 1821; quit rent, £1, commencing from 9th January 1826 (Mount Terry) Granted by Lachlan Macquarie. Conditions: To cultivate 100 acres, and not to sell for five years.
- Kangaroo Ground (Exmouth) - 800 acres granted to Richard Brooks on or before 21st February, 1821; quit rent, £1. Granted by Lachlan Macquarie; Not to sell for five years.
- Coolangatta - 10,000 acres, granted to Alexander Berry and Edward Wollstonecraft, county of Camden; registered date of grant, 30th June, 1825. Granted by Sir Thomas Brisbane.
- Numbaa - 2,000 acres granted to Alexander Berry (Portion 8) on 30th June, 1825.
- Brundee and Numbaa, granted to William Elyard the younger, on 23rd April 1841, (Portion 4 - Brundee) being the land promised to William Elyard the elder, on or before 23rd April, 1829.

There was also a transfer of land at Greenwell Point from William Elyard to Alexander Berry, which was an exchange under government supervision, Berry taking the Greenwell Point property in exchange for Brundee. Anyone interested could possibly find the particulars in the Mitchell Library, where many of those peculiar transactions are stored.

The first grant of land on the south side of Lake Illawarra was given by Governor Macquarie to Lt-Col. Thomas Davey (1758-1813), generally known as 'Mad Davey,' situated at Barrack Hill, Shellharbour, in January of 1817, with others following:[25]

- Macquarie Rivulet (Macquarie's Gift) - 1,500 acres granted to George Johnston Esq., senr., on 24th January 1817; quit rent, £1.10s; quit rent commences 24th January, 1822, situated on the northern bank of the Macquarie Rivulet and later part of the estate known as 'Johnston's Meadows.'
- Macquarie Rivulet (Waterloo) - 700 acres granted to Allan Andrew, situated on the south bank of the Macquarie Rivulet, opposite the 'Macquarie Gift' grant.
- The Dunlop Vale Estate, near Lake Illawarra, was a grant from the Crown to Mr. John Wyllie, bearing date 1822. It comprised 2000 acres. It was approved by Governor Ralph Darling on 13th October, 1829, about which date Mr. Wyllie had it somewhat improved and stocked with many valuable Ayrshire cattle. Mr. Wyllie then went into the employ of Mr. Alexander Berry at Coolangatta, Shoalhaven.

Up to 1820, the last year of Macquarie's government, 400,000 acres had passed into the hands of private individuals. Macquarie was generous to his friends, and from him the settler frequently obtained with his grant, the use of a government gang, who not only cut down, but rolled the logs into piles and burnt and cleared the timber off land that would not pay the settler to clear with hired labour.[26]

Governor Macquarie's replacement Sir Thomas Brisbane (1773-1860) granted 180,000 acres at a yearly quit rent of 2/- per 100 acres. Between December 1824, and the 19th May 1825, he sold 369,050 acres at 5/- per acre, giving long credit, with, in addition, 2/- per 100 acres, and he also granted in two years between 1823 and 1825, 573,000 acres at 15/- annual quit rent per 100 acres. But it must be noted that all these grants and purchases were accompanied by an allowance of a certain number of convicts per 30 acres to clear and till them, and that these convicts, as well as the settler and his wife, were rationed for a limited period at the expense of the government.

Governor Sir Ralph Darling (1772-1858), who ruled the convicts with a rod of iron, arrived as the new governor in December 1825, when the times of the 'first fleeters,' the irresponsible floggers, and the short allowance of coarse food were revived, and carried out in Illawarra. Some authorities have stated that his six years administration was singularly and deservedly unpopular. He was a man of forms and a precedent of the true red-tape school, and he continued to rule until the year 1831.

All the same, for years afterwards there were long lists of floggings ordered by the several naval and military magistrates who visited, first at Red Point, Port Kembla, then later at Wollongong and from thence south to Kiama, and then on Alexander Berry's Coolangatta Estate.

By 1830, the South Coast of New South Wales had been transformed from a rugged frontier into a patchwork of pastoral settlements, where European settlers carved out farms, built homesteads, and forged uneasy relationships with the land and its original custodians. The once-isolated coastline was now dotted with the odd whaling station, timber camp, and sheep run, as new arrivals sought their fortunes in an unfamiliar world.

But for some, the journey to this distant shore was not one of choice, but of punishment. Among them was a young Irishman, by the name of John Frawley, whose fate was sealed not by ambition, but by misfortune. Born in Limerick around 1816, John's life took a fateful turn when, while still just a teenager, he was convicted of stealing clothes, an offence that saw him torn from his family and sentenced to exile on the other side of the world. In 1833, he arrived in Sydney in chains, condemned to seven years of servitude, where the next chapter of his settlement in the great south land would begin.

References

1. The Sydney Gazette & NSW Advertiser, 8th June 1811, p.1.
2. McLachlan, N. D. (1967). 'Macquarie, Lachlan (1762-1824)', Australian Dictionary of Biography, Melbourne University Press. (ISSN 1833-7538 - via National Centre of Biography, Australian National University).
3. Davison, G., Hirst, J.B., & MacIntyre, S. (1998). 'The Oxford Companion to Australian History' (revised ed.). Melbourne, Vic: Oxford University Press, p.405 (ISBN 9780195515039).
4. Ward, R. (1975). 'Australia: a short history' (rev ed.). Ure Smith, p.37-38. (ISBN 978-0-7254-0164-1).
5. Molony, J.N. (1987). 'The Penguin History of Australia,' Ringwood, Vic: Penguin, p.47 (ISBN 978-0-14-009739-9).
6. Ibid, p.28.
7. Ibid, p.30.
8. Australian Dictionary of Biography - George William Evans [https://adb.anu.edu.au/biography/evans-george-william-2029].
9. The Sydney Gazette & NSW Advertiser, 17th April 1813, p.2.
10. Ibid.
11. McAffrey, Frank (1922). 'The History of Illawarra & Its Pioneers,' Sydney, John Sands Ltd., p.22.
12. McCaffrey, Frank (1922). op. cit., p.25.
13. Heritage Shoalhaven - Shoalhaven in the 19th centurey: Kangaroo Valley [https://heritageshoalhaven.wordpress.com/2018/01/23/shoalhaven-in-the-19th-century-2/].
14. Ibid.
15. McCaffrey, Frank (1922). op. cit., p.23-24.
16. Journeys in Time - "Snapper" from List of Ships [https://www.mq.edu.au/macquarie-archive/journeys/ships/list.html#s].
17. McCaffrey, Frank (1922). op. cit., p.24.
18. Organ, Michael (1990). 'Illawarra & South Coast Aborigines 1770-1850. Aboriginal Education Unit, The University of Wollongong, p.48.
19. Dowd, B.T. (1977). 'The First Five Land Grantees and the Grants in the Illawarra', Illawarra Historical Society, Wollongong, p.2.
20. Ibid.
21. Jervis, James, (1942). 'Illawarra: A Century of History' JRAHS, XXVIII, p.86.
22. Jervis, James, (1942). op. cit., p.65-6.
23. First Settlers of Jamberoo (The Kiama Independent and Shoalhaven Advertiser, 5 Aug 1939, p.2).
24. McCaffrey, Frank (1922). op. cit., p.26.
25. McCaffrey, Frank (1922). op. cit., p.27.
26. McCaffrey, Frank (1922). op. cit., p.26.

5

AN UNWILLING PIONEER

The waves that had carried settlers and fortune-seekers to the south coast of New South Wales also bore the unwilling, the exiled, and the condemned. Among them was our ancestor John Frawley, a boy of barely seventeen, whose journey to this distant land was not driven by ambition, but by punishment.

Born in Limerick, Ireland, John's life was forever altered by a single act of desperation, a theft of clothes that saw him branded a criminal and wrenched from his family. His sentence was unforgiving: transportation across the seas to the convict colony of New South Wales. In 1833, he stepped off a prison ship onto the sun-scorched shores of Sydney, a world away from the damp green fields of his homeland. But exile was only the beginning. Assigned to the sprawling Coolangatta Estate on the South Coast, John Frawley would find himself thrust into the brutal rhythms of servitude, forging a life in a land both foreign and untamed. Though he had arrived in chains, the choices he made in this strange new world would shape not only his fate, but that of the generations to come.

John Frawley of Limerick

John Frawley was born and baptised a Catholic in Limerick, in Ireland.[1] Unfortunately, no birth or baptism records have been found, but information ascertained from his convict, marriage and death records mark his birth year to be around the year 1816.[2] A number of records attest to John's age and place of birth,[3] but the information he himself supplied on his second marriage certificate in 1894 substantiate this and would likely be most valid.[4]

Details about John Frawley's parents and early years are scarce. His father worked as a clerk and likely valued education, as John was able to read and write. He spoke the Limerick dialect, known for its sharp, nasal quality, which was often mocked for sounding rough.

Life in early 19th-century Limerick was harsh, and survival often required desperate measures. Like many others, young John likely took whatever work he could find. By the time of his arrest, he was employed as an errand boy.[5]

The City of Limerick

At this time, Limerick, located 125km west of Dublin, was and still is the principal city in the southwest of Ireland and is the Irish Republic's third largest city with it's most striking feature being the River Shannon, flowing majestically beneath the city's three bridges. The city received its charter in 1197, and is divided into three principal areas: English Town, on King's Island; Irish Town lying to the south of the river, which includes the oldest part of the city dating from the 9th century Norse settlement; and Newtown-Pery, to the south of Irish Town, dating from 1769. Historically Limerick is a city of many contrasts, containing a medieval core with a later Georgian addition. Of particular importance are King John's Castle, built on the orders of King John in the year 1200, and the cathedral, built about 1172.[6] Dominating the King's Island, which is the oldest part of Limerick City, is the enormous St. Mary's Cathedral, founded by the King of Munster, Donal Mor O'Brien, on a site where his palace once stood.

In view of the especially desperate and difficult situation many Irish folk found themselves in at this time, it is not surprising that young John Frawley fell upon difficult times. About the age of 16 he may have fallen in with a disreputable gang, or more likely found himself in a desperate situation. While the reasons why he committed his offence, without any former convictions, are unclear, evidence reveals that he was arrested, tried in court and convicted of 'stealing clothes' in Limerick, on the 5th of March 1833.[7]

During the course of the 18th century, when the death penalty came to be regarded as too severe a punishment for certain categories of capital offences, as an alternative there was frequent recourse to the transportation of convicts to colonies outside of Britain and Ireland. Initially, convicts were transported to North America, but after the American War of Independence, New South Wales was preferred as the first Australian penal colony.

Legislation to permit the transportation of convicts from Britain to New South Wales was passed in 1784. Equivalent Irish legislation, enacted in 1786 and with further legislation in 1790 to make transportation from Ireland more effectual, permitted the transportation of convicts from Ireland from 1791. Until the termination of the transportation system in 1853, some 160,000 persons were transported to Australia, approximately 26,500 of whom left from Ireland.[8]

In accordance with the strict laws of the time, crimes involving possessions or property were heavily dealt with and despite this being his first ever conviction, John Frawley's case was of this nature. For the crime of stealing clothes, he was duly sentenced to seven years penal service in the colony of New South Wales. Along with other convicted criminals, he was speedily transferred under guard by goal wagon from Limerick to the city of Cork in preparation for his transportation.

Cork City, County Cork

The city of Cork dates from a religious settlement founded there in 622AD by Saint Finbar, and is the seat of the county of Cork, located on the Lee River, at the head of Cork Harbour inlet and today, is the second largest city in Ireland. During the 11th century the Danes made it a trading station encircled with walls, then in 1172 Cork was subsumed into the Angevin Empire by King Henry II of England. By 1649 the city fell to Oliver Cromwell, Lord Protector of England during the English Civil War. The town changed hands once more in 1689 when it was captured by John Churchill (1650-1722), 1st Duke of Marlborough, for the English crown by forces loyal to King James II.[9]

Transportation to New South Wales

However, John Frawley wouldn't have spent much time in Cork as he was quickly embarked aboard the convict ship "Java", which was loaded with 206 male convicts and that ship sailed from Cork on the 24th July, 1833.[10]

Convicts under transportation were routinely handed over to the master of a ship for the duration of the journey at the beginning of the voyage, and formally transferred at the other end, into the custody of the governor of the colony that was receiving them. Indents, or 'Indentures', were the documents used to record the transactions of transferring the convicts on arrival.

Although the convicts of the First Fleet arrived in relatively good condition, the same cannot be said for the many ships that followed over the next 60 years. The lengthy voyage, cruel masters, harsh discipline, scurvy, dysentary and typhoid fever often combined to result in a substantial loss of life. During the voyage, convicts were housed below decks on what was known as the 'prison deck' and often further confined behind bars. In many cases they were restrained in chains and were only allowed on deck for fresh air and exercise. Conditions were very cramped and like the sailors, they mostly slept in hammocks. While little information is available about the usual layout of the convict ships, a few books do contain artist's impressions and reproductions of images held in library collections.[11]

After the English authorities began to review the system in 1801, convict transports were despatched twice a year, at the end of May and again at the beginning of September, to avoid the huge seas and dangerous winters of the southern hemisphere. Surgeons employed by the early contractors had to obey the master of the ship and on later voyages were replaced by independent Surgeon Superintendents, whose sole responsibility was for the health and well being of the convicts. As time went on, more successful routines were adopted and surgeons were supplied with explicit instructions as to how life on board ship should be organised. By then the charter operators were also paid bonuses if convicts were landed safe and sound at the end of the voyage.

By the time exiles were being transported in the 1840's and onwards, a more enlightened routine was in place, which even included the presence on board of an onboard Religious Instructor to educate the convicts and attend to their spiritual needs. The shipboard routines on some of the Western Australian transports during the 1860's have been transcribed in detail and are worth reading.

Another point of confusion that often arises with convict voyages is the route they sailed. The convict shipping lists usually indicated if a ship travelled via other ports. That was especially so in the early days when ships were smaller, took longer and had to put in for supplies and repairs along the way. In later years, after other Australian settlements had been established, the transports often stopped at more than one destination to land convicts. From England the transports may have stopped off at Gibraltar, a port in the West Indies, South America, the Cape of Good Hope and any one of the Australian penal settlements.

Voyage of the "Java" (1833)

Captain John Todd commanded the "Java", while Surgeon Superintendent Robert Dixon maintained a 'Medical and Surgical Journal' from June 30 to December 3, 1833. On July 22, 1833, 200 convicts were hastily embarked at the Cove of Cork. Alongside them, three free settlers, John McNamara, Michael McNamara, and Patrick McNamara also boarded. Additionally, six military convicts were taken on, including Robert Deighton, Michael Fox, James Fraser, Hugh McQuiggan, and Edward Standford.

The "Java" set sail from Cork on July 24th, just two days after embarkation. Among the convicts, three were already ill. A 13-year-old boy, John Sullivan, was also in poor health, but eventually recovered enough to be landed in a stable, though still fragile, condition. Surgeon Dixon attributed the high number of bowel complaints during the voyage to abrupt changes in temperature, from dry heat to cold moisture and excessive perspiration. He also believed that Irish convicts, being less well-fed than their English counterparts, were more susceptible to illness during the long passage and shifting climates. Several convicts did not survive the journey. Thomas Adams, aged 15, died on October 17; Patrick Burke on October 8; Robert Polly, 19, on October 11; James Crawley, 19, on October 30; and Michael Bercury on October 15.

After a 117-day voyage, the "Java" arrived in Port Jackson on November 18, 1833. The ship's guard comprised 29 rank-and-file soldiers from the 4th, 17th, and 21st Regiments, accompanied by five women and four children, all under the command of Lieutenant Wrixon of the 21st Regiment. Passengers included Mrs. Wrixon, Ensign Codd, and John Wrixon. The "Java" was scheduled to sail for Madras and Calcutta in December 1833.

The "Java", on which John Frawley journeyed, was built in 1813 in Calcutta and was a barque of 411 tons, the master being Jn. Todd.[12] During the voyage John Frawley reported to the ships surgeon with a complaint on the 21st August 1833. The ship's surgeon, Mr. Robert Dickson diagnosed him with having contracted pneumonia, which lasted until 25th August when he was discharged:

> Between the 24th day of July and the 3rd day of December, 1833. John Frawley, aged 17, pneumonia, from 21st to 25th August, discharged.
>
> *Journal of the "Java", Convict Ship* [13]

He apparently made a full recovery as no other mention of John Frawley was made on the voyage. The captain of the "Java" held regular Sunday church services for the convicts and all ships company on the way to Port Jackson. At journey's end the medical superintendant submitted his journal, as he was required to keep throughout the voyage.

> On the 22 July 1833 at the Cove of Cork, embarked on board, John Todd, master, 200 convicts, six military convicts and four free settlers, total 210, of whom three namely Daniel Sheehan, Patrick Burke and John Sullivan, did not appear in health. However, Sheehan landed at Sydney; Sullivan, the only person (a boy of 13 years) whom I objected to, after several physical attacks, rallied and landed in health; but of exceedingly delicate habit, Burke died. The embarkation of the convicts was more hurried than the surgeon had wished. The surgeon attributed the cause of so many bowel complaints to the sudden change from dry heat to cold moisture, choking perspiration and determining to the intestines. Also mentioned was that the Irish convicts, as these were, being so ill fed in their own country, do not bear the long passage or the vissitudes of climate so well as their more pampered neighbours. Included in the remark is the surgeon's [Robert Dickson] opinion of the way in which several naval surgeons have boasted of their great success in taking out convicts without losing a man, and instead of filling this journal with a repetition of successful cases the surgeon [Robert Dickson] inserted the most severe, and most fatal cases.
>
> *Surgeon's General Remarks from the "Java", 1833.*[14]

However, a critique was added to this journal by the inspector who checked it in Sydney.

> "This is a very ill-written journal and by no account creditable in any respect to Mr. Dickson".[15]

After the penal colony of New South Wales became well established and permanent buildings had been erected, a routine for handling newly arrived convicts was set in place. Most convicts were assigned to settlers and emancipated convicts after an application for a convict servant or worker was lodged with the governor. Some married convicts were even assigned to their free spouses. Very few assignment registers have survived, but the Assignment Registers of 1821 to 1824 do exist. Martin Cash described his arrival in 1828 as follows:

> "On the 10th February, 1828, we arrived at Sydney, and on landing we were drafted to Hyde Park Barracks, which formed the general depot at that time for receiving prisoners. The assignment or hiring-out system had then come into operation, and myself, together with eighteen or nineteen of my companions in misery, were forwarded to different masters in Richmond."
>
> *Martin Cash, Convict* [16]

The worst type of convicts were assigned to hard labour in iron-gangs and set to work on the roads. Road gang reports (1827-1830) supplied convict number, name, ship, job, casualties, discharge details, the place stationed and the overseer. State Archives hold other records for Iron Gangs and Road Parties, and there is also a list of men in irons on Norfolk Island and Moreton Bay (1839-1840).

Musters, or head counts of prisoners were needed to keep a check on supply and demand upon the Government Stores. Usually they recorded the name, ship, sentence and residence of the convicts. Some also included the children of convicts and free persons. The 1828 Census of New South Wales is the most detailed and best surviving record of its type and is kept in most major libraries.[17] Divorce was not available to commoners until the late 1800's and was both scandalous and expensive. However, previously married convicts were permitted to remarry after seven year's separation as long as their spouse was abroad, even if they were still living. The government encouraged marriage between convicts as it was seen as a means of rehabilitation and more desirable than de facto relationships.

In the latter half of the voyage they experienced much wet, foggy weather, which saturated the decks, clothes and everything that moisture could reach. It was amidst the confusion of this convict driven society that John Frawley arrived in Port Jackson on the 18th of November 1833, after a journey of 117 days at sea. The prisoners were mustered on board the "Java" on the 22nd November 1833, which revealed that of 206 male convicts that embarked in Cork, five had died at sea and four were sent on shore sick, on arrival at Sydney.

Upon disembarkation in Sydney all convicts were recorded by the authorities in the Convict Indents and the listing for John Frawley contains his details.[18] Oddly there were two convict indent listings for John Frawley with the only difference being the reported age of 17 in one and 19 the other. The other feature is that he is listed as being John Frawley Jr, so he obviously had a father, who was called John Frawley Sr.[19]

After being processed by the authorities, convicts were then either allocated to government service or assigned to the care of free settlers and land owners, who were required to support them in return for their work. This support included the provision of housing, clothing and food. After being held for a short stint in the Hyde Park Barracks, John Frawley was perhaps fortunate to be assigned to an established estate at Shoalhaven on the mid South Coast of NSW.

Hyde Park Barracks, Sydney

Mention must be made of Hyde Park Barracks, Sydney,[20] a heritage-listed former barracks, hospital, convict accommodation, mint and courthouse and now museum at Macquarie Street in the Sydney central business district of Sydney. Originally built from 1811 to 1819 as a brick building and compound to house convict men and boys, it was designed by convict architect Francis Greenway (1777-1837).

After his arrival in Sydney, Governor Macquarie had become increasingly disturbed by the male convicts' behaviour in the streets after work, who had been allowed to find their own lodgings. However, Macquarie thought that barracks accommodation would improve the moral character of the men and increase their productivity. To this end, he requested convict architect Francis Greenway to design a barracks for 600 men. Constructed by convicts, the foundation stone was laid by Macquarie on the 6th April 1817 and the barracks were completed by 1819. Macquarie was so impressed by Greenway's design that he granted him a full pardon shortly after its completion.[21] Convicted of forging signatures, Greenway was also known for his architectural skills and quickly advertised himself in the local places. The barracks were officially opened on the 4th June 1819, when 589 convicts were admitted.[22]

Internally, the four rooms on each floor were hung with two rows of hammocks, with a 0.9-metre (3-foot) passage. The room allowed for each hammock was 2.1 by 0.6 metres (7 by 2 feet). In this way, the long eastern rooms could sleep 70 men each, while 35 men slept in the smaller western rooms.[23]

Macquarie was happy to note that since the confinement of the male convicts to the Barracks at night "not a tenth part of the former Night Robberies and Burglaries" occurred.[24] Commissioner John Bigge (1780-1843), however, complained that the congregation of such a large number of "depraved and desperate characters" in one area had just condensed the problem.[25] Stealing was rife within the Barracks with items being passed over the walls to waiting accomplices for disposal. In an attempt to curb the thefts convicts were searched at the gates and broad arrows were painted on their items of clothing and bedding.[26]

The accommodation soon proved inadequate as up to 1400 men were being housed in the Barracks at any one time. It has been estimated that perhaps 30,000 men and boys passed through the Barracks between 1819 and 1848.[27] The convict response to the Barracks was somewhat mixed: those that were able to pay for lodgings by working on Saturday were not happy about the confinement; others were happy to have a roof over their heads. In 1820, in order to ease the pressure on the crowded Barracks the reward of being allowed to live outside the facility was extended. Convicts found gambling, drunk, engaged in street violence or other unseemly behaviour had this freedom revoked and were returned to live in the Barracks - it had become a form of punishment. Loitering or idling on a Saturday was also punishable by confinement to the Barracks. Convicts had a peculiar mix of detention and freedom, they had to work for the government during the week, but were allowed to work for their own benefit on Saturdays. This was a privilege Governor Macquarie did not like to see abused.[28]

From 1830 convicts were brought to the site for sentencing and punishment by the Court of General Sessions sitting in northern perimeter buildings. Punishments handed down included floggings, which were carried out onsite, or terms on the treadmill or chain gangs. While one of the first agencies to encroach on the Barracks, but not the last - the Board for the Assignment of Servants operated from the Barracks between 1831 and 1841.[29]

Today, the Hyde Park Barracks is also known as the Mint Building and Rum Hospital; Royal Mint - Sydney Branch; Sydney Infirmary and Dispensary; Queen's Square Courts; and Queen's Square. The site is managed by the Sydney Living Museums, an agency of the Government of New South Wales, as a living history museum open to the public.

The site is inscribed on the UNESCO World Heritage List as one of 11 pre-eminent Australian Convict Sites as amongst "the best surviving examples of large-scale convict transportation and the colonial expansion of European powers through the presence and labour of convicts",[30,31] and was listed on the Australian National Heritage List on the 1st August 2007,[32] and on the New South Wales State Heritage Register on 2 April 1999.[33] The historic site was closed in January 2019 for $18 million restoration work to transform it into "a rich new, immersive visitor experience like no other in Australia" and reopened in February 2020.[34,35]

This property known as 'Coolangatta', was more than just a backdrop to John Frawley's seven years of servitude, it was a vast and ambitious estate shaped by one of early Sydney's most influential figures, Alexander Berry.[36] Understanding Berry's background and motivations provides crucial insight into the world Frawley inhabited, as it was here that he likely honed the skills and gained the experience that would shape his future. But how did this remote expanse of land become one of New South Wales' first great rural enterprises? And what obstacles did Berry overcome to bring his vision to life? Before we continue on John Frawley's journey, we must first uncover the story of Coolangatta and the man who built it.

References

1. NSW State Archives & Records. (1833). 'John Frawley off the "Java", arrived Sydney, 18th Nov. 1833, in 'Convict Indents.' (Fiche #706, p.181; Film #907, Shelf #X635) & (NSW Archives Convict Indents Fiche #688, p.202; Film #906, Shelf #4/4018).
2. Ibid.
3. John Frawley - Christening held on the 27th October, 1811 (International Genealogical Index (2000).
4. Queensland Dept of BDM. (1894). Marriage Certificate for John Frawley & Rose Emily Curtis, 27th February 1894, #1894/C/1672).
5. NSW State Archives & Records. (1833). 'John Frawley off the "Java," op. cit.
6. Wikipedia - Limerick [https://en.wikipedia.org/wiki/Limerick].
7. NSW State Archives & Records. (1833). 'John Frawley off the "Java," op. cit.
8. National Archives, Ireland [https://www.nationalarchives.ie/wp-content/uploads/2019/03/Ireland-Australia-transportation_DB.pdf].
9. Wikipedia, 'History of Cork.' [https://en.wikipedia.org/wiki/History_of_Cork]. Retrieved 8th June 2021.
10. Convict Records, 'Departure of the "Java", 24th July 1833.' [https://convictrecords.com.au/ships/java]. Retrieved 2nd March 2020.
11. Hawkins, I. (1977). 'Shipping Arrival and Departures Sydney, 1826-1840: Volume 3.' Canberra, Roebuck.
12. Bateson, C. (1974). 'The Convict Ships, 1787-1868.' Sydney, Reed.
13. Medical Journal of the "Java" convict ship from 30 June to 3 December 1833 by Robert. Dickson.The National Archives, Kew. (Public Record Office, 3198/ADM, 101/36.)
14. Ibid.
15. Ibid.
16. Cash, Martin (1961).The Bushranger of Van Diemen's Land in 1843-4: A Personal Narrative of His Exploits in the Bush and His Experiences at Port Arthur and Norfolk Island, Hobart. Convict Letters, Mitchell Library, Sydney.
17. NSW State Archives & Records.(1828). "1828 Census, New South Wales." Mitchell Library, Sydney.
18. NSW State Archives & Records. (1833). 'John Frawley off the "Java," op. cit.
19. NSW State Archives & Records. (1833). 'John Frawley off the "Java," op. cit.
20. Wikipedia - Hyde Park Barracks, Sydney [https://en.wikipedia.org/wiki/Hyde_Park_Barracks,_Sydney].
21. "Mint Building and Hyde Park Barracks Group". New South Wales State Heritage Register. Department of Planning and Environment. H00190. Retrieved 13 October 2018. Text is licensed by State of New South Wales (Department of Planning and Environment) under CC-BY 4.0 licence.
22. ondinee (4 June 2019). "On this day: an 'excellent institution' opens". Sydney Living Museums. Retrieved 27 June 2019.
23. "Mint Building and Hyde Park Barracks Group", op.cit.
24. Cumberland County Council (1962). Historic Buildings: Central Area of Sydney, Volume II. 1962, p.6.
25. Cumberland County Council (1962). Historic Buildings: op.cit.
26. "Mint Building and Hyde Park Barracks Group", op.cit.
27. Lynn Collins, ed. (1994). Hyde Park Barracks, p.19.
28. "Mint Building and Hyde Park Barracks Group", op.cit.
29. "Mint Building and Hyde Park Barracks Group", op.cit..
30. "Australian Convict Sites". World Heritage Convention. United Nations. Retrieved 10 October 2015.
31. "Australian Convict Sites". Department of the Environment. Australian Government. Retrieved 10 October 2015.
32. "Hyde Park Barracks, Macquarie St, Sydney, NSW, Australia (Place ID 105935)". Australian Heritage Database. Australian Government. 1 August 2007. Retrieved 7 December 2018].
33. "Mint Building and Hyde Park Barracks Group", op.cit.
34. "'Work in progress': Hyde Park Barracks closes for $18 million transformation". The Sydney Morning Herald. 10 January 2019.
35. Dow, Steve (20 February 2020). "'Designed to wake people up': Jonathan Jones unveils major public work at Hyde Park barracks". The Guardian. Retrieved 20 February 2020.
36. NSW State Archives & Records. (1833). John Frawley, Assigned to Alex Berry at Shoalhaven 'Coolangatta.' Convicts Arrived, 1833-1834.

6

BERRY'S COOLANGATTA HOMESTEAD

Nestled just north of the Shoalhaven River, the towering hill known as 'Cullunghutti' to the Jerrinja people offers a breathtaking lookout, providing expansive views over the surrounding landscape. In 1822, Alexander Berry, along with his partner Edward Wollstonecraft (1783-1832), who managed affairs in Sydney, set out to establish the first private European settlement on the South Coast of New South Wales. They chose a site beneath a mountain in the Shoalhaven as the site for their ambitious project. The sprawling property, named 'Coolangatta,' would become more than just a land transaction, it would develop into a pioneering estate, shaped by the vision and influence of one of early Sydney's most notable figures, the Scotsman Alexander Berry.

Berry's background and motivations offer crucial insight into the world in which John Frawley lived and worked during his seven years of servitude. And it was on this land, transformed by Berry's ambition, that the likes of John Frawley would gain the skills and knowledge that would define their future. But who was Alexander Barry? And how did this remote stretch of land, far from the bustling life of Sydney, evolve into one of New South Wales' first great rural enterprises?

Alexander Berry

For initiative, courage and sheer wild adventure there would be few careers to rival that of Alexander Berry (1781-1873). Born at Cupar in Fifeshire, Scotland, on St. Andrews Day 1781, his father planned for him to become a surgeon and to that end sent him to St. Andrews and Edinburgh Universities. While studying, his thoughts turned to a life at sea and he accepted a commission with the East India Company, and made a number of voyages as a ships surgeon to China and India. Whilst on the job he taught himself navigation and business principles, but resigned from this role soon after as he was determined to follow a future in commerce.

The "City of Edinburgh"

After his first commercial venture to the Cape of Good Hope in 1807, he heard of a serious shortage of food in New South Wales. Investing all his resources in the purchase of a ship, which he renamed the "City Of Edinburgh" and stocking it with provisions, he set sail for Sydney on 4th September 1807. The voyage took 14 weeks and the ship was twice dismasted in furious seas, but it eventually limped into Sydney on the 14th January 1808. Berry had offloaded most of the cargo at Port Dalrymple and the remainder was mostly spirits. This apparently aroused the anger of Governor Bligh as the Rum Rebellion was in full swing in Sydney at this time.

Following a trip to Norfolk Island and Van Diemans Land, Berry set out for New Zealand seeking spars and sandalwood. Attacked by hostile Maories in Koroaika, he left for Tevenuni in the Tongan Group.

Here he almost met with disaster and it was only quick thinking that saved him and his crew from becoming the main course at a cannibal feast. Loading sandalwood in Fiji, the "City Of Edinburgh" reached the Bay of Islands where Berry heard of a British ship being attacked and the crew taken prisoners at Whangaroa. With two armed boats he set out at once and found the remains of a convict transport ship "The Boyd", which had been returning to England and learned from local tribesman that the ships company were being eaten at a rate of two per day. Berry was able to arrive just in time to rescue four survivors.

A month later in January 1810 saw Berry enroute for England via Cape Horn. Approaching the notorious passage, terrific storms played havoc with sails and steering gear, and the "City Of Edinburgh" drifted helplessly for several days. In his reminiscences, Berry tells of opening a Bible and reading the passage in Ecclesiastes 9: "Whatever thy hand findeth to do, do with all thy might." This he took as a message for him to act and not to despair. His changed attitude had its effect on a crew on the point of mutiny and with only a makeshift rudder and rig they finally reached Callao in Chile, where his ship was repaired.

With his ship ready for sea again and loaded with produce, he set sail for Cadiz in Spain and this time rounded Cape Horn in safety only to meet such constant bad weather in the Atlantic that the vessel became water-logged and foundered not far from the equator. Two boats were launched, but only that carrying Berry and his party reached safety in the Cape Verde Islands, from where he eventually reached Lisbon and then Cadiz. Here, a bout of yellow fever nearly cost him his life, and on recovery Berry signed on as a crew member of a ship bound for England only to be captured by a privateer! After more adventures and much journeying Berry eventually found himself back in Lisbon where he met his future partner and friend Edward Wollstonecraft, son of a London lawyer and the nephew of Mary Wollstonecraft, wife of the poet Percy Bysshe Shelley (1792-1822).

Reaching London in 1815 Berry stayed with the Wollstonecrafts at Greenwich for three years. Having established a legal partnership with

Edward they chartered the "Admiral Cockburn" and took a cargo to Sydney, which arrived in July 1819. Berry wasted no time in getting the business going and built a wharf and commenced trading in timber, wool, sealskins and whale oil at what is now Berry's Bay, North Sydney.

While the business grew Berry explored the coast as far as the Hunter River and inspected the Bong Bong (Southern Highlands) district. They returned to London and applied for a grant of land in the colony, which was refused because only permanent residents were eligible. Berry and Wollstonecraft therefore decided to return to Sydney to fulfil the condition and sailed on the "Royal George" along with Governor Macquarie's successor, Sir Thomas Brisbane.

Berry faced numerous challenges in realizing his dream. From managing the vast property to navigating the difficulties of establishing a European settlement in such an isolated location, his journey was far from easy. However, his determination and foresight led to the creation of a thriving estate, which played a significant role in the early agricultural development of the region. The story of Coolangatta is more than just a tale of land acquisition, it is a testament to the pioneering spirit that helped shape the future of Australia's rural landscape.

Foundation of the Coolangatta Estate

Alexander Berry, a Scottish-born ship's surgeon, merchant, and explorer, sought a government land grant to develop an estate on the mid-south coast of New South Wales, alongside the Shoalhaven River. Berry applied to the NSW Government for a grant of 10,000 acres and 100 convicts, and Wollstonecraft was granted 500 acres in the Sydney suburb that now bears his name. Wollstonecraft built a house on a hill overlooking the harbour called 'Crows Nest Cottage', which is today on the site of the current North Sydney Public School. Not surprisingly, the government approved both requests, estimating that by maintaining 100 convicts, Berry and his partner, Edward Wollstonecraft, would save authorities £16,000 over the next ten years.

Notwithstanding the trail-breaking role of the aforementioned explorers, Berry became the first European to establish a settlement in the Shoalhaven District. Early in 1822, at the request of the governor, Berry explored the south coast in the "Snapper", under the command of Lt. Robert Johnston, as they entered every inlet between Wollongong and Bateman's Bay. His reports of the surrounding country were both accurate and interesting, but the area in the vicinity of Shoalhaven impressed him so much that he decided to settle there. Six months later he was sleeping at the foot of the hill he called 'Cullengatty" and began erecting buildings.

On the morning of June 22, 1822, Alexander Berry embarked from Sydney Cove aboard the small, single-masted wooden ship "Blanche". He was heading to the northern bank of the Shoalhaven River to take up his government land grant. Alongside the crew, there were convicts, whom Berry insisted be called "government men", explorer Hamilton Hume, and an Aboriginal man named 'Charcoal Will', who was familiar with the area. The ship also carried provisions, tools, and eight pigs. He chose a site at the base of Coolangatta Mountain on the northern side of the Shoalhaven River, where he built his homestead that became the headquarters of his Coolangatta Estate.

As the "Blanche" attempted to enter the Shoalhaven River, the large waves and shallow, narrow river mouth proved treacherous. A small boat sent out to assess the conditions capsized, resulting in the loss of two men. Berry then took command of the ship and sailed south to the Crookhaven River, where they anchored for the night.

Berry's Canal

The next morning, Berry had the convicts commence digging a channel through a sandbar between the Shoalhaven and Crookhaven Rivers, with the aim of joining the rivers to make navigation easier. This remarkable project, overseen by Hamilton Hume, kept the convicts busy for 12 days. The channel, known as 'Berry's Canal', became the first navigable canal in Australia and is still in use today. It altered the dynamics of the Shoalhaven River, making the original entrance to the river at Shoalhaven Heads accessible only during major floods. The canal also separated a landmass, creating Comerong Island. It became an essential route for transporting goods and people to Sydney.

Encounters with Aboriginal People

Upon arrival, Berry found the local Aborigines to be ferocious and initially had to be driven away by the sawyers and woodcutters. Several weeks after the first arrival of the party at Shoalhaven about 20 came down and camped near Berry's settlement, and for a year or two they stole maize and potatoes. Their two chiefs were Wagin, chief of Numba or Shoalhaven, and Yager, chief of Jervis Bay. Berry later took these two on as part of the crew of a cutter in which he voyaged to Sydney and return. Berry recalled the following account of that initial settlement period:

> "I went to Shoal Haven in June 1822 in order to form an establishment. At that time the Natives at that place bore a very bad character and were considered very hostile to the whites. Some years previously the Shoalhaven River was frequented by cedar cutters from Sydney. In the end the natives either killed all the sawyers or forced them away."
>
> One day my friend James Norton thus addressed me... "I hear you are going to take a farm near Jervis Bay. Is it true?" I replied in the affirmative. "Are you mad," he retorted. "The natives will eat you."
>
> Alexander Berry [1]

Despite the initial conflicts, Berry later employed local Aboriginal people on his estate, integrating them into his workforce alongside convicts, free settlers, and indentured laborers. Some Aboriginals took on key roles in timber cutting and farming, helping to shape the estate's success. Their involvement in estate operations was complex, blending cooperation and tension as they navigated a rapidly changing landscape.

The date 22nd June 1822 has since been recognised as the first European settlement on the South Coast of NSW. Alexander Berry wrote:

> "For my headquarters I fixed on the north side of the river at the foot of a hill called by the natives 'Collungatta'. I located the 10,000 acres grant in this locality."

'Collungatta' was the Aboriginal word for fine view, a description that Berry found difficult to dispute. On 1 July 1822, Alexander Berry climbed Mt. Coolangatta to view his vast estate. He spent the night atop this ancient mountain, pondering the future of his settlement and possible uses for its fertile land.

The Homestead

A homestead was swiftly established, and despite allegations of harsh treatment towards his convicts, Berry always insisted that "only mild measures and moral influences were of use in controlling men." Significantly, many of his workers remained with him on the estate even after the expiration of their penal terms, indicating a fair level of treatment.

Berry's approach to estate management was both methodical and innovative. He implemented a structured system where convicts were assigned specific tasks based on their skills. Blacksmiths, carpenters, and agricultural labourers worked in designated sections, ensuring the estate's rapid development. This system not only benefited Berry, but also allowed convicts to gain valuable skills, increasing their chances of a better life post-sentence. The government monitored the estate's progress, recognizing Berry's methods as a model for penal settlements across the colony. As a result, Coolangatta became a hub of economic and agricultural activity, setting a precedent for future landowners who sought to develop self-sustaining estates.

Berry's initial years at Coolangatta were filled with challenges, including sourcing materials, managing labor, and establishing reliable transport routes. Despite these difficulties, he successfully developed a thriving agricultural and timber enterprise. As the estate expanded, its influence grew, shaping the broader economic landscape of the developing Shoalhaven region.

Evolution of the Coolangatta Estate

As time flowed on, Berry sought to combine his merchant business with farming, drawing on his farming roots in Fife, Scotland. To prepare the land for farming, his laborers cleared trees to open up grazing land. In the early 19th century, red cedar (Toona ciliata), a native deciduous tree, grew abundantly along the New South Wales coast. This valuable wood was used for building, furniture, and boat construction, much of it being exported to Europe. Knowing that cedar was scarce around Sydney, Berry saw an opportunity to profit, as timber from his land was exempt from government taxes. On the return journey of the "Blanche" to Sydney, it carried a load of cedar wood bound for Europe.

Berry was drawn to the area by its rich alluvial soils, ideal for farming and grazing, though much of the low-lying land was swampy. To make the land productive, he devised a drainage system to channel water from the swamps into the river. Convicts, using basic tools, dug channels between one and three meters deep. The main channel draining Coomondery Swamp into the Shoalhaven River is still in use today and runs through the village of Shoalhaven Heads, parallel to Bolong Road. By the end of the work, around 200 kilometers of drainage channels had been dug.

Later in 1822, Hamilton Hume brought cattle to the area, marking the beginning of the district's primary industry. Mills and workshops were established, where tradesmen worked on cask-making, building repairs, leather treatment, condensed milk, gelatine, and shipbuilding. By 1824, the first vessel they called "Coolangatta" had been launched, and his influence was such that the town of Coolangatta in Queensland was even named after this first schooner, which was wrecked there in 1846.

Berry married Elizabeth (1781-1845), the sister of his business partner, Edward Wollstonecraft, on September 21, 1827. They established their headquarters at the foot of Coolangatta Mountain, north of the river, surrounded by tools, provisions, and mostly convict laborers who formed the first community. With further land purchases from the Crown and private transactions, the Coolangatta Estate expanded, eventually covering land from Gerringong in the north to

Jervis Bay in the south, and even beyond the town of Berry to the west. The Coolangatta Estate village, at the base of Coolangatta Mountain, grew into a self-sustaining township with up to 600 people. The community included builders, carpenters, blacksmiths, stonemasons, tinsmiths, bootmakers, and livestock keepers for pigs, sheep, and cattle. The estate also bred thoroughbred horses for export to India. The partners employed both convict labor and free workers to drain swamps and grow crops such as tobacco, maize, barley, and wheat, as well as raise pigs and cattle for hides, milk, and cheese. These products were transported to Sydney via ships purchased or built by the estate.

Coolangatta Estate's produce was sold in Sydney, and the estate's shipbuilders constructed vessels for transportation. The estate also supplied salt beef to the government and exported cedar to Europe. In 1823, the estate's first tobacco crop brought in substantial profits, as it was highly sought after in the Sydney market. The estate was home to a diverse population of convicts, ex-convicts, free settlers, and Aboriginal families, and his distribution of free goods to many of these helped improve their morale.

John Frawley at Coolangatta

By 1833, convict assignment had become a fairly efficient process, enabling John Frawley to be placed under Alexander Berry's charge. This likely required him to embark on another voyage, though a much shorter one south from Sydney to the Shoalhaven. The voyage would only have taken around a day or two and the vessels, which were plying this minor route at that time were smaller coastal sailboats. To be selected by a respected member of the colony at the time in the identity of Alexander Berry, proved to be providential for John Frawley in more ways than one. By the time John Frawley arrived at Berry's Coolangatta homestead in late 1833, the estate had already been functioning for 11 years, so so accommodation and out-buildings had already been erected and daily routines firmly established.[2]

On the Berry Estate most of the day to day operations were recorded and live on today in the 'Berry Papers', which are held at the Mitchell Library, at the State Library of New South Wales, Sydney. Entries for all workers including assigned servants on Berry's Estate were listed alphabetically, with the initial arrival entry for John Frawley making for interesting reading.³

A 'Flash' Reputation

Upon his arrival at Coolangatta in December 1833, John Frawley would no doubt have been surprised at the beauty of the rural property. He gave his age as 17, which confirms the information given by him on the Convict Indents, and fixes his birth year as somewhere in the year 1816. The other notable feature was that the convict overseers at Coolangatta categorised John Frawley as a 'free, flash gambler', with the added note that he was 'very lazy'!⁴ Undoubtedly, this attitude and work ethic would have to change if he was to survive in his new environment.

> **'FLASH'**
> Convicts of the early colony had their own 'flash' language, made up of slang words developed by criminals in London. Outsiders couldn't understand the language, so convicts were often able to undermine the authorities with their own jargon.

Discipline and Punishment

After 18 months of work, often enduring harsh treatment, John likely became quite familiar with the Coolangatta homestead, the work routine and life in general. However, he was slow to change his habits and his old reputation soon snagged more difficulties with the estate overseers. Infringements of any kind on Berry's Estate were noted, and John Frawley is recorded in the 'Berry Estate Punishment Book' on three separate occasions during 1835.

He received 36 lashes on the 30th November, for 'disobedience of orders and insolence', which certainly would have made a psychological and physical impression on him, as there is no further mention of punishment for John Frawley thereafter.⁵ Furthermore, signs that

John's run of bad lack was drawing to a close became apparent when he was scheduled to receive his Certificate of Freedom in March 1840, although his actual certificate has not been found to date.

Following ten years of constant urging, Alexander Berry's three brothers, John, William and David as well as his two sisters, arrived from Scotland to reside at the Coolangatta Homestead. Berry now left much of the daily running of the homestead to his brothers, although how much this affected the labourers is not known.

In 1837 the New South Wales Government conducted a General Return of Convicts in an attempt to accurately locate the whereabouts of the convict population at that time. John Frawley is recorded in the return as residing and working with Alexander Berry in 'Illawarra'.[6] The day to day work continued on the Berry Estate, but resources were always scarce, especially in regard to supplies handed out to the convicts. The masters of the day recorded all transactions in the Assigned Servants 'Day or Slop Book,' where John Frawley is recorded as receiving a number of items of clothing and supplies over the period from 1834 to 1840.[7]

The "Coolangatta" & The Town

Most people have no idea that the Queensland Gold Coast township of 'Coolangatta' was named after Alexander Berry's ship, the "Coolangatta", which was built in 1843 on the Coolangatta Estate in Shoalhaven, New South Wales. The Coolangatta was a topsail schooner, measuring 83 feet (25 meters) in length and weighing 88 long tons. It was built by John Blinksell for Alexander Berry at his property, Coolangatta Estate, which bordered Coolangatta Mountain on the northern bank of the Shoalhaven River. The ship primarily transported produce to Sydney for sale.

The unfortunate vessel met its fate just three years after it was built, being wrecked on Kirra/Bilinga Beach near a creek during a storm in 1846.[8] The story of how that came about was that on the 6th July 1846, under the command of Captain Steele, the "Coolangatta" departed from Brisbane, carrying two convict prisoners, George Craig (in irons) and William George Lewis. The ship was bound for the Tweed River to collect red cedar logs for transport to Sydney. However, upon arrival, Steele found the river entrance blocked by a sandbar and he was forced to anchor the ship in the lee of Point Danger off Kirra Beach. Since the logs could not be loaded directly onto the vessel, they were hauled overland from Terranora Inlet and rafted out from the beach. But despite six weeks of constant effort, fewer than half of the contracted 70,000 feet of cedar had been loaded, while five other ships remained trapped inside the river due to the bar.

On August 18, while Captain Steele was ashore, a southeast gale struck. His boat was damaged in the surf, leaving him stranded as he watched the storm intensify. As conditions worsened, the "Coolangatta" began dragging anchor. Realizing the ship was doomed, the prisoners were freed, and the crew abandoned ship, swimming to shore just before it broke apart and was wrecked on what would later be called 'Coolangatta Creek'.

The survivors then embarked on a grueling six-day, 110-kilometer trek north to Amity Point. Along the way, they were provided food each night by various groups of friendly Aboriginals before being rescued and transported to Brisbane aboard the "Tamar". Over time, the wreckage of the Coolangatta was buried by sand, and in 1883, the area was officially named in its honour.

The Coolangatta Estate After 1850

After convict transportation to New South Wales ceased in 1850, labour shortages worsened, compounded by the gold rush of the 1850s, when many workers left for the goldfields. To address this, Berry began bringing immigrant workers from China and Germany as indentured laborers and also employed local Aboriginal people and some Pacific Islanders.

In the mid-1800s, Berry began leasing small farms, requiring tenants to clear and fence the land. By 1863, the estate had expanded to over

40,000 acres. By 1869, there were around 370 tenant farmers, many of whom were the pioneer settlers who contributed to the development of the Shoalhaven District.

Alexander Berry passed away in 1873, leaving an estate valued at £1,252,975. His brother David, who had been managing the estate since 1836, inherited it. To cover three large bequests left by Alexander, David was forced to sell much of the land. The sale began in 1892, starting with the Gerringong farms and eventually including other estates.

By the late 1870s, most of the cedar had been harvested, and the estate turned increasingly to dairying to supply products like cheese and butter to the Sydney market. Dairy farming was further encouraged by the failure of wheat crops due to rust disease.

Upon David Berry's death in 1889, the estate passed to his cousin, Dr. John Hay, and later to his half-brother, Alexander Hay. Under their management, the estate became a Government Stud Farm and school in 1900. Dr. Hay traveled to Europe to study the latest methods in dairy production and imported the best dairy cattle breeds to improve milk yield. In 1895, Dr. Hay established the Jersey Milk Company at Shoalhaven Heads to produce tinned milk, which was exported to markets including China, Africa, and New Zealand. The factory was known for its strict hygiene standards, with workers required to bathe daily.

Dr. Hay died in 1909, and Alexander Hay continued managing the estate until his death in 1941. His son, Alexander Berry Hay, inherited the estate, but under their management, it declined into neglect. Buildings fell into ruin, and by 1946, a fire destroyed the homestead, along with much of the estate's history. The fire was considered suspicious, and the estate was insured.

Following the fire, his second wife Elizabeth Hay began selling off the property. Over the years, Col Bishop, born on a neighbouring farm, bought parts of the estate, ultimately restoring the remaining buildings. In 1950, he purchased the former servant's quarters and made it his family home. By the 1960s, Col and his wife, Norma, had acquired all 300 acres of the estate.

In 1968, the Bishops began restoring the property for commercial use, transforming it into accommodation. Col financed the restoration himself, purchasing furniture from the Metropole Hotel in Sydney, which was due for demolition. The Coolangatta Historic Village Motel opened in 1972, on the 150th anniversary of Alexander Berry's arrival.

Today, the Coolangatta Estate remains a picturesque site overlooking the ocean and surrounded by vineyards, preserving its historic legacy amidst modern development. For further details of the founding of the settlement at Coolangatta and to read Berry's fascinating account of his interactions with the Aboriginals, read the "Reminiscences of Alexander Berry', (*see Appendix D*).

Few lives could match the initiative, courage, and sheer adventure of Scottish born Alexander Berry, who trained as a surgeon but soonafter turned to trade and exploration, embarking on daring ventures across the Pacific. Eventually, he settled in New South Wales, where he became a prominent landowner and entrepreneur.

In 1822, Berry established the first European settlement on the Shoalhaven River, securing an enormous land grant of 10,000 acres, five times the typical allocation. The grant came with a strict condition: he had to employ, feed, and clothe one convict for every 100 acres for a decade, meaning he was responsible for 100 convicts. Many of these men had been sentenced to transportation for life due to serious crimes. The arrangement, however, benefited both parties, reducing the government's burden while supplying landowners with much-needed labour.

Berry's sharp business instincts and resilience enabled him to build immense wealth, but his later years were overshadowed by legal battles and personal tragedies. He passed away in 1873, leaving a lasting mark on Australian colonial history.

For John Frawley, life as a convict at Alexander Berry's Coolangatta estate was one of toil and hardship. Sentenced to a life far from his homeland, he laboured under the harsh conditions of colonial New South Wales, shaping the very land that would become his reluctant home. The days were grueling, the work unending, and his hope of freedom a distant dream. Yet, in the midst of his struggles, fate had something unexpected in store.

However, as the year 1838 drew to a close, John's world changed with a single glance. Among the convicts toiling on the estate was a young Irishwoman, someone who, like him, had been torn from her homeland and sentenced to an uncertain future on the far side of the world. She was Mary Ann McGarry, a fellow Limerick native, and like John, she carried the weight of exile on her shoulders. Their shared pasts, their shared loss, and the bond of their homeland forged an unbreakable connection.

But who was Mary Ann McGarry before she became a convict? What circumstances led her to this distant shore? To understand her journey, we must turn back the pages of history and uncover the story of her ancestors, a tale that begins far from the rugged coast of Shoalhaven and deep in the heart of Ireland.

References

1. Bayley W. A. (1965). 'Shoalhaven: History of the Shire of Shoalhaven', pp.24-25.
2. Anderson, J. (ed.). (1990). 'Guide to the papers of the Berry, Wollstonecraft and Hay Families.' Mitchell Library, Sydney.
3. Berry Papers. John Frawley, in 'List of Assigned Servants'. Mitchell Library, Sydney (MSS-315/62).
4. Ibid.
5. Berry Papers. John Frawley in 'Assigned Servants Punishment Book.' Mitchell Library, Sydney (MSS-315/62).
6. John Frawley in 'General Return of Convicts in 1837.' Mitchell Library, Sydney, p.227.
7. Berry Papers. John Frawley, off the 'Chafer' [sic. "Java"] in 'Assigned Servants Day (Slop) Book.' Mitchell Library, Sydney.
8. Gold Coast Bulletin,'Could Coolangatta's History Be Rewritten If A Maritime Mystery Is Solved?,' by Andrew Potts, 29th March 2014, p.1.

7

THE McGARRY ANCESTORS

Although Mary Ann McGarry was not born until 1813, her story begins long before then, shaped by the turbulent history of Ireland and the struggles of her ancestors. The period between 1780 and 1838 was one of profound change in Ireland, particularly in County Limerick, where her family resided. This era witnessed major events that reshaped Irish society, affecting the political, economic, and social conditions that would ultimately influence Mary Ann McGarry's path and her fate as a convict.

One of the most significant events of this period was the Act of Union (1801), which formally united Ireland with Great Britain, dissolving the Irish Parliament and intensifying tensions between Irish nationalists and the British Government. The economic hardships that followed were exacerbated by lingering effects of the Penal Laws, which disproportionately impacted Catholic families like the

McGarrys. These restrictive laws suppressed Catholic rights, limiting land ownership and access to education, thereby perpetuating poverty and social division.

Limerick, a key city in western Ireland, was deeply affected by these national struggles. The Napoleonic Wars from 1803 to 1815, had both positive and negative consequences for the region. While they created temporary economic opportunities through military recruitment and increased demand for goods, they also led to trade disruptions and greater hardship for rural communities. In response to economic distress and oppressive landlord policies, secret agrarian societies such as the 'Whiteboys' and the 'Rockites' emerged, engaging in resistance against landlords and British authorities. This period of unrest and rebellion reflected the desperation of many Irish families who faced eviction, starvation, and persecution.

Within this historical backdrop, this chapter delves into the origins of the McGarry surname and explores Mary Ann McGarry's earliest known ancestors, who were farmers in County Limerick. Their lives, shaped by agricultural traditions and the changing political landscape, provide vital context for understanding the world Mary Ann was born into. By examining their struggles and resilience, we gain deeper insight into the circumstances that led to her eventual transportation as a convict.

Ireland in the 16th & 17th Centuries

The McGarry ancestors lived through turbulent times including the American Revolution, which ignited strong sympathy in Ulster, particularly among the Presbyterians. Having been denied the right to hold public office, they sought widespread emancipation that included Roman Catholics. In 1778, the Irish Parliament responded by passing the Relief Act, easing some of the harshest restrictions imposed by the Penal Laws. Meanwhile, Irish Protestants, using the pretense of protecting the country from a potential French invasion, formed volunteer militias, swelling to nearly 80,000 members. Empowered by this force, they demanded legislative independence for Ireland. This push for autonomy gained momentum when British statesman Charles James Fox successfully moved for the repeal of Poynings' Law and significant anti-Catholic legislation. However, despite these advances, the Irish Parliament remained firmly under Protestant control and resisted extending voting rights to Catholics.[1]

The Protestant Ascendancy

The Protestant Ascendancy,[2] often referred to simply as the Ascendancy, was the political, economic, and social dominance of Ireland by a small Protestant elite from the 17th to the early 20th century. This ruling class consisted mainly of wealthy landowners, Protestant clergy, and professionals, all of whom belonged to the Church of Ireland or the Church of England.

The Ascendancy systematically excluded most of the Irish population, primarily Roman Catholics, but also Presbyterians and other religious minorities, including Jews, from political power and high society. Even the majority of Irish Protestants were largely excluded due to property requirements that prevented them from voting until the Reform Acts (1832–1928). The privileges enjoyed by the Ascendancy were widely resented, particularly by Irish Catholics, who made up the majority of the population.

The dispossession of Catholic landowners in Ireland occurred gradually, beginning in the reigns of Queen Mary I and her Protestant half-sister, Elizabeth I. A series of unsuccessful Irish uprisings against English rule, including the Nine Years' War (1595–1603), the Irish Rebellion of 1641–53, and the Williamite Wars (1689–91), resulted in widespread land confiscation by the Crown. These lands were then granted or sold to individuals deemed loyal to the English monarchy, most of whom were English and Protestant. Over time, English soldiers, traders, and landowners formed a new ruling class. The wealthiest among them were elevated to the Irish House of Lords and eventually gained control over the Irish House of Commons. Collectively, they became known as the Anglo-Irish.

By the 1790s, the term Ascendancy took on different meanings depending on political perspective. For Irish nationalists, who were mostly Catholic, it became a symbol of oppression and resentment. For unionists, who were predominantly Protestant, it evoked a sense of lost prestige and influence. The vast majority of Ireland's population were Catholic peasants, many of whom lived in extreme poverty and had little political influence during the 18th century. Some Catholic leaders even converted to Protestantism to avoid severe legal and economic penalties. Despite this, a growing Catholic cultural awakening was beginning to take shape.

Tensions eventually erupted in the Irish Rebellion of 1798, culminating in the Battle of Vinegar Hill on June 21, 1798. In this decisive conflict, more than 13,000 British troops attacked Vinegar Hill, near Enniscorthy in County Wexford, which served as the largest camp and headquarters of the Wexford United Irish rebels. The battle, which took place both on Vinegar Hill and in the streets of Enniscorthy, marked a turning point in the rebellion. It was the last major attempt by the Irish rebels to hold and defend territory against the British military.

The influence of the French Revolution found its most fervent supporters in Ireland through the Society of United Irishmen, who orchestrated the 1798 Irish Rebellion. Though poorly armed, Irish peasants rose in Wexford, staging a valiant effort that briefly threatened Dublin. However, they were ultimately defeated by Crown forces at Vinegar Hill. A French force of 1,100 men later landed at Killala Bay, but their arrival came too late to turn the tide. Observing the unrest, British Prime Minister William Pitt the Younger concluded that only a legislative union between Great Britain and Ireland, alongside Catholic emancipation, could stabilize the situation. To achieve this, he employed a mix of financial incentives and political patronage, persuading the Irish Parliament to pass the Act of Union.

In 1800, both the Irish Parliament and the Parliament of Great Britain passed the Act of Union, which came into effect on the 1st

January 1801. This abolished the Irish legislature and merged the Kingdom of Ireland with Great Britain to form the United Kingdom of Great Britain and Ireland. The Union Flag was modified to include Saint Patrick's Cross, which was counterchanged with Saint Andrew's Cross to symbolize Ireland's inclusion. However, King George III vehemently opposed Catholic emancipation, forcing Pitt to abandon his promise and resign in frustration.[3]

The 1801 Act of Union

At the start of the 19th century, Ireland was still reeling from the aftermath of the 1798 Irish Rebellion. Prisoners were being deported to Australia, and sporadic violence continued in County Wicklow. Another failed uprising, led by Robert Emmet, took place in 1803. The Act of Union,[4] which formally merged Ireland with Britain, was largely an effort to address the grievances behind the 1798 rebellion and to prevent future unrest from threatening Britain or inviting foreign intervention.

In 1800, both the Irish Parliament and the Parliament of Great Britain passed the Act of Union, which came into effect on the 1st January 1801. This abolished the Irish legislature and merged the Kingdom of Ireland with Great Britain to form the United Kingdom of Great Britain and Ireland. The Union Flag was modified to include Saint Patrick's Cross, which was counterchanged with Saint Andrew's Cross to symbolize Ireland's inclusion.

The act's passage in the Irish Parliament, like the 1707 Acts of Union between Scotland and England, was ultimately secured through widespread bribery. Many Irish MPs were granted British peerages and other incentives in exchange for their support.

During this period, Ireland was governed by officials appointed by the British government. The Lord Lieutenant of Ireland, who represented the King, and the Chief Secretary for Ireland, appointed by the British Prime Minister, were the key figures. Over time, as the British Parliament assumed more executive power from the monarchy, the Chief Secretary gained prominence, while the Lord Lieutenant became largely symbolic. With the abolition of the Irish Parliament, Irish representatives were now elected to the United Kingdom's House of Commons at Westminster.

The British administration in Ireland, often referred to as "Dublin Castle," remained dominated by the Anglo-Irish elite until its withdrawal from Dublin in 1922.

Post-union Irish history was dominated by the struggle for civil and religious freedom, as well as the ongoing desire for independence from Britain. Dissatisfaction with the union quickly boiled over, leading to the armed rebellion of July 23, 1803, led by Irish nationalist Robert Emmet. The uprising was swiftly crushed, and for a time, armed resistance subsided. However, the fight for Catholic rights continued through peaceful means. In 1823, the Catholic Association was founded, relentlessly advocating for full emancipation. Their efforts bore fruit in 1828, when Catholics were granted the right to hold local office, followed by the landmark 1829 decision allowing them to sit in Parliament.

With religious restrictions easing, attention turned to another major grievance, the compulsory tithes paid to support the Anglican Church of Ireland. The so-called "Tithe War" erupted as Irish Catholics resisted these unjust payments. Violent clashes ensued, with atrocities committed by both sides. Alongside the tithe protests, the call for repealing the Act of Union grew louder, giving rise to various nationalist groups, including the Ribbon Society, which operated on the fringes of law and order.[5]

The 1832 reform of the British Parliament brought a modest victory for Ireland, increasing its parliamentary representation from 100 to 105 seats. More significantly, it empowered the middle class, weakening the dominance of the pro-English aristocracy. In 1838, Parliament passed a bill converting tithes into rent charges paid by landlords, momentarily easing tensions over the issue.

Just as one struggle seemed to settle, a catastrophic disaster reshaped Ireland's landscape. Between 1845 and 1850, a devastating famine struck, caused by widespread potato crop failure. The impact was catastrophic, millions either perished from starvation or fled the country. Emigration to America surged, with entire communities uprooted in search of survival. It is estimated that Ireland's population declined by over two million due to famine and forced displacement.

Amidst this period of upheaval, the McGarry ancestors endured. Coming from the southwestern city of Limerick, they lived through these turbulent times, witnessing firsthand the fight for Irish independence, religious equality, and economic survival. The reforms of 1838 had briefly alleviated tensions, but the famine's devastation overshadowed any progress, leaving an indelible mark on the history of Ireland and its people.

The resilience of the Irish spirit, tested through centuries of struggle, would continue to shape the nation's history in the years to come. Through rebellion, reform, and resistance, Ireland's long road to self-determination was far from over.

In weaving this family history with Ireland's historical past, this chapter sets the stage for Mary Ann McGarry's journey. Whether by forced exile, voluntary migration, or transportation as convicts, countless Irish laid the foundations for new communities in Australia. Mary Ann McGarry, the 'colleen' from Limerick, was part of this story of Irish resilience and survival. What better way to begin this section than by tracing the origins of the McGarry name and uncovering the history of the ancestors and family that came before her?[6]

The McGarry Ancestors

The McGarrys were the paternal ancestors of Mary Ann McGarry, but unfortunately, little is known about them. The earliest confirmed mention of Mary McGarry's paternal ancestors was written into her 1889 death certificate, registered in Queensland. On that document, Mary's father was identified as Patrick McGarry, who was a farmer likley working in and about Limerick. While we face the same frustrating lack of information about John Frawley's ancestors, we can nevertheless dive into the origins of the McGarry surname and uncover its history.

The Surname of McGarry

The surname of McGarry is found in various spellings which include MacCarry, McHarry, McGarrie, McGarry, MacAree, M'Garry and Megarry. This latter form is a strange anglicised corruption, which resulted from the similarity of the sound 'Mac an Ri', meaning 'the son of king', although there is no logical connection.[7] It is said that the McGarrys form part of the clan MacHugh of Leitrim and Roscommon, although again this has not been proven as the derivation of the surnames are quite different. Examples of recordings for this complex surname include Grizzel McHarry at Killyleagh, County Down, on April 28th 1742; Mary McGarry, christened at Downpatrick, County Down on July 8th 1779; and Mary McCarry, who was a passenger on the ship "Marmion of Liverpool", which sailed from Belfast to New York on May 25th 1846, during the 'Great Famine' of 1846-1848.[8]

The first known recorded spelling of the family name of McGarry may be that of Nickolas Magheree, which was dated September 28th 1625, at the church of St John the Evangelist, in Dublin, during the reign of King Charles I (1625-1649), otherwise known as 'The Martyr'.[9]

Famous & Notable McGarrys

The surname McGarry, has been associated with a number of notable individuals across various fields. Some distinguished bearers of the McGarry name (all from Wikipedia) are:

Seán McGarry (1886–1958, no known relation): An influential Irish nationalist and politician, Seán McGarry was a senior member of the Irish Republican Brotherhood (IRB) and served as its president from 1917 to 1918. He played a significant role in Ireland's struggle for independence, participating in the 1916 Easter Rising and later serving as a Teachta Dála (TD) in the Irish parliament.

Bill McGarry (1927–2005, no known relation): An English international football player and manager, Bill McGarry had a notable career in football, both on the field and from the sidelines. These individuals exemplify the diverse achievements of those bearing the McGarry surname, making significant impacts in their respective fields.

The Heffernan Ancestors

The Heffernans were the maternal ancestors of Mary Ann McGarry. The Heffernan family crest came into existence many centuries ago. This ancient Irish name of Heffernan is an Anglicized form of the Gaelic surname "O'hIfearnain", the "O" prefix indicating "male descendant of", and the personal name "Ifearnan", being a diminutive formation from the nickname "Ifreannach", or demon, being from "ifreann", or hell.[10]

The Surname of Heffernan

There is some confusion as to the meaning of this name, but some believe it to mean Horse-Lord, or 'eachearnan', where 'eich' was 'horse' and 'Thigearnán' meant lord' and that the name Aherne, who are from the same area is the anglicised variation of this name. Traditionally, Irish family names were taken from the heads of tribes, or from some illustrious warrior, and were usually prefixed by "O", as above, or "Mac", denoting "the son of." The original territory of the Heffernan sept was near Corofin in County Clare, called Muintirfernain after them, but they established themselves early on in eastern County Limerick, on the Tipperary border, and were chiefs of Owneybeg. The O'Heffernans are still found mostly in those areas. Old manuscripts such as the "Book of Rights" describe the O'Heffernans as one of the "four tribes of Owney", the others being MacKeogh, O'Loingsigh (Lynch), and O'Calahan. The modern surname of Heffernan can be found recorded in a number of variations such as Heffernan, Hiffernan, Heffernon and Hefferan.[11]

Famous & Notable Heffernans

A notable bearer of the name was William Dall O'Heffernan (1715-1802), the Gaelic poet. One of the first recorded spellings of the family name is shown to be that of Aeneas O'Heffernan, the Bishop of Emly, which was dated 1543, during the reign of King Henry VIII (r.1509-1547), otherwise known as "Bluff King Hal," of England. Notable persons with the Heffernan surname include the following...[12]

William Daniel Heffernan (b.1943), more commonly known as Bill Heffernan, is a former Australian politician who was a member of the Liberal Party in the Senate representing the state of New South Wales, and serving from 1996 to 2016. Christy Heffernan (b.1957) is an Irish retired hurler who played as a full-forward for the Kilkenny senior team. William J. Heffernan (1872-1955), was an American politician and member of the New York State Senate (5th District) from 1913 to 1918, sitting in the 136th, 137th, 138th, 139th and 140th New York State Legislatures.[13]

Beyond the Heffernan surname, no further details are known about Mary McGarry's maternal ancestry at this time.

Patrick McGarry & Mary Heffernan

Around 900 years before the McGarrys and Heffernans set foot in Limerick, the region was known as 'Luimneach.' It encompassed the general area along the banks of the Shannon Estuary, then referred to as 'Loch Luimnigh.' The earliest recorded settlements on King's Island during the pre-Viking and Viking eras were called 'Inis Sibhtonn' and 'Inis an Ghaill Duibh' in historical annals.[14]

Mary Ann McGarry's parentage is fortunately well-documented. Her death certificate, recorded at the Dunwich Benevolent Asylum in Queensland in 1889, lists her parents as Patrick MacGarry, a farmer, and Mary Heffernan of Limerick, County Limerick, Ireland.[15] However, due to the lack of surviving records, tracing her ancestry beyond this point remains an exceedingly difficult task.

A 2014 blog post by 'GenealogyBank' titled "Why Do You Love Genealogy?" highlighted the widespread passion for family history research. Bu the sub-question, "what most frustrates people about genealogy", resonated with my own experiences of hitting research roadblocks. The post received over 200 responses, many of which echoed my own struggles with the Frawley and McGarry lines, dead ends, missing information, and the occasional inaccuracy in shared genealogical data.[16]

As the daughter of Patrick MacGarry and Mary Heffernan, Mary Ann McGarry was undoubtedly a native of Limerick. Her parents likely had other children, and records from the International Genealogical Index (IGI) list Patrick McGarry (1821-1878) and Michael McGarry (born 1833) as potential siblings. Michael married Johanna FitzGerald, daughter of James FitzGerald, on February 25, 1865, in Croom, County Limerick.

Patrick McGarry, the Patriarch

Little is known about Mary's father Patrick MacGarry, who was likely born around 1790. Mary Ann recorded his occupation as a farmer and noted that the McGarry family hailed from Limerick, or possibly from Loughmore, slightly to the south. A death registration in the IGI lists a Patrick McGarry of Aghalust, born around 1788, but there is no way to confirm whether he was Mary Ann's father.

Mary Heffernan, the Matriarch

Similarly, very little is known about Mary Heffernan, Patrick MacGarry's wife, and Mary Ann McGarry's mother. She was probably born around 1790 and resided in County Limerick. One possible record in the IGI lists a Mary Heffernan of Mitchelstown, County Cork, about 60 kilometers south of Limerick, born around 1790. However, there is no definitive proof linking her to Mary Ann McGarry.

A baptism record for a Maria (Mary) Heffernan was discovered on the FamilySearch website, dated July 4, 1790, at St. Mary's Church in Clonmel, close to Mitchelstown, and this record lists her parents as Joannis (John) Heffernan and Catharine Hennessy, with William Meehan and Maria Kelly as godparents. However, this connection requires verification.[17]

At this stage, further investigation into the McGarry and Heffernan family lines has been unproductive. Although multiple birth registrations exist for individuals named Patrick McGarry and Mary Heffernan, none provide definitive proof of lineage. Rather than clarifying the picture, the available data only deepens the mystery, leaving the search for Mary Ann McGarry's ancestors an ongoing challenge.

Patrick McGarry and Mary Heffernan's legacy carried on through their children, including a daughter born in Limerick around 1813. Named after her mother, young Mary's life took a devastating turn when she was convicted of 'receiving stolen goods', a crime that ripped her from her home and condemned her to exile on the far side of the world.

In 1838, she arrived in Sydney aboard the convict transport "Diamond", sentenced to seven years of servitude. But as the ship's anchor dropped, her true journey was just beginning. Forced to navigate the brutal realities of a fledgling colony, Mary's story became one of resilience, survival, and fate's unexpected twists.

In the next chapter, we uncover the trials she faced, the choices that shaped her destiny, and how the ghosts of her past would forever shape the woman she would become.

References

1. Wikipedia - History of Ireland (1801-1823) [https://en.wikipedia.org/wiki/History_of_Ireland_(1801–1923)].
2. Wikipedia - Protestant Ascendancy [https://en.wikipedia.org/wiki/Protestant_Ascendancy].
3. Ibid.
4. Wikipedia - Acts of Union 1800 [https://en.wikipedia.org/wiki/Acts_of_Union_1800].
5. Ibid.
6. Ancestry - McGarry Family History [https://www.ancestry.com.au/name-origin?surname=mcgarry].
7. SurnameDB - McGarry [https://www.surnamedb.com/Surname/McGarry].
8. Ibid.
9. Ibid.
10. Wikipedia - Heffernan [https://en.wikipedia.org/wiki/Heffernan].
11. SurnameDB - Heffernan [https://www.surnamedb.com/Surname/Heffernan].
12. Ibid.
13. Wikipedia - Heffernan, op. cit.
14. Wikipedia - History of Limerick [https://en.wikipedia.org/wiki/History_of_Limerick].
15. Queensland Dept of BDM. (1889). Death Certificate for Mary Frawley (nee McGarry) at Dunwich Benevolent Asylum, 1889/3633-1695.
16. Harrell-Sesniak, Mary, (2014). 'Your Top Genealogy Challenges & Frustrations', GenealogyBank Blog, October 28, 2014.
17. Possible baptism for Mary Heffernan on the 4th July 1790 at St Mary's, Clonmel, co. Tipperary, Ireland. (Catholic Parish Registers, 1655-1915, Waterford and Lismore - St Mary´s, Clonmel 1790 - 1797).

8

MARY ANN McGARRY
THE CONVICT

ary Ann McGarry's journey began in the heart of Ireland, likely around the year 1813, in the bustling city of Limerick.[1] Born to Patrick McGarry and Mary Heffernan, she was one of many caught in the tides of hardship that swept through early 19th-century Ireland.[2] While little is known of her childhood, by the mid-1830s, she was working as a housemaid in Limerick, a position that offered stability, but little protection from the grinding realities of life.

Fate, however, had a different path in store for Mary. In July 1837, she found herself standing in a courtroom, accused of receiving stolen goods, a crime that, minor as it seemed, carried severe consequences in an era of unforgiving British law. It wasn't her first run-in with the authorities; records indicate a previous conviction that had already landed her behind bars for three months. Whether out of desperation or misfortune, Mary had crossed a line that the judicial system did not take lightly.³ The verdict? Transportation beyond the seas, a seven-year sentence to the penal colony of New South Wales.

Desperate to alter her fate, Mary took the only option available to her, she petitioned for clemency.⁴ Her plea landed on the desk of none other than Richard Wellesley (1760-1842), 1st Marquess Wellesley, the Lord Lieutenant of Ireland, and elder brother of the Duke of Wellington.⁵ In a time when mercy was rarely granted, prisoner petitions were meticulously reviewed, their merits weighed by judges, constables, and gaol governors. Mary's petition, however, was sparse. She claimed to be just sixteen years old, perhaps an attempt to evoke sympathy, but beyond that, there was little to strengthen her case.⁶,⁷

With the weight of the British judicial system against her and her fate hanging by a thread, Mary's journey was only just beginning. What lay ahead was a world unknown, one of hardship, resilience, and the unyielding will to survive.

Transportation

Unfortunately, the appeal was unsuccessful and Mary was transported under guard in a gaol wagon along with other prisoners from Limerick to Dublin, and was later embarked on board the female convict ship "Diamond", which was then moored in Kingston Harbour.

The "Diamond" was a relatively new and large schooner of 573 tons, having been built in 1835 on the Isle of Man, the master being James F. Bissett.⁸ The ship was loaded with 162 female prisoners and 27 of their children, who were received from the Penitentiary at Dublin, probably in October or early November of 1837.

There was also 18 female passengers aboard the "Diamond", most of whom were the free wives of convicts already in New South Wales together with 36 of their children. One cabin passenger also came aboard in Mr. Goodwin.9 The newspapers reported that the ship was to depart at the first opportunity, however their actual departure was delayed from Kingston Harbour until the 29th November 1837, and sailed just a day after the "William Jardine".

> "Two hundred female convicts have been embarked on board the Diamond convict-ship, now in Kingston Harbour, for New South Wales. She sails on the first fair wind."
>
> *The Morning Post, 15th November 1837* [10]

Mr. William McDowell, the surgeon superintendent, who was going out on his third such convict voyage, was required to keep the ships journal.

> "Receipts for convicts, clothes etc received on board, 16 November 1837; Memorandum of convicts families recommended to be sent to New South Wales at Public expense, with observation on character, situation etc; List of Free Settlers embarked; Scale of the Proportion of Medicines and Necessaries for 200 Convicts for voyage (printed); Manifests of Stores received; Return of names and ages of the children of Convicts embarked; and List of money belonging to Convicts given into the charge of the Surgeon Superintendent."
>
> *William McDowell, Surgeon* [11]

McDowell kept the medical journal from the 20th October 1837 to 20th April 1838. However, it seems few if any unusual events confronted any of the female convicts, the ships company or the ship itself en route to New South Wales.

> "I beg leave to acquaint you agreeable to my instructions that the number of female convicts embarked on board the ship Diamond for a passage to New South Wales were in all 162 received from the Penitentiary in Dublin all in tolerable good health with twenty-seven of their children of different ages."
>
> *William McDowell, Surgeon* [12]

Once at sea, the women suffered severely from seasickness and constipation during the voyage, with Mr McDowell supposing this was made worse by the great change they experienced in their rations and lack of exercise. According to the surgeon's sick book, McDowell remarked that there were seven confinements, which expended most of the medical comforts and hospital clothing, with three deaths on the voyage, although only one was a prisoner, and considered that illnesses aboard were otherwise "mostly trifling." A violent gale blew up on the 14th December during which the prisoner Catherine Raygan (Regan), was injured by a cask rolling about the deck, and she was afterwards treated by the surgeon for almost six weeks for her sufferings.

According to the masters log on route, the "Diamond" spoke with the "Hyacinth", bound for the Cape of Good Hope in latitude

4°6' north and longitude 18°15' west. Also on the 1st February the "Duchess of Northumberland" from London to Sydney in latitude 32°5', and longitude 21°30' west, near the Cape of Good Hope; and on the 3rd January exchanged numbers with the "Alacrity", 30 days out from London in latitude 5° north, and longitude 18°40' west, bound for Port Jackson.[13]

The "Diamond" arrived at Port Jackson on the 28th March 1838 after a voyage of 114 days. However, the women were kept on board for almost two weeks before being landed on Thursday 12th April, but at Fort Macquarie instead of at the dockyard. Fort Macquarie was designed by Francis Greenway, and built in 1817, but was demolished in 1901. The superlative site then became a tram shed until the 1950s when Jan Utzon won a competition to design the world famous Sydney Opera House that occupies the site today.

Just six months later, Caroline Chisholm (1808-1817) arrived in Sydney with her husband Captain Archibald Chisholm, who had been granted a two-year furlough from Madras, India on the grounds of ill health. Rather than return to England, the Chisholms decided the climate in Australia would be better for his health so they set sail for Sydney, aboard the "Emerald Isle", and arrived at Port Jackson in September 1838, later settling at Windsor.[14]

Upon disembarkation on the 12th April 1838 the female convicts were recorded by the authorities in the Convict Indents and the listing for Mary Ann McGarry was very informative. A committee of ladies was in attendance at Fort Macquarie for the purpose of pointing out to the newly arrived prisoners the necessity of their behaving themselves in the different situations they may be placed in, so as to merit any future indulgence. Governor Sir George Gipps (1790-1847) was also in attendance, and exhorted the women to behave themselves in their new capacities. They were also addressed by the Bishop before being distributed to various people who had applied for convict labour.[15]

The 'Sydney Monitor' carried the following news on the 16th April 1838...

NEWS OF THE DAY

"At the time of landing the women by the "Diamond", at Fort Macquarie on Wednesday last, a circumstance occurred which is likely to give employment to some of our gentleman learned in the law. The matter of dispute was between two gentlemen well known in the town, and both holding Government appointments. As the facts will most probably come to light in the Supreme Court, we abstain from at present mentioning names or particulars."

The Sydney Monitor, 16th April 1838.

Although we know not the exact reason, the dispute was apparently between Colonel Wilson and the clerk to the Superintendant of Convicts at the time, and a Mr. Thomas Ryan, which involved the distribution of two of the women who disembarked the "Diamond".[16]

Details taken directly from Mary McGarry's 'indent' show that she declared herself to be a Catholic, and was working as a housemaid prior to her arrest in Limerick.[17] However, an interesting feature of Mary's information was that despite her 'Prisoner Petition,' which was submitted in Ireland just nine months earlier, stating her age to be just 16, her true age may actually have been as high as 28, according to her 1889 certificate of death.[18]

The Female Factory

Most female convicts were directly assigned to a colonist for work as a domestic servant, while the more troublesome, hardened or 'useless' prisoners were mostly sent to the 'Female Factory' in Parramatta, as it was then known. Although some convict women were classed as depraved and irredeemable prostitutes, most had been in domestic service in England and had simply stolen from their employers or shops, and were therefore being transported for the most menial of crimes. Upon arrival, the system of selection of servants often meant that the gentry and officers could choose the prettiest young convict girls, while others had to take up prostitution to survive.[19]

After being processed by the authorities, Mary Ann McGarry was not officially recorded as an inmate of the Female Factory at Parramatta, but she may very well have spent a short time there or nearby. The first 'Female Factory' was built at Parramatta in 1804 and initially consisted of a single long room with a fireplace at one end for the women to cook on. Women and girls made rope, spun and carded wool. Their accommodation was very basic and they often slept on the piles of wool. An upgraded three-storey barracks and Female Factory was built in 1821, which was mainly used to house women convicts who had committed local offences, or women with children and convict girls who were unsuitable for work with the settlers. In time, the work done in the Female Factory transformed to be less difficult with needlework and laundry becoming the main duties. Some women consigned to the Female Factory did not actually take up residence in the Parramatta building itself, but resided nearby and came in every day to work. Many also remained only for a day or so before being assigned to free settlers or even emancipated convicts, while others were very quickly married off.

One if the Female Factory's moralistic features was that any man could apply to marry one of the girls. The procedure involved the women being lined up at the Factory while the men would walk along the line and drop a scarf or handkerchief at the feet of his woman of choice. If she picked it up, the marriage was virtually immediate... so much for getting to know one another! Children of convict women either stayed with their mothers or were moved to an orphanage.[20]

Convict women generally left little trace of themselves, and their movements in early Sydney were rarely if ever recorded. This was most certainly the case for Mary, so after disembarking from the "Diamond," where did she go and what did she do? A few clues reveal snippets of evidence that better piece together Mary's movements from the time she arrived in Sydney in April 1838 until her marriage at Wollongong in July 1840.

To Coolangatta Estate

Records show that our ancestor Mary McGarry, was selected by Alexander Berry for his Coolangatta Estate by pure chance, where she was either put to work as a housemaid, or given the regular supplies of fabric she withdrew from stores, she may also have worked as a seamstress. It was almost certain to have been at Coolangatta where Mary met and developed a relationship with her future husband John Frawley, which was likely a case of mutual attraction that could very well have come from their both being natives of the same town.

However, being of similar age, it is also possible that Mary McGarry and John Frawley already knew one another from Limerick. If this were the case, might it have also been possible that John Frawley somehow knew of her impending arrival in the colony, in which case he could have somehow played a part in having her assigned to Coolangatta? We may never know the answer to this question, but all options remain a possibility.

Mary was soon placed on board a coastal vessel from Sydney to the Shoalhaven wharf and then brought to Berry's Estate by wagon. At Coolangatta the day to day operations were recorded in the Estate journals with all workers on Berry's Estate being listed alphabetically.

The initial entry for Mary McGarry recorded little information, perhaps because she was later returned to the government. Why this initial Coolangatta Estate entry in the records that Mary Ann McGarry was 'returned to the government' is unclear, but if she was returned, it couldn't have been for long as she is soon after listed as receiving supplies at the Berry Estate, in records kept in the supply (slop) books.[21]

Although no evidence of her assignment has been found, it appears that Mary McGarry arrived at Coolangatta sometime between her disembarkation from the "Diamond" in Sydney in April, and the 5th July 1838, as it was then that she was first recorded in the 'Assigned Servants Day (Slop) Book', and began to regularly draw supplies of cotton, calico and flannel from the Estate stores.[22]

But the Berry Estate entries for Mary McGarry concluded on the 3rd January 1839, when she was transferred to the service of the Rev. Matthew Devenish Meares (1800-1878), in Wollongong. This assignment was confirmed by Mary herself, and recorded on her death certificate that about this time she worked for a period of 18 months at Wollongong, in the service of the Rev. Meares,[23] the first Anglican Minister of the Illawarra-Shoalhaven District.[24]

Rev. Matthew Devenish Meares

Matthew Devenish Meares (1800-1878),[25] was born in 1800 in Meares Court, Westmeath, Ireland, the son of William Devenish and Deborah Coghlan and the brother of John Devenish Meares (1795-1875). Matthew married his cousin Georgina Augusta Devenish (c.1802-1881) on 23rd June 1822 in St. Anne's Church, Dublin, County Dublin, Ireland.[26] Their oldest child was born in Dublin Ireland, which at that time was part of the United Kingdom.

Matthew emigrated aboard the "Mariner" which arrived Sydney, in the colony of N.S.W. on the 10th July 1825. Matthew was accompanied by his wife and two children, William being under two years old and their daughter Elizabeth who was born enroute.[27] Matthew had graduated in Arts at Trinity College, Dublin, Ireland and later qualifying for Holy Orders. The family lived at Windsor, NSW for about 2 years then moved to Pitt Town, where he performed weekly services at Wilberforce. On every other Sunday he held service at Pitt Town and Sackville and every three months at Wiseman's Ferry. He moved the family to Wollongong in 1837 where he stayed until 1858 when he resigned his position and moved to Sydney to become Rector of St. Thomas' Enfield until he retired about 1860. The following was printed in the Sydney Gazette on the 14th July 1825.

"KNOW YE, that we have nominated and appointed, and do hereby nominate and appoint, Our trusty and well loved Matthew Devenish Meares, Clerk, to be one of our Chaplains within our said colony; he, the said Matthew Devenish Meares, being a Priest in holy order of the established church of England and Ireland, And it is Our Will, that the said (Matthew) shall hold such his office during our pleasure, and no longer, And We do further direct and command, that the said (Matthew) so long as he shall retain his office, shall officiate as a Minister of the Church."[28]

Rev. Meares was the first incumbent of the Illawarra-Shoalhaven District where he served from 1838-1857.[29] He died on the 5th December 1878 in Olivia Terrace, Bourke Street, Surry Hills, New South Wales,[30,31] at age 78, and was buried in St. Thomas' Anglican Cemetery, Enfield, New South Wales.[32,33] His wife Georgina was born in 1802 in Dublin, Ireland, United Kingdom and died on 28 June 1881 in Sydney, Colony of New South Wales at age 79. Their children were William Devenish Meares, Elizabeth Devenish (Meares) Ellis, Henry Douglas Devenish-Meares, John Devenish Meares, Alfred Devenish-Meares, Catherine Ann (Meares) Ellis, Augusta Ann Devenish (Meares) Osborne, Alexander Sparke Meares, Frederick Potter Devenish-Meares and Thomas Barker Septimus Meares the younger.

Meares was a fervent anti-papist, but despite railing against the Catholics and taking issue in 1840 at the building of a Catholic Church by outright refusing them the use of a quarry on his property, he was evidently happy to select Mary McGarry, a Catholic from Limerick, as a house servant. Following a raft of back and forth correspondence on the Wollongong Catholic Church issue, the final say of the colonial Catholics was poisonous... and may have even had something to do with Mary's eventual departure:

> "On this subject we trust we are 'sans peur et sans reproche' (without fear and without reproach), but we do not see the necessity of carrying the war into the heart of the peaceful Protestant camp, because a few of the 'awkward squad' have the folly to batter their heads against our ramparts. Mr Meares' own letter was the most terrible blow that he could give his own reputation, a blow which could not be strengthened by any comment of ours.
>
> *Australasian Chronicle, 4 June 1840, p.2*

We know that Rev. Meares was in the habit of making regular visits to Coolangatta for the 'moral and spiritual improvement' of the assigned servants there.[34] Although as a covict she couldn't marry without permission, and couldn't write, Mary likely received letters from her suitor John Frawley, at Coolangatta via her 'master.' Or she may even have accompanied him on occasion, with the intersection of these circumstances providing every possibility of visiting her future husband.

Mary McGarry's early years in the colony had been filled with hardship, but as time passed, her fortunes began to change. Having been assigned at Coolangatta, and later worked in the service of Rev. Meares in Wollongong, she had carved out a place for herself in the growing settlement of Wollongong. After just two years in New South Wales, life for Mary looked much brighter than it had since she first stepped off the convict ship. But a new chapter was about to begin, one that would transform her life completely.

At the same time, another figure in Coolangatta's convict ranks was reaching a turning point. John Frawley had served his full seven-year sentence on the Berry estate, with his last recorded entry on January 4, 1840. By then, he was a well-known figure in the settlement, possibly granted a cottage or even promoted within the estate. But freedom meant change. No longer bound to the estate without pay, he was likely no longer needed. Yet, instead of moving on immediately, John remained at Coolangatta a little longer. Perhaps it was because something, or someone, was keeping him there.

And so, as he stood at the threshold of his new life, John Frawley found freedom and a new future all at once. In March of 1840, he and Mary Ann McGarry applied for permission to marry in Wollongong, marking the beginning of a life together, one of the earliest unions in the town's history. Their story, and the challenges and triumphs that lay ahead, is the subject of the next chapter...

References

1. Queensland Dept of BDM. (1889). Death Certificate for Mary Frawley (nee McGarry) at Dunwich Benevolent Asylum, 1889/3633-1695.
2. NSW State Archives & Records. (1838). Mary McGarry off the "Diamond," arrived Sydney 28th March 1838, in 'Convict Indents.' (Fiche #735, p.226; Film #908; Shelf #X641).
3. NSW State Archives & Records. (1838). Mary McGarry, op. cit.
4. The National Archives. (15/11/1837). 'Prisoner Petition for Mary McGarry of the "Diamond."' [http://www.nationalarchives.ie/cgi-bin/naisearch01]. The National Archives, Kew, Surrey. (Record 10 of 17/PPC - TR2, p.77).
5. Wikipedia. 'Richard Wellesley.' [https://en.wikipedia.org/wiki/Richard_Wellesley,_1st_Marquess_Wellesley]. Retrieved 8th June 2021.
6. The National Archives. (15/11/1837). 'Prisoner Petition for Mary McGarry of the "Diamond," op. cit.
7. National Archive of Ireland, 'Convict Reference Files and Prisoners' Petitions and Cases', [https://www.nationalarchives.ie/topics/transportation/transp8.html].
8. Jen Willetts. (1838). 'Convict Ship "Diamond." [https://www.freesettlerorfelon.com/convict_ship_diamond_1838.htm]. Retrieved 9th June 2021.
9. Jen Willetts. (1838). 'Convict Ship "Diamond." op. cit.
10. Departure of the "Diamond" (The Morning Post, 15th November 1837).
11. The National Archives. (1838). Journal of William McDowell off the "Diamond." UK Royal Navy Medical Journals, 1817-1857, The National Archives, Kew, Surrey.
12. The National Archives. (1838). Journal of William McDowell off the "Diamond," op. cit.

13. The National Archives. (1838). Journal of William McDowell off the "Diamond," op. cit.
14. Australian Dictionary of Biography - Caroline Chisholm [https://adb.anu.edu.au/biography/chisholm-caroline-1894/text2231.
15. Jen Willetts. (1838). 'Convict Ship "Diamond," op. cit.
16. 'Police Incidents'. The Sydney Gazette and New South Wales Advertiser, 19 Apr 1838, p.2.
17. Convict Indent for Mary Ann McGarry, off the "Diamond", March 1838. (NSW Archives Convict Indents Fiche# 735, p.226; Film# 908, Shelf# X641).
18. Queensland Dept of BDM. (1889). Death Certificate for Mary Frawley (nee McGarry), op. cit.
19. Nicholas, T. H. (2019). The Place That Had No Heart: a Memoir. Parramatta Factory Precinct Memory Project.
20. Cobb, J. E. (1958). The History of the Female Convict Factory at Parramatta. Published by The Author.
21. Mary McGarry in the Berry Papers, op.cit. (MSS-315/37).
22. Berry Papers. Mary McGarry, off the "Diamond" in 'Assigned Servants Day (Slop) Book. Mitchell Library, Sydney.
23. Queensland Dept of BDM. (1889). Death Certificate for Mary Frawley (nee McGarry), op. cit.
24. Davis, Joseph L. (2019). 'The Spotless Reputation of the Reverend Matthew Devenish Meares, 1800-1878 At Wollongong' [www.academia.edu/39765539/].
25. Wikitree - Rev. Matthew Devenish Meares [https://www.wikitree.com/wiki/Meares-316].
26. Matthew Devenish Meares & Georgiana Augusta Devenish marriage licence, 1822 ("Dublin, Ireland, Probate Record and Marriage License Index, 1270-1858").
27. New South Wales And Tasmania: Settlers And Convicts 1787-1859. (From... FindMyPast). First name(s): Richd M. D. - Last name: Meares - Age: 28 - Birth year: 1797 - Arrival year: 1825 - Ship name: "Mariner" - Occupation: Clergyman - Residence: Pitt Town, New South Wales. With... Georgiana Meares (Age: 28, born 1797); William Meares (Age: 5, born 1820); Elizabeth Meares (Age: 3, born 1822); Henry Meares (Age: 1/2, born 1825).
28. By Appointment of the King: "Appointment by King George the Fourth: GIVEN at Our Court, at Carlton-house, this Twentieth Day of December, One thousand eight hundred and twenty-four, in the Fifth Year of Our Reign."
29. Memorial: "Rev Meares started St Michael's Anglican Church: In April 1938, at St Michael's Anglican Church, a special service was held to unveil a memorial plaque in honour of the Reverend Matthew Devenish Meares and his wife. This memorial recognises that Rev. Meares was the first incumbent of the Illawarra-Shoalhaven District from 1838-1857." (By Carol Herben, OAM, in the 'The Illawarra Mercury', 10th Nov 2014).
30. NSW Dept of BDM. (1878). Death certificate for Matthew Devenish Meares, # 2170/1878.
31. Death Notice: Rev. Matthew Devenish Meares - December 5, at Olivia-terrace, Bourke-street, in the 79th year of his age (The Sydney Morning Herald (NSW) Sat, 7 Dec 1878, p.1).
32. Burial: Rev Matthew Devenish Meares - Birth: 1800 Meares Court, Westmeath, Ireland - Death date: 5 Dec 1878 (aged 77–78) - Place: Surry Hills, New South Wales, Australia - Burial: St. Thomas Anglican Cemetery, Enfield, Burwood Municipality, New South Wales, Australia - Portion: 11 Row, 15 (Find A Grave: Memorial #123534395).
33. FamilySearch, Australia Cemetery Inscriptions (1802-2005). Name: M. D. Meares, Death date: 05 Dec 1878; Age: 78; Burial Place: Enfield St Thomas; Spouse's Name: Georgina Augusta, citing Jim and Alison Rogers (Various cemeteries, Australia; FHL microfilm).
34. Rev. Meares at Coolangatta (The Colonist, 11 July 1838, p.2).

JOHN FRAWLEY & MARY ANN McGARRY

As the year 1840 began, John Frawley had reached a turning point in his life at Coolangatta. For seven years, he had laboured on the estate, becoming a familiar figure within its operations. However, the records of his service begin to wind down from the beginning of that year. What became of him afterward remains unclear, perhaps he was granted a cottage elsewhere on Alexander Berry's vast property, or maybe he was elevated to a managerial role. Yet, the most plausible outcome is that, having completed his term and now entitled to wages, his continued employment was no longer required.

Despite the common perception of convict servitude as brutal and oppressive, life on the estate was more nuanced. Referred to as 'government men,' the assigned convicts were not shackled, dressed in prison garb, or regimented into tightly controlled work units. They were not supervised by soldiers, nor were they subjected to the inhumane conditions often associated with penal labor. Nevertheless, discipline was strictly enforced. Infractions were met with corporal punishment or deprivation, and oversight fell to former convicts who had firsthand knowledge of the tricks and tendencies of reluctant labourers.

Alexander Berry, often accused of treating his convict workforce with excessive severity, consistently defended his methods, claiming that mild measures and moral persuasion were the key to maintaining order. His assertions hold some merit, as evidenced by the number of men who chose to remain in his employ even after earning their freedom. John Frawley Jr.'s continued presence at Coolangatta beyond his term suggests that, while the system was undoubtedly one of control, it was not entirely devoid of opportunity or choice.

The Aboriginal Population at Shoalhaven

The years 1833-42 are some of the historically richest, in terms of the study of Illawarra and South Coast Aborigines, for during this period the first census information of the local Aboriginal inhabitants was compiled in connection with the issue of blankets. This survey revealed a great deal of personal information on the native population. Though blankets had been issued earlier, it is only from 1833 that returns have survived for the Illawarra and South Coast people. With such detailed information many of the Aborigines mentioned in the historical accounts were brought to life for the first time *(see Appendix C)*. The family history value of this material is also significant, as Aborigines were not again included in Australian census returns until the 1960s.

While most Europeans found their customs abhorrent, the Aboriginal people were just as often revolted by some of the customs of the Europeans. Aboriginal methods of punishment for example seemed to be barbaric, especially the act of spearing, while Aboriginals were horrified by some of the white man's ways of punishing offenders like flogging.

This period also saw the issue of a significant collection of reminiscences on the Aboriginals of Shoalhaven, by Alexander Berry *(see Appendix D)*. But it was their nomadic lifestyle, and their lack of ingenuity that made them easy targets for colonisation:

> "...at no stage did Aboriginal civilisation develop substantial buildings, roadways or even a wheeled cart... I would strongly make the point that rightly or wrongly dispossession of the Aboriginal civilisation was always going to happen."
>
> *Tim Fischer (Deputy PM, 1995)*

John Frawley's Freedom

John Frawley was just a small cog in the vast machine that was the Coolangatta Estate, where the whole was truly greater than the sum of its parts. As one of many convicts assigned to the estate, he played his role in the daily operations, likely performing hard labour under the oversight of the Berry family's strict management. Yet even within the rigid structure of convict life, personal connections and aspirations for a better future still flourished.

It was in this environment, sometime in 1838, that John Frawley either met or reconnected with his fellow Shannonsider, Mary Ann McGarry. Their paths may have first crossed at the Coolangatta Homestead, where she might have been employed, or perhaps in Wollongong, where they could have encountered one another while running errands or attending church services. Whatever the circumstances, a bond formed between them, strong enough that they soon agreed to marry.

But John's situation was still uncertain, as records indicate that he remained at the Berry Estate until at least early 1840. His last documented mention at Coolangatta comes from a routine but telling request, another pair of boots from 'slops,' the convict clothing and supplies store. This suggests that as of that moment, he was still under the control of the estate and had not yet secured his freedom. However, John Frawley was well aware that liberty could be obtained through several legal avenues, each with its own restrictions and conditions.

Convicts in the colony had four primary paths to freedom:

- TICKET OF LEAVE, allowed early release but restricted the convict's movements to a designated area within the colony. Holders of a Ticket of Leave were still required to report regularly to local authorities and, whenever possible, attend divine worship on Sundays.

- CERTIFICATE OF FREEDOM, was issued once a convict completed their full sentence. This document confirmed they were no longer under any penal obligations and granted them unrestricted travel within the colony and beyond. While some ex-convicts chose to return to the United Kingdom or Ireland, doing so was often financially difficult. Those who managed to make the journey back frequently found the "convict stain" to be a far heavier burden in their homeland than in Australia, where former prisoners could more easily integrate into society.

- CONDITIONAL PARDON, granted to convicts serving life sentences. This allowed them freedom within the colony but forbade them from ever returning to the United Kingdom. For many, this was an acceptable trade-off, as Australia provided opportunities unavailable to them in their homeland.

- ABSOLUTE PARDON, was the most coveted form of clemency. It granted complete freedom, lifting all restrictions and allowing the former convict to travel wherever they pleased, including back to Britain if they wished.

Regardless of the method of release, all ex-convicts were required to carry their discharge papers at all times. Failure to present a Ticket of Leave, Certificate of Freedom, Conditional Pardon, or Absolute Pardon when demanded, particularly at muster time, could result in being classified as a 'Prisoner of the Crown' once more and returned to government service. These documents essentially functioned as passports for former convicts, proving their legitimacy as free individuals in a society where their past was never entirely forgotten.

Although no direct records confirm the exact manner of John Frawley's release, circumstantial evidence strongly suggests that he obtained either a Ticket of Leave or a Certificate of Freedom before mid-March of 1840. His likely window of release falls between January, when he would have completed his required sentence at Berry Estate, and March, when he formally submitted a "request to marry," an official declaration of his free status. This process would have required legal documentation proving he was no longer bound by the constraints of servitude, reinforcing the likelihood that his freedom had been secured just weeks or months prior.

Meanwhile, Mary Ann McGarry's circumstances in the lead-up to their wedding remain somewhat unclear. The marriage certificate records her residence as Shoalhaven, which suggests she was likely working at Coolangatta at the time. However, it is also possible that she remained in the employ of the Reverend Meares, a situation that could have extended even beyond her nuptials. Domestic service was one of the most common occupations for women in colonial Australia, and if she had been working in a household such as that of Reverend Meares, she would have had some stability, though likely little personal freedom.

For John, the reunion with Mary Ann and the transition from convict to free man would not have been without its challenges. To reach her, he would have needed to make his way from Shoalhaven to Wollongong, an arduous journey by any means available. He could have booked passage aboard a small coastal cutter bound for Kiama or Wollongong, a common but often unpredictable mode of transport along the colony's rugged eastern coastline. Alternatively, if no boat was available or if he lacked the necessary funds, he would have been forced to make the grueling 60-kilometer overland trek on foot.

At the time, no proper roads connected Shoalhaven to Wollongong, only a series of rough coastal tracks carved through dense bushland and treacherous terrain. These paths were not for the faint-hearted, requiring careful navigation and considerable endurance. He would have had to traverse forests, cross rivers, and contend with the unpredictable elements of the Australian wilderness, all while carrying whatever meager belongings he possessed. For a man recently freed from servitude, it was perhaps a small price to pay for the promise of a new life with Mary Ann.

Though many details of John Frawley's journey remain lost to history, one thing is certain, by mid-1840, he had successfully left his past as a convict behind. Whether by land or by sea, he reached his destination, claimed his freedom, and prepared to embark on the next chapter of his life as a husband and, eventually, a man free from the constraints of his past.

> "By 1849 a new road was cleared from Kiama to Gerringong to replace the old track along the beaches and headlands. It rose to a point midway up the hillsides winding around the spurs to meet the top of the range at Mt. Pleasant. After descending to the south of Mt. Pleasant it crossed the flats and rose to the village site of Gerringong on the hill and then almost straight along the ridge to Crooked River near Black Head."[1]

Marriage of John Frawley & Mary Ann McGarry

As Mary was still serving her sentence in the months leading up to their July 1840 wedding, the couple had to wait for official approval to marry. Their application for 'permission to marry' was submitted to Governor Sir George Gipps on March 26, 1840.[2,3] At the time, Mary had five years remaining on her sentence and was listed as 'bonded' for seven years aboard the "Diamond", while John Frawley was recorded as 'free.'

The next documented reference to the couple is their marriage, which took place on July 6th, 1840, in the Roman Catholic Parish of Wollongong. Their marriage certificate states that Father John Rigney of Wollongong, who was then the priest for Illawarra certified the wedding of John Frawley and Mary McGawly [sic. McGarry] both of Shoalhaven. The ceremony was witnessed by Dudley Morris and Patrick Keogh and signed by both the bride and groom.[4] Early governors and clergy encouraged marriage due to its 'presumed reformatory and moral advantages.' For female convicts, marriage provided a path to respectability, as they were assigned to their husbands and allowed to live freely, provided they maintained good behavior. Additionally, land grants were offered to married convicts, with extra land allocated for each child born.

Given the circumstances, John and Mary likely traveled back to Coolangatta by boat from Wollongong or Kiama. At the time, Kiama was a small but developing port.[5] Although a few houses existed there as early as 1829, the first land purchase wasn't recorded until 1840, followed by the establishment of the Post Office on January 1, 1841. Over time, Kiama grew into a modest yet productive regional port. While mail was transported overland, local produce was shipped to Sydney two or three times a month via small coastal sailing vessels, with each trip taking one to two days. Ships such as the "Bee", "Charles", "Pedlar", and "Dolphin" all regularly traveled the route before 1847, though sailors had been navigating those waters long before then.

The region's first steamer, the "Tamar", arrived from Sydney in 1841, but did not operate for long. Until the 1850s, smaller sailing vessels remained the primary means of transport for settlers in the area.[6]

Beginnings of Wollongong

During their years at Shoalhaven, John and Mary Frawley would have been witnesses to the development of the town of Wollongong. On 26 November 1834, the town of Wollongong was first gazetted and George Brown erected the first court house. The main road down the escarpment through through Westmacott Pass later renamed Bulli Pass was built by convict labour in 1835–6, although other passes were built during the 19th century as well, such as O'Briens Road and Rixons Pass. By 1836, a small wooden church with seating for 250 people was built for the Catholics of Wollongong. Shortly afterwards, the pioneer priest, Monsignor John Rigney established St Francis Xaviers Church in 1838, and that structure remains the oldest church of any denomination in the Illawarra region.[7]

While the first settlers in the Illawarra in the early 19th century were cedar cutters, they were followed by graziers in 1815 when Charles Throsby established his stockman's hut near Wollongong.[8] By 1830, a military barracks had been constructed near the harbour, and with further settlers constantly arriving, the town of Wollongong was first gazetted on the 26th November 1834.

In 1831 the "Sophia Jane" became the first steamship to visit Wollongong and in 1839 the first regular service commenced from Sydney with the establishment of the Illawarra Steam Packet Company. Mr. Thomas Shadforth (c.1771-1862), an ex-soldier and trustee of the company, bought the paddlesteamer "Maitland" from Edye Manning (1807-1889), and she began sailing to the South Coast on the 15th June

1839.⁹ While the newly formed company commenced the Wollongong service with the "Maitland", it later added the "William The Fourth", both of which were built in New South Wales on the Williams River.¹⁰ Just three months after its inception, the Illawarra Steam Packet Company merged with the Brisbane Water Steam Passenger Co. to become the General Steam Navigation Company,¹¹ and that company then serviced the Hunter River along with the South Coast.¹²

By 1841 the Census of that year revealed that there were 468 males and 296 females residing in northern Illawarra, 637 males and 294 females in Wollongong, 233 males and 143 females on the small farms around Dapto whilst the Lake Illawarra area had a sizeable population of 588 males and 340 females.¹³ The 1841 Census listed 659 houses in Illawarra of which 571 were of wood and 88 of brick.¹⁴ The road from Sydney to Wollongong began in 1843, and traversed to the south via Georges River.

The first coal mine in the Illawarra was opened at Mt Keira by Mr James Schoobert in 1849, and some of these coal mines built jetties so that the coal could carried by horse and loaded directly onto ships before being sent to other places within Australia or other countries.

Most travellers and settlers to Wollongong either walked or journeyed by horse from Liverpool, Campbelltown or Appin along rough tracks before reaching the dangerous Illawarra escarpment. Others came by paddlesteamer as by the 1850's there were two steamers running almost daily between Sydney and Wollongong. In 1852 a new road was built from Appin through Broughton's Pass down Mount Keira to Wollongong, on which carriages could drive for the first time. The Illawarra Mercury newspaper was established by Thomas Garrett and W. F. Cahill in 1855.

By 1858, a court house had been built, a horse-drawn tramway from Mount Keira to the harbour was completed in 1861, and in 1862 a telegraph line was opened between Wollongong and Bellambi. By 1865 the first gas supply in Wollongong was provided from a gas plant in Corrimal Street, and in 1868, extensions to the harbour were opened.

Return to Coolangatta

After returning to Coolangatta, records indicate that John Frawley began drawing more heavily on estate provisions and supplies.[15] He partnered with B. Smith to carry out "burning off" operations, accumulating an account of £14.9.1 by the end of 1840. The clearing work continued into 1841, but their demands on estate supplies nearly tripled, placing an even greater strain on resources.

Their first child, John Frawley Jr., was born on May 7th, 1841, while they were still residing at Coolangatta. He was baptized in Wollongong by Father John Rigney on May 19th, with Martin Grealis and Bridget Leary serving as sponsors.[16] That same year, the New South Wales Government conducted a colony-wide census. Although not listed individually by name, John, Mary Ann, and their infant son were recorded as part of the total in return #618 for the County of Camden, Illawarra District, under the household of John Berry (brother of Alexander) at the Coolangatta Homestead. Berry provided the census information to officials on March 13th, 1841.[17]

While the census does not specify their identities, it is not difficult to deduce where John and Mary Ann were recorded. They were a married couple, aged between 21 and 45, Roman Catholic, and either privately employed or holding a ticket of leave. Based on John's later occupation, it is likely that he worked as a shepherd or stockman at the homestead, a theory supported by evidence that he handled horses while at Coolangatta.[18]

The Berry Estate ledgers record that sometime after August 19th, B. Smith absconded. Meanwhile, John Frawley was allowed to leave the homestead, as his debts were mounting daily. One final reference to John Frawley appears in the Berry Papers for 1842, though its precise details remain unclear. However, it appears to be of a financial nature, possibly related to his departure from the Coolangatta Estate.[19]

The Frawleys' exact movements between late August 1841 and September 1842, the month their daughter Ellen was born at Warragaberra on the far South Coast, are unclear. They may have either have traveled south to Twofold Bay or remained in the Shoalhaven or Illawarra District, possibly finding work there.

During his last days and weeks at Coolangatta, John Frawley likely heard of new opportunities on the far South Coast, where labourers were being drawn in increasing numbers. Ever resourceful, he somehow secured employment before September 1842, with the Imlay Brothers at Warragaburra Station.[20]

By the summer of 1841, the Frawleys had become accustomed to a life at Coolangatta that was a far cry from their convict beginnings. The once-untamed land had been transformed into an ordered, civilised community, with the comforts and stability that came with hard-earned progress. They had grown familiar with the solid buildings, regular routines, and the ease of a life now firmly rooted in the colony's growing prosperity.

Yet, as they left Coolangatta behind, they were about to step into a starkly different world, a world where civilization had not yet touched the land. Ahead lay the untamed wilderness of the far South Coast, a region so remote that few dared to dream of settling there. The Frawleys would soon find themselves surrounded by dense forests, wild rivers, fierce Aboriginal tribes and vast expanses of isolation that would challenge everything they had come to know.

With the comforts of Coolangatta fading into the distance, they faced an uncertain future. Would the wilderness prove to be a new beginning, or would it be a harsh reminder of the very hardships they had hoped to escape? The life they had left behind might have been comfortable, but the true test of their resolve was only just beginning.

References

1. Bayley, W. A. (1960) Blue Haven: Centenary History of Kiama Municipality NSW. Kiama Municipal Council, Halstead Press.
2. NSW State Archives & Records. (1840). John Frawley and Mary McGarry in 'Convicts Permission to Marry 1826 to 1856.'
3. NSW State Archives - John Frawley & Mary McGarry, 'Convicts Applications to Marry 1825-1851' (NRS 12212 [4/4510 p.045]; COD 13; Reel 713; Fiche 786-788 | Place: Wollongong).
4. NSW Dept of BDM. (1840). Marriage Certificate for John Frawley & Mary McGarry, 6th July 1840 at Wollongong, #25/123.
5. Bayley, W. A. (1960) Blue Haven: Centenary History of Kiama Municipality NSW. op. cit.
6. Ibid.
7. Piggin, Stuart., et al. (1984). Faith of Steel: a History of the Christian Churches in Illawarra, Australia. University of Wollongong.
8. Wikipedia - Wollongong [https://en.wikipedia.org/wiki/Wollongong].
9. Kolsen, Helmut (1959). 'Company Formation in NSW: 1828-1851,' Bulletin of the Business Archives Council, Vol. 1, No. 6.
10. Inglis, Brian (2000). "Transport". In Fellows of the Australian Academy of Technological Sciences and Engineering (ed.). Technology in Australia 1788-1988. Melbourne: Australian Science and Technology Heritage Centre. ISBN 0-908029-49-7. Retrieved 1 February 2009.
11. Coroneos, Cosmos (2005). "Steamer Bega (1883–1908): Conservation Plan" (PDF). Parramatta, New South Wales: NSW Heritage Office. Retrieved 1 February 2009.
12. Ibid.
13. Henderson, K. & T. (1983). 'Early Illawarra - People, houses, life', History Project Inc, Canberra, p.19 & 24.
14. Jervis, James, (1942). op. cit., p.273.
15. NSW Dept of BDM. (1841). Birth & Baptism Certificate for John Frawley Jr., op.cit..
16. NSW Dept of BDM. (1841). Birth & Baptism Certificate for John Frawley Jr, #1450/1841 (V18411450 121A).
17. NSW State Archives & Records. (1841). '1841 Census of the Colony of NSW: John & Mary Frawley in 'Return #618 for Coolangatta.' County of Camden, District of Illawarra.
18. Berry Papers. John Frawley in 'Assigned Servants Punishment Book.' Mitchell Library, Sydney (MSS-315/62).
19. Berry Papers. John Frawley in 'Index to Persons on the Berry Estate - Financial Records.' Mitchell Library, Sydney (MSS-315/62).
20. NSW Dept of BDM .(1842). Birth & Baptism for Ellen Frawley, 2nd Sept 1842 at Warigubera, #1772/1842 (V18421772 62).

10

THE MANEROO & TWOFOLD BAY

The Frawley family's journey to the remote and largely unexplored region of the Maneroo in 1842 marks a pivotal chapter in the history of early Australian settlement. Having already carved out a place for themselves in the growing colonies of Shoalhaven and the Illawarra, they had witnessed the transformative power of civilization and progress in areas like Berry's Coolangatta Estate and the township of Wollongong. These settlements, though still young, were already imbued with the trappings of colonial life: government infrastructure, established roads, and the steady rise of European influence in the region. In contrast, the path the Frawleys were now embarking upon would take them far beyond the safety and structure of these burgeoning communities.

Their move into the Maneroo, an area largely unknown to the wider population of New South Wales in 1842, would place them on the frontier of European settlement. At this time, the Maneroo was still a wild and untamed land, dominated by dense forests, rugged terrain, and Indigenous peoples whose presence and way of life had remained largely undisturbed by European settlers. To understand the significance of the Frawleys' decision to venture into this unknown wilderness, it is essential to explore the origins of the Maneroo region itself, its early exploration, and the challenges it presented to those daring enough to settle there.

This chapter delves into the early history of the Maneroo, examining its geographical, cultural, and historical significance within the context of colonial expansion. By understanding the region's origins and the motivations behind the Frawleys' bold move, we gain a deeper appreciation of the challenges they faced, as well as the pioneering spirit that drove them to push further into the frontier.

Twofold Bay & The Maneroo

Prior to European settlement the local Aborigines, the Katungal of the Thawa tribe who were part of the Yuin language group, had lived in the area for thousands of years. But the first European to sight Twofold Bay was Lt. James Cook in April, 1770.

The first known white men to pass through the South Coast and Bega district on foot were a group of 17 survivors from the wreck of the "Sydney Cove", which was beached on what became known as Preservation Island in Bass Strait, on the 9th February 1797. The small group had been despatched by their captain in a longboat to seek help, but were themselves wrecked in a storm west of Point Hicks. They had to trek nearly 500 miles (800km) north to Sydney, through completely unknown, often dense bush and across numerous rivers, lakes and around other obstacles including mountain ranges and hostile natives. Only three of the original party managed to reach Sydney. However, little more was heard about this area of New South Wales for another 30 years.[1]

Hearing the reports of the survivors, George Bass, travelled down the coast in December of 1797. On his return in early 1798 he entered

Twofold Bay and named Snug Cove, where Eden wharf now stands, because he believed it was suitable as a resting place for passing vessels. Later in 1798, Bass with Matthew Flinders headed south to Van Diemen's Land. This time a more detailed and accurate survey of Twofold Bay was made and the duo made contact with the local Aborigines. Flinders recounted an amusing and friendly incident where he offered a local some biscuits and in turn the local offered Flinders some fat. After tasting the fat Flinders explained that while "watching an opportunity to spit it out when he should not be looking, I perceived him doing precisely the same thing with our biscuit".

The Whalers

As early as 1791 whalers were seen in the area, which was the reason the area was initially settled. The migration, mostly of right whales, to and from the Antarctic resulted in large numbers passing Twofold Bay between May and November. The first European whaler in Twofold Bay was evidently Capt. Thomas Raine (1793–1860), in 1828, and although whaling stations were already set up on Van Diemen's Land and Kangaroo Island, he established the first shore-based whaling station on the Australian mainland. The Twofold Bay area became a well known whaling ground and the bay was a natural harbour for ships.[2]

Then in 1829, some Braidwood squatters came down Eurambene Mountain into Wandella and the Maneroo to explore the kangaroo grasslands and open forests. William Duggan Tarlington (1806-1893), found a route down to the sea at Bermagui, and later that year pushed through from Cobargo to Biggah (Bega).[3] Tarlington chose Cobargo for his run and returned with cattle in 1832. Other squatters included John Campbell, Henry Badgery, Captain Raine, Thomas Cowper, Major William Elrington, the Pollack Brothers, the Alsops, and Dr Thomas Braidwood Wilson, who did not settle in the valley. Other squatters followed and soon a second party was sent from Thomas Cowper's 2,000 acre squattage at Braidwood with 300 head of young cattle to take up Brogo.[4] Cowper's squattage expanded rapidly to include

Yarranung, and Tarraganda on the north east side of the Bega River, and Brianderry on the north western side of the river about two miles due west and opposite the present site of Kingswood. Joseph Bartley with Michael Dunn as hut-keeper took up the land on the south west side of the river below the eventual site of the Bega township, on behalf of Henry Badgery and this squattage became known as 'Warragaburra'. Otherwise the entire region was basically unpopulated.[5]

The 'Maneroo' was the early reference for what is now known as the far South Coast region of New South Wales. By the early 1830s the Imlay Brothers had also started whaling at Twofold Bay, and trained local Aborigines to become whalers. Peter Imlay (1797–1881), arrived at Twofold Bay around 1833 and decided to settle. Unfortunately the depression of the 1840s destroyed the family financially. The Imlays and others reported considerable activity between Twofold Bay and Wolumla, about 10km south of Brianderry and 16 km south of Bega.

The year 1834 saw the visit of Governor Bourke, which was followed soonafter by the arrival of the Imlay brothers. They acquired over 65,000 acres of land by squatting and began permanent settlement of the 'Biggah' region, which included a few assigned convict servants, who became the district's pioneers. But the area was so remote that Governer Bourke recognised the futility of collecting the government 20/- per 100 acre squattage fee and did not enforce it. Bourke actually visited the district twice in 1834 and was so impressed by its fertility that he recommended to the Colonial Office that the land be made available for sale, and that a town be built at Twofold Bay. Soon after Bourke's visits, Eden was gazetted as a town in 1836.

The Imlay Brothers

George (1794–1846), Peter (1797–1881), and Alexander Imlay (1800–1847),[6] were Scottish landowners and speculators born in Aberdeen. They were the sons of Alexander Imlay, a farmer and merchant, and his wife, Agnes Bron.

Alexander, an army surgeon, arrived in Sydney in December 1829 aboard the "Elizabeth" and was appointed to the colony's medical staff in March 1830. Peter, a naval surgeon, reached Hobart Town in February 1830 on the "Greenock". George arrived in Sydney in February 1833 as the surgeon superintendent of convicts on the "Roslyn Castle" and later joined Alexander at the Sydney Infirmary.

In 1832, Alexander explored the South Coast and County of Argyle with Governor (Sir) Richard Bourke. By the following year, he held 1,280 acres (518 ha) on the Breadalbane Plains. That same year, Peter visited Twofold Bay and saw potential for shore-based whaling and stock-raising. He soon settled there, and in 1835, George joined him. Despite managing pastoral interests, George remained in his naval post until 1841. Meanwhile, Alexander resigned from his army medical post in 1833 after ten years of service. He moved to Hobart in January and became primarily responsible for the brothers' properties in Van Diemen's Land.

In 1834, Alexander secured support from Governor Bourke and Lieutenant-Governor (Sir) George Arthur for his plans to develop trade in cattle and salted provisions between Twofold Bay and Van Diemen's Land. He also proposed introducing steam navigation and expanding the wool trade from the Monaro district. The brothers acquired several properties in Van Diemen's Land, including a 2,560-acre (1,036 ha) grant on Forestier Peninsula, the site of one of their whaling stations. Despite government objections to their use of convict labour, the Imlays were among the top six producers of whale products by 1837. In 1841, Alexander attempted to diversify their interests by drilling for coal on his New Town property near Hobart, but the effort was unsuccessful.

In January 1838, Alexander transported 120 cows from Twofold Bay to Adelaide by sea. Shortly after his arrival, he traveled across the Mount Lofty Ranges to the Murray River with a servant and an Aboriginal guide. His journey diary was later published in the 'Adelaide Register' in June and July 1838. David McLaren, manager of the South Australian Company, found the expedition significant enough to report it to his London headquarters.

The Imlay brothers' most substantial holdings were in the Bega district, where George and Peter managed pastoral and whaling operations. Peter also expanded their trade into New Zealand, acquiring land at New Plymouth. Despite holding 1,500 square miles (3,885 km²) of prime land, their financial fortunes collapsed. By late 1844, they had surrendered most of their holdings to creditors, retaining only four runs totaling 37,400 acres (15,135 ha) near Bega and Cobargo. In November, Alexander attempted to sell his Forestier Peninsula property to the government, but Lieutenant-Governor Sir John Eardley-Wilmot declined the offer. The following year, all their Van Diemen's Land properties were put up for sale as Alexander prepared to join his brothers at Bega.

The Imlay brothers prospered at Twofold Bay, where they diversified from whaling into the pastoral industry, and in the process they obtained an extensive land holding across south eastern New South Wales.

They established themselves at Panbula and extended their Bega holdings, which were used as pastoral properties for grazing sheep and cattle. However, drought and bushfire in 1839 and 1840 caused grave problems and dealt them a serious financial setback. Fortunately, they were saved from financial ruin by bankers in Hobart Town by the name of James, Sydney and Edward Walker, who were wealthy men at the time. With backing from the Walkers, the Imlay brothers prosperity again increased such that by 1844 they owned 72,500 acres of land (30,000 ha) in the immediate district. This holding was part of a total of 960,000 acres that they held between Twofold Bay and the Clyde River.[7]

The Imlay brothers' biggest interests were in the Bega district, where George and Peter controlled the pastoral and whaling activities. Peter also opened up trade with New Zealand where he had acquired land at New Plymouth. Although he and his brothers held 1500 sq miles (3885 km²) of the colony's best land, their fortunes once again declined disastrously. By the end of 1844 they had surrendered to their creditors all their land except four runs totalling 37,400 acres (15,135 ha) around Bega and Cobargo.[8]

These early settlements were all outside and well beyond the 'limits of location' for settlement as decreed by Governor Sir Ralph Darling (1772-1858), in 1824, which meant there was no military protection against the Aborigines, no land survey provided and no deeds to land, so disputes over boundaries were frequent. Slab huts with stringy bark roofs were erected and generally occupied by two shepherds or stockmen and a hut keeper. They took the sheep or cattle to pasture in the morning and returned them to pens at night to prevent their straying and becoming lost in the bush, or being killed by natives.[9]

> Imlay, George (per P. Imlay). Name of run: Bega. Estimated area: 20,000 acres. Estimated grazing capabilities: 640 cattle, 4,000 sheep. Bounded on the north and east by Mumbla Range; on the south by Bega River and Grossis Creek, being the boundary lines with the Warragaburra and Brichago stations occupied by William and James Walker; and on the west by a swamp running parallel to the east side of the Numbugga swamps and nearly joining the Double Creek.

Prior to 1840, the only practical way in and out of Twofold Bay and Eden was by ship. Later attempts were made overland from Braidwood and a Mr. Nicholson gave an account of his trip over the coast ranges from Broulee to Maneroo in 1841, which hitherto, had been considered impassable:

> "It gives me great pleasure in being able to inform you of the full success of my trip from Broulee to Maneroo, over the heretofore considered impassable coast ranges. I started on the 26th ult, from the coast, with a team of eight bullocks, containing nearly fourteen hundred weight, I reached Braidbo on the ninth instant, four days out of which was occupied in resting the bullocks, so that my journey would have been completed in 11 days, had it not been for the density of the scrub, and live and dead timber which we had either to cut down or remove from the road.
>
> I had, when I left the range on the New Country, upwards of ten hundred weight on the dray, and the bullocks drew it over easy enough, owing much to the management of the drivers. The possibility of bringing a dray over the ranges is now set at rest. The Maneroo people are willing to cooperate with the Broulee folks, as it will save a distance of 100 miles; even now, twelve or fifteen hundred weight of dry goods can be easily conveyed between these two places by drays."

> Mr. Nicholson, Driscoll's Inn, Maneroo, 16 Sept 1841 [10]

However, tragedy struck in July 1846 when Peter's chartered vessel, the "Breeze", was shipwrecked at Upolu while traveling from Tahiti to New Zealand in search of oil. Later that year, on 26 December, George, who was unmarried and suffering from an incurable disease, took his own life atop a mountain overlooking Bega, now known as Dr. George Mountain.

Alexander married Sophia Atkins in Hobart, and they had a son born in New Town on 2 September 1843. However, the child died in March 1847, and Alexander passed away later that year.

Peter, the last surviving brother, migrated to New Zealand in 1851. He married Jane Maguire at St. Andrew's Church, Sydney, on 23 February 1853, in a Presbyterian ceremony. Settling in Wanganui in 1857, he oversaw trading interests in the southwest Pacific. He died there on 8 March 1881, survived by Jane and three daughters.

The Township of Eden

The Australian botanist, Allan Cunningham (1791-1839), landed at Snug Cove in December 1817 so that he could collect botanical specimens from the district.[11] However, Peter Imlay and his brothers George and Alexander Imlay are credited with erecting Eden's first building, a small bark slab hut at Snug Cove. Sketches of the hut were made by Sir Oswald Brierly in 1842 and by Captain Owen Stanley from "HMS Rattlesnake" in 1843.[12]

The graziers, who had taken up squattages in the Monaro district inland from Twofold Bay, were seeking a better way to transport their cattle to Hobart, Tasmania. It was therefore decided to establish cattle-handling facilities and an accompanying township on an appropriate site at Twofold Bay.[13] Thus the government authorised the captain of "HMS Alligator" to seek an appropriate site for a settlement at Twofold Bay.[14] Early in 1835 the governor of New South Wales, Sir Richard Bourke, visited Twofold Bay and the site of the proposed new settlement on board "HMS Hyacinth".[15]

Permission was given by the governor to establish a town at

Twofold Bay in 1834, when Eden was named after George Eden (1784-1849), 1st Earl of Auckland, the British Secretary for the Colonies.[16] The area for the proposed town of Eden was surveyed in 1842 by Mr Thomas Townsend, the government surveyor. The main thoroughfare was named after the Imlay brothers who were honoured as the earliest pioneers to the district. Other streets were named after Lieutenant Flinders, George Bass, Queen Victoria and her consort, Prince Albert. A wharf was built out into a cove, now named Cattle Bay, from a site on the western edge of Eden, where cattle could be grazed prior to their being loaded onto the ships. Cattle were also grazed on Lookout Point until 1853, but was later subdivided for housing.[17] After the town plan was finalised the first blocks were auctioned off on 9th March 1843, when the land was sold to Thomas Aspinall, Benjamin Boyd, S. Clinton, Lewes Gordon, W. Hirst, James Kirwan, J.P. Robinson and T.A. Townsend.[18]

The first postmaster was appointed in 1843, but the first post office did not officially open until 1847. The first customs officer was appointed in 1846, but he was located at East Boyd initially, until the customs house was constructed in 1848. Eden grew in the 1850s following the decline of nearby Boydtown, and the discovery of gold in Kiandra, which led to the 1859–1860 gold rush.

The discovery of alluvial gold at Kiandra in 1859-1860 led to the development of Eden as a port for prospectors heading to the goldfield. At one point there were some 4,000 people living in the town. But the rush ended by 1866 when the port failed to develop. Around 1900 Eden was even mooted as a possible future national capital. This was partly because it was recognised at the time as having the third deepest natural harbour in the world. Whaling died off in the late 1920s and slowly replaced by other industries. There was a need for wattlebark, a source of tannin, and dairying, timber and brickmaking became important. Today tourism, commercial fishing, and the woodchip industry are the town's economic base.

The Arrival of Ben Boyd

Benjamin Boyd (1801-1851) was a Scottish entrepreneur born on August 21, 1801, in Penninghame, Wigtown, Scotland. He was the second surviving son of Edward Boyd, a London merchant from Merton Hall, Wigtownshire, and his wife, Janet Yule of Wheatfield, Midlothian. By 1824, Boyd had established himself as a stockbroker in London and held an interest in the St. George's Steam Packet Company.

In October 1840, Boyd wrote to Lord John Russell, outlining his ambitious plans to develop the resources of Australia and its surrounding islands. He believed that efficient communication between settlements required large steamships and informed Russell that he had already dispatched one to New South Wales, with another soon to follow. Seeking official support, Boyd requested permission to select five or six coastal locations for harbors and coaling stations, along with the right to purchase nearby land. While he was assured of assistance for his navigation proposals, the Colonial Office remained non-committal regarding his broader plans for the Pacific Islands.

Boyd's ventures were financed by the Royal Bank of Australia, established in London in 1839 with a nominal capital of £1,000,000. He personally carried £200,000 in debenture sales to Australia. Additionally, in November 1841, he formed the Australian Wool Company, depositing £15,000 of its debentures with the Royal Bank. Boyd, a director of the bank, was supported by his brother Mark, who served as its manager.

It was toward the end of 1842 that Benjamin Boyd arrived at Twofold Bay, and established Boydtown in late 1842. He also took up large holdings in the Monaro District in addition to establishing his own whaling station on the south side of Twofold Bay, away from the Imlay's smelly try-works on the northern shore. Boyd had sound financial backing from London and established such a strong settlement that by 1848 the immigrant ship "Bermondsey" sailed directly from Plymouth to Twofold Bay, bringing 111 immigrants into the district.[19]

Sailing from Plymouth aboard his schooner, "Wanderer", a vessel of the Royal Yacht Squadron, Boyd arrived at Port Phillip on June 15, 1842, and reached Port Jackson on July 18. His arrival generated much excitement, with crowds gathering to witness the "Wanderer" and a welcoming salute from the schooner "Velocity". Among his passengers were his brother James, marine artist Oswald Walters Brierly, and future whaling captains Adam Bogue and Downes. Boyd's steamers had begun arriving ahead of him, with "Seahorse" in June 1841, Juno in March 1842, "Velocity" in May, and "Cornubia" in June, all bringing supplies for his enterprises.

Wasting no time, Boyd launched multiple ventures. Partnering with Joseph Phelps Robinson, he established the Sydney office of the Royal Bank at Church Hill, offering financial services, including Scotch Bank acceptances payable in London. His steamships primarily serviced the southern route to Twofold Bay and Hobart Town. By May 1844, Boyd had become one of the colony's largest landholders, controlling fourteen stations in Monaro and four in the Port Phillip District, covering 426,000 acres (172,398 ha). His pastoral holdings, often purchased from previous owners, were described by Governor Sir George Gipps as "well-watered and in the best parts of the Colony." By 1844, he managed 20,000 sheep and 10,000 cattle in Monaro.

Governor Sir George Gipps mentioned in a dispatch dated 17th May 1844 that Boyd had become one of the largest squatters in the country, with 14 stations in the 'Maneroo' district and four in the Port Phillip district, amounting altogether to 381,000 acres (1,540km²) of land. At about the same period the firm of Boyd and Company had three steamers and three sailing ships in commission. Large sums of money were also spent on Boydtown at Twofold Bay, with the building of a jetty 300 feet (91m) long, and a lighthouse tower of some 75 feet (23m) in height.

Boydtown featured a Gothic church with a spire, commodious stores, well-built brick houses, a whale watch tower, and "a splendid hotel in the Elizabethan style." At this time Boyd had up to nine whaling ships working out of Twofold Bay. He was also elected to the

New South Wales Legislative Council for the Electoral District of Port Phillip in September 1844, a position he held for just 11 months.[20]

The Royal Bank, or Boyd & Robinson, oversaw more than 160,000 sheep and controlled over 2,500,000 acres (1,011,715 ha) in Monaro and Riverina, secured at minimal annual license fees. However, Boyd struggled to recruit suitable labor. In testimony before the select committee on immigration on September 27, 1843, he revealed that he employed around 200 shepherds and stockmen but saw the colony's prosperity as dependent on cheap labor. He advocated lowering shepherd wages to £10 per year with rations, excluding luxuries such as tea and sugar. Despite his claims of concern for the unemployed, critics like Samuel Sidney saw Boyd as representative of a "haughty, gentlemanly, selfish class."

With labour shortages persisting, Boyd proposed using convicts with tickets-of-leave from Van Diemen's Land in New South Wales, but the government rejected the idea. He then turned to the Pacific Islands, recruiting approximately 200 laborers from Tanna (New Hebrides), Lifu (Loyalty Islands), and other islands in 1847. However, most were sent back by year's end following protests from workers and humanitarian objections. Allegations arose that some islanders had been brought against their will, but a subsequent investigation by the attorney-general found no evidence of wrongdoing.

Boyd selected Twofold Bay as his coastal base, facilitating the shipment of livestock, wool, and tallow from Monaro. He planned two townships: Boyd Town, featuring a hotel, church, houses, stores, salting and boiling-down works, a jetty, and a lighthouse, and East Boyd, where he established a whaling station. He also set up facilities in Port Jackson, including ship fittings at Mosman Bay and a wool-washing establishment at Neutral Bay.

As tensions over land policy mounted in the 1840s, Boyd sought to protect his interests by entering public life. In 1844, he became president of the newly formed Pastoralists' Association, which sent Archibald Boyd to London to advocate their cause. From September

1844 to September 1845, Boyd represented the Port Phillip District in the Legislative Council.

However, his complex and opaque financial dealings led to overextension and financial difficulties. In 1846, he lost a costly legal battle over a £25,000 insurance claim for his damaged steamer, "Seahorse". He misrepresented financial reports to London investors, inflating profits to £36,071 for 1845. Suspicious shareholders ousted him in 1847 in favor of his brother William Sprott Boyd, who also failed to stabilize affairs. In 1849, the Royal Bank of Australia entered liquidation.

Following his financial collapse, Boyd sought fortune in the Californian goldfields. Departing on "Wanderer" on October 26, 1849, he lamented the loss of an anchor on departure, calling it a "parting legacy" to a colony where he had "hoped for much, succeeded in part, but ultimately failed." His American ventures proved unsuccessful, and he turned to the Pacific Islands, envisioning a "Papuan Republic or Confederation."

In June 1851, "Wanderer" and its tender, "Ariel", left San Francisco for the Hawaiian Islands before reaching Guadalcanal in the Solomon Islands. On October 15, Boyd went ashore to hunt but never returned. His companions heard two gunshots and later searched in vain. Concluding he had been killed by locals, they retaliated before sailing for Australia. Less than a month later, "Wanderer" was wrecked in a gale off Port Macquarie on November 12, 1851.

Rumors that Boyd had survived persisted, prompting expeditions by "Oberon" and "H.M.S. Herald" in 1854, but no trace was found. In May 1864, his estate, valued at under £3,000, was granted to the London manager of his creditor, the Royal Bank of Australia.

Boyd was known for his striking appearance and charisma. Artist Georgiana McCrae, who dined with him in 1842, likened him to Rubens and recalled how he once attended a masquerade as the painter. In his prime, Boyd entertained lavishly in Sydney and Boyd Town. A visionary and adventurer, he constantly devised new business or pleasure pursuits. He never married, and the remnants of his ventures now stand as ghost town relics, the only enduring testament to his grand ambitions in Australia.

Twofold Bay became a focal point of settlement in the early 19th century, its deep harbour and abundant whale populations drawing enterprising settlers to the region. The Imlay brothers, Alexander, Peter, and George, arrived in the 1830s, establishing vast pastoral holdings and a thriving shore-based whaling operation. By the late 1830s, they were among the colony's leading producers of whale oil and baleen, despite government restrictions on convict labour. Their success helped lay the foundations for the small but growing settlement of Eden, which emerged as a crucial hub for maritime trade and industry.

In the early 1840s, Scottish entrepreneur Benjamin Boyd arrived with grand ambitions, expanding the whaling industry, establishing Boydtown, and attempting large-scale commercial ventures. However, his reliance on indentured South Sea Islander labour and speculative investments led to financial collapse, leaving his once-promising empire in ruins.

Amidst this landscape of booming industry and shifting fortunes, John Frawley and his family arrived on the far South Coast in 1842, and was hired to work on the Imlays' remote pastoral property, 'Warragaburra'. As they stepped onto this rugged frontier, they found themselves in a land of opportunity and hardship, where fortunes could be made, or lost, on the whims of the sea and the struggles of the land. Their journey into this untamed world was just beginning.

References

1. Jeffreys, Max. (1997). The Wreck of the 'Sydney Cove.' New Holland Publishers Pty Ltd.
2. History Cooperative. (2 March 2017). 'History of Whaling in Twofold Bay.' [https://historycooperative.org/history-whaling-twofold-bay/]. Retrieved 9th June 2021.
3. Bayley, W.A. (1942). History of Bega. Sydney, Brooks, p.10.
4. Weebly, "A Brief Early History of Bega Valley", [https://begapioneersmuseum.weebly.com/a-brief-early-history-of-bega-valley.html.
5. Higgins, J. (1982). Pambula's Colonial Days: A short history of the period 1797-1901. The Merimbula – Imlay Historical Society.
6. Wellings, H.P. (1967). 'Imlay, Peter (1797–1881)', Australian Dictionary of Biography, National Centre of Biography, Australian National University, published first in hardcopy 1967, accessed online 18 May 2016. [http://adb.anu.edu.au/biography/imlay-peter-2259/text2887].
7. Swinburne, H. & Winters, J. (2001). 'Bega Valley Shire: Pictorial History.' Kinsclear Books & Bega Valley Shire, p.19.
8. Australian Dictionary of Biography - Peter Imlay, by H.B. Wellings [https://adb.anu.edu.au/biography/imlay-peter-2259].
9. Parbery, D.G. (1992). Fabric Of A Family. Self-Published. Mont Albert, Vic.
10. Mr. Nicholson's Overland Trip to Maneroo (Sydney Monitor & Commercial Advertiser, 24 Sep 1841, p.2)
11. Wellings, H.P. (1996). 'Eden and Twofold Bay: Discovery, Early History and Points of Interest 1797–1965' (Second ed.) [ISBN 0-646-29410-5].
12. Ibid.
13. Aussie Towns - Eden, NSW [https://www.aussietowns.com.au/town/eden-nsw].
14. "HMS Alligator" at Twofold Bay (The Australian, 3 June 1834).
15. Gov. Bourke Visits Twofold Bay (The Australian, 13 February 1835 & 13 March 1835).
16. "Eden, New South Wales" Travel (Sydney Morning Herald, 8 February 2004).
17. Wellings, H.P. (1996). 'Eden and Twofold Bay, op. cit.
18. Wellings, H.P. (1996). 'Eden and Twofold Bay, op. cit.
19. Bayley, W.A. (1942). History of Bega, op. cit., pp.16-17.
20. "Mr Benjamin Boyd (1803-1851)". Former members of the Parliament of New South Wales. Retrieved 7 April 2019.

11

WARRAGABURRA HOMESTEAD

The year was 1842, and John Frawley, his wife Mary Ann, and their infant son, John Jr., stood on the deck of their ship as it sailed into Twofold Bay. The vast, untamed Australian coastline stretched before them, a world apart from the familiar landscapes of their homeland. Growing up in Ireland, they had walked the stone streets of Limerick, where the grandeur and comfort of King John's Castle and St. Mary's Cathedral stood as towering reminders of a medieval past. Seven centuries of history had shaped those structures, their stone walls echoing the footsteps of countless generations. Now, as they disembarked, they faced a stark contrast, a land where the comforts of civilization were exchanged for the crude bark slab huts and dirt floors of New South Wales settlers.

The Frawleys had come in search of opportunity, a future carved out of the unforgiving wilderness. Their journey overland would take them from the sleeping hamlet at Twofold Bay to the remote Imlay brothers' 'Warragaburra Station', a place where survival required resilience and determination.

Like many who ventured into the frontier, they were met with formidable challenges. The harsh Australian landscape was as merciless as it was beautiful, searing heat, relentless bushfires, and devastating floods tested their endurance at every turn. Even more perilous was the ever-present tension between settlers and the Aboriginal inhabitants, who fiercely resisted encroachment on their ancestral lands.

John Frawley and his wife, Mary Ann, likely arrived on the far South Coast in response to an advertisement from the Imlay Brothers, who were seeking a husband-and-wife team or a shepherd for their pastoral property, called Warraguburra. With the skills and experience John had gained at the Coolangatta homestead, he was probably hired as a general hand or hutkeeper. Meanwhile, Mary likely took on essential domestic duties such as sewing, mending, laundry, and cooking, tasks highly valued by the other workers.

For the Frawleys, there was no turning back. They were true pioneers, battling the harsh realities of survival while building a new life in an unfamiliar and grueling land. Their story is one of hardship and adversity but also of resilience, courage, and determination.

In the early days of settlement, the region surrounding Eden and Bega was completely devoid of roads, making transportation of supplies an arduous challenge. Even the most basic necessities had to be carried by pack-bullocks, significantly limiting access to essential goods. Twofold Bay, located 332 kilometers south of Sydney, was remote and difficult to reach. While no direct records confirm their exact route, the Frawley family likely traveled by ship from the Illawarra to Sydney, then continued on another vessel to Twofold Bay after a brief stopover.

In 1842, the port of Eden had a population of only about 30 people, and the idea of a South Coast road had not yet been considered. Traveling beyond the officially designated 'Limits of Location' was not only difficult but also extremely dangerous. The Bega Valley, in particular, posed significant risks, with deaths from snake bites, starvation, exposure, and conflicts with Aboriginal groups being harsh realities of life.¹ Early settlers in the Maneroo region faced extreme isolation and had to rely entirely on the land for survival until they could cultivate their own food. Their homes were simple huts made from slabs of stringy bark, and they often encountered hostility from Indigenous groups. Without roads, public transport, regular mail, or church services, self-reliance was essential for survival.²

Due to the dangers of the wilderness, settlers were only allowed to take up land within the officially gazetted 'Nineteen Counties', the designated boundaries of the colony. These limits had been established in 1826 by Governor Ralph Darling in accordance with an order from Henry Bathurst (1762-1834), 3rd Earl Bathurst, the Secretary of State. Counties had been used for administrative purposes since the very first year of settlement, with Cumberland County, the first being officially proclaimed on June 6, 1788. William Baker's map provides data on the grazing district of Maneroo. Since Maneroo lay beyond the 'Limits of Location' in 1841, its statistics were not drawn from the census but instead compiled for an 1840 report to the Legislative Council of New South Wales regarding proposed boundaries within the colony.

The Spearing Of Michael Dunn

Prior to 1850 on the far south coast, and throughout the Bega district, the pioneers struggled to co-exist with the Aboriginals. Not least among their problems was the ferocity of the local 'Jellat Jellat' tribe of Aborigines near Bega, whose camp was nearby to both Warragaburra and Brianderry Stations. The murder of Michael Dunn at Warragaburra in 1835 served to illustrate the dangers of remote living:

> "The men from these two stations went around together for mutual protection. One day in 1835 when Bartley had left Warragaburra to visit Brianderry, the blacks attacked the hut at Warragaburra, speared Dunn to death and threw his body into a waterhole. When Bartley returned he found the hut ransacked, blood on the floor

and Dunn missing. He barricaded himself in and spent a worried but quiet night. The following day when Bartley tried to leave, the tribesman again attacked the hut preventing him from doing so. Later in the day he again attempted to leave and succeeded only after sooling his dog onto the nearest warriors. He made for a white man's camp at Wandella, north west of Cobargo, about thirty miles away and the Badgery settlement was subsequently abandoned. Higgs and a party from Brianderry buried Michael Dunn in an unmarked grave the following day."

D. G. Parbery [3]

Coastal Shipping

Coinciding with the relocation of John Frawley and family to Warraguberra, who likely knew little of its history, was the arrival of the intrepid Benjamin Boyd with his various enterprises. While Boyd sailed into Port Jackson in his yacht "Wanderer" on the 12th July 1842,[4] John, Mary and their infant son John Frawley Jr. were preparing to sail out, taking the momentous step of accepting a pioneering position in the Maneroo District.

Realistically, the Frawleys could have arrived at Warraguberra anytime after the birth of their son John Jr. on the 7th May 1841, until the birth of their daughter Ellen on the 2nd September 1842, which was is an unaccounted window of some 18 months.

From 1841, Broulee was increasingly becoming the preferred port for loading and unloading of goods on the South Coast, with an average of 2.3 ships arriving and departing from there each month. However, Twofold Bay had been the preferred port for the Imlay's since the early 1830s, with their ships mainly transporting livestock, and by 1841, it also began to receive commercial ships from Sydney. Considering the overland track from Broulee to Warragaburra was 140km, it made more sense for the Frawleys to sail south via Twofold Bay, which meant only a 53km journey to Warragaburra. Interestingly, that route passed right by Imlay's 'Panbula Station', which was to become the future township of Pambula. We don't know exactly when the Frawleys sailed south from Sydney, but there were then a few vessels operating the Sydney to Twofold Bay route in 1842.

In an attempt to identify the actual ship the Frawleys might have sailed on, evidence reveals that there were only three possible vessels that sailed from Sydney to Twofold Bay in 1842. So the Frawleys were either aboard the "Brothers", "Industry", or most likely, the "Mary Hay", the latter of which, departed from Sydney on the 21st July, and carried on board one of the owners of 'Warragaburra', in a Mr. Imlay.[5]

Frawleys Arrive at Warragaburra

Exactly when John and Mary Ann Frawley, and their infant son John Jr. arrived at 'Warragaburra' is uncertain, but the "Mary Hay" arrived in mid-winter at Twofold Bay, around the 23rd July 1842. Whichever route they travelled, the Frawleys evidently arrived safely at Warragaburra after what would have been quite a journey. Mary Ann, who was heavily pregnant at the time, and her husband, likely set themselves up in nothing more than a tent in the wilderness, or a dirt floored slab hut if they were fortunate. The property was situated exactly at the tidal extent of what was later named the Bega River, so travel to and from was often conducted by navigating the river. Above the tidal limit was fresh water, which was used to irrigate crops, making Warragaburra an excellent place to situate the original hut in the mid 1830s.

The term 'warragaburra' is a mild corruption of the aboriginal word 'warragubbra', which means, 'the turning of the tide'.[6] Warragaburra, has been variously spelt as 'Warragubera', 'Warragubra', 'Warigubra' and even 'Warigaberra'. That property today is situated around 5kms southeast of today's town of Bega, and was located precisely at the point on the Bega River, where the flow becomes tidal and then empties into the sea just north of today's town of Tathra.

The Frawleys likely arrived at Twofold Bay about six weeks prior to the birth of their second child Ellen Frawley, which occurred at 'Warigubara Station' on the 2nd of September 1842,[7] with her father working as a labourer. Consequently, Ellen is believed to be one of the first, if not the very first white child born on the far South Coast.

Until 1862, squatters occupied all the land in the Monaro and coastal districts except for some land sold near government townships.

So far as the white population was concerned, the area was almost entirely occupied by squatters, their assigned servants and employed persons. However, few immigrant families ventured into the district of Twofold Bay until the 1840s. Indeed, the family of James Kirwan's wife objected to their Elizabeth accompanying James to the Monaro, at that time, because there were no white women there.

First White Child Born in the Monaro

In those early days, the hardships and privations borne by these worthy pioneers was really indescribable, but here arises the disputed issue as to who was the first white child born in the Monaro District. Ellen Frawley was one amongst a shortlist of contenders, but if she wasn't the very first white child born in the region, there was obviously only a short space of time between her and the rival claimants.

> There are many claims regarding which European women and which child was first born in the isolated areas. A white woman, a widow named Ritchie, was reported to be with the Imlays at Twofold Bay, in 1840, after her husband, a ship's carpenter died there. When the Anglican Rev E. G. Pryce visited Bega in 1844, he baptised Henry the son of Thomas and Jane Underhill born there in 1842. William Bartley was born at Dry River in 1841. Father Michael Kavanagh of Queanbeyan baptised a child at Kiah in 1844 and also John Jr. andEllen Frawley at Warrigubura. From this information it can be deduced that the first family groups entered the district in the 1840s. Reporting on conditions in the Queanbeyan - Canberra districts in 1839 Rev. Pryce stated, "There is no school of any description in the district... here is no church, no school, no place where the decencies of public worship can be observed.' Concerning Twofold Bay which he referred to as the 'Untouched District' he wrote:
>
> "The popular neighbourhood of Braidwood and all the country as far as Bateman's Bay are I believe unprovided for. Menaroo also, extending 150 miles in another direction, beyond the limits with a scattered population of 1600 is totally without the means of grace."
>
> *John B. Cornell* [8]

Ellen had been preceded in her family by her older brother John Frawley Jr, but he had been born in May of the preceding year, and baptised while the Frawley's were still working at Alexander Berry's Coolangatta homestead. In any case, by November of 1843, John and Mary Ann Frawley's third child, James Frawley, had arrived at Warragaburra.[9]

Although the Frawley's had by now become accustomed to the rigours of the untamed Australian bush, this attribute hadn't yet extended to other members of colonial society and in particular the clergy. Indeed it wasn't until the 18th March 1844 that Father Michael Kavanagh, the roving parish priest for Queanbeyan and the Monaro District, arrived for the very first time, to administer to the outlying Catholic pioneers. Baptismal record state that John Jr., Ellen and James Frawley were all baptised at that time, with the ceremonies being conducted in 'Parish Unnamed' in the County of Murray and in the District of Manaroo (aka Monaro) of New South Wales. The father, John Frawley was recorded as working as a labourer and living with Mary (McGarrey) at Warragaburra, with Twofold Bay being the nearest settlement.[10]

> "When Bishop Polding [1794-1877] came to Sydney in 1835, he set up parishes to cover the populated areas of the country. Among them was Queanbeyan, with Father Heston in charge in 1842. The Bega Valley was in this vast Parish, which stretched from west of the Dividing Range to the sea, and from Moruya to south of Twofold Bay. So Catholics who had come down with William Duggan Tarlington from Braidwood or made their way from Ben Boyd's camp in Twofold Bay belonged to the Queanbeyan parish. Once a year Rev. Michael Kavanagh, who was appointed to Queanbeyan in 1843, visited the coastal fringe of the Queanbeyan parish. On the 18th March 1844 he baptised John Jr. [Ellen & James] Frawley of Warrigubura...So the Sacraments were administered and probably the Holy Sacrifice offered in somebody's slab hut."
>
> *Gerard Monaghan* [11]

The fact that their oldest child John Frawley Jr. had already been baptised in 1841, didn't seem to matter... as in the wilderness, they likely concluded that "the more protection, the better." While the actual record of his baptism has not been accessed, the Queanbeyan baptismal records for both Ellen (18 months) and James Frawley (5 months), provide sufficient information.

Reminiscences of a Bush Family

The book "Recollections of the Early Days of Moruya", by Mrs Celia Rose of 'Gundary', Moruya, mirror similar experiences of the Frawley family at Warragaburra, and she gives an account of her interactions with the Aborigines of that district, after she had arrived there as a child with her family in the late 1830s...

> "There was only one sailing vessel, named the "Waterwitch", that called at Broulee about once a month, bringing provisions from Sydney, and the shortage was acute. Aboriginals saved the settlement several times from starvation by supplying fish and oysters. I think the Aboriginals numbered about four hundred. They were quiet and harmless, and the elders of them were very kind, and would put their hands on our heads and say, "Buderree", or fellow white picanniny. There were no other white children but my brother and myself, and we used to play with the blacks, and were never frightened of them. My mother was the only white woman here at the time. The first hotel was built on the northern bank of the Moruya River, and when the blacks got drunk there they would fight and kill each other, and now there is not one full-blooded black left in this district."
>
> Mrs Celia Rose of 'Gundary', Moruya [12]

The Walker Brothers

The year 1844 brought the collapse of the beef industry, and having over-extended themselves the Imlay brothers were unable to repay their debts. The combination of a severe drought and depression saw the foreclosure of the Imlay properties by their bankers, the Walker brothers. Consequently, the Imlays were forced to sell-up most of their holdings with ownership of 'Warragaburra' passing to William Walker & Co.

William Walker (1787-1854),[13] merchant, was the second son of Archibald Walker, the laird of Edenshead, Fife in Scotland, and his second wife Isabel, daughter of the laird of Falfield. In 1803 William joined the London branch of a Scottish bank and after a few years joined Fairlie, Ferguson & Co., merchants, whose headquarters were in Calcutta. He was soonafter sent to Calcutta and in July 1813 voyaged to Sydney in the "Eliza" as agent for his firm, with the immediate task of collecting debts owed to it by Robert Campbell (1769-1846). After sailing back to Calcutta, Walker resigned from the firm and in March of 1820 he returned to Sydney in the "Haldane".[14]

William's eldest brother James, a half-pay naval officer, followed him to Sydney on the 24th September 1823,[15] joining two nephews, Thomas and Archibald Walker, who were also in the colony as shareholders. Walker had already formed William Walker & Co., and their firm became engaged in coastal shipping and whaling, and operated out of their wharf and warehouse at Dawes Point in Sydney. William received a grant of 1000 acres (405 ha) from Governor Lachlan Macquarie in 1821 and in 1825 another 1000 (405 ha) from Governor Sir Thomas Brisbane at Lue, near Mudgee. James received 2000 acres (809 ha) at Wallerawang and settled there in 1824.

In May 1826 William sailed in the "Mangles" for London. On his return to Australia in the "Numa" in July 1828 he brought 160 Saxon merino ewes from Stettin. On the 20th October 1828 in Sydney he had married Elizabeth Kirby; they had nine sons and two daughters. While in England he had applied for an increased grant as he now had capital of approximately £25,000 invested in the colony. He was given another 1000 acres (405ha) and later obtained more land in the central west of NSW and at Twofold Bay. In February 1831 both brothers chartered the "Forth" and returned to London to establish the firm of Walker Bros. & Co., which during the late 1830s exported large quantities of wool to London. Their men moved stock to the upper Castlereagh River and squatted on several runs. David, William and Thomas Archer, sons of William Archer and Julia Walker, daughter of William's half-brother Archibald, had arrived at Wallerawang and remained there from 1834-38 when David Archer began managing the Walkers' properties. News of losses in the depression and drought brought William Walker to Australia again in 1843, but his permanent residence remained in England until he died on the 8th July 1854.

William Walker played an active part in public life during his long residence in New South Wales. He was a director of the Bank of New South Wales in 1820-24, a member of committees appointed to examine the bank's affairs in 1844 and 1845, and was on its first London board in 1853-54. He was president of the Chamber of Commerce and treasurer of the Agricultural Society, a strong supporter of the Scots Church and a subscriber to charitable institutions.

Settlers with capital were favoured by the land and immigration regulations of the 1820s, since these 'capitalists' could support themselves and relieve the government of expenditure by employing convicts. As a result, half-pay navy and army officers and well-to-do middle-class merchants and farmers formed an increasing proportion of the population at that time. In addition, the first part of Commissioner Bigge's report on the state of the colony in New South Wales, had aroused a great deal of interest in Britain.[16] Following the publication of William Charles Wentworth's (1790-1872) book in London in 1819,[17] which glowingly described the colony and emphasised the prospects for men of capital regarding the farming of sheep, James Walker joined his younger brother William, who was then prospering in New South Wales. James Walker's career had been in the navy until 1822, when he was retired on half-pay as Britain reduced the armed forces, following its long drawn-out wars against France.[18]

But James Walker made up his mind to become a pastoralist in New South Wales rather than to join his brother in commercial life. He was then thirty-seven years old with no experience of agriculture, but he brought with him a free labourer named Andrew Brown who had been born at 'Tibbermuir' near Perth, Scotland, who was then 25 years old.[19] By 11th November 1824 James Walker was back in Sydney and had received from Governor Brisbane a promise of the usual grant of 2,000 acres (809 ha),[20] at the site he had selected, which was known by the Aboriginal name of 'Wallerawang', near Lithgow.[21]

By 1844, the Walkers were the third largest share holders in the Bank of New South Wales, so when they foreclosed on the Imlay's, they took most of their land in the process. This left George and Alexander Imlay only with 'Tarraganda Station', which Peter Imlay, who later moved to New Zealand, re-purchased following the death of his brothers in 1846-7.

The Birth of Pambula

On the South Coast, James Walker established his head station at 'Kameruka' with a series of out-stations like 'Warragaburra', while his younger brother Edward established a grand residence in Pambula, known as 'Oaklands House'.²² The Oaklands property was originally owned by the Imlay brothers (1833-1844), who transferred it, with the manor house built by William Walker & Co, to the 'sleeping partnership' of Edward Walker (1844-1853). Ownership was transferred again to the Twofold Bay Pastoral Association from 1853 to 1863, whose proprietors included William Montagu Manning (1811–1895), James A.L. Manning (1814–1887), Edye Manning, Thomas Sutcliffe Mort (1816–1878), John Croft (1792–1863), Robert Tooth (1821–1893) and Edwin Tooth (1822–1858).

The Walker's continued with the Imlay's practice of exporting cattle to Sydney and Hobart Town. The procedure used by the shepherds and graziers to get these cattle to market at that time was rather unique:

> "For loading, the cattle had a sling placed around them and were then forced into the sea off a shallow beach at Cattle Bay and led by a horseman to the side of a ship, often the "Aron", where sailors hooked onto the sling and winched the beast aboard".
>
> D. G. Parbery ²³

Essentially the Imlay Brothers, followed by Ben Boyd and the Walker Brothers were the first developers to draw settlers and employees to the region, and the dealings of these land barons no doubt coincided with and affected the lives of the Frawley family. And so, as living in almost complete isolation at Warragaburra would have been extraordinarily difficult, John and Mary Ann Frawley likely looked around and took on work wherever it presented itself, so that within a few years of Ellen's birth, they had moved into the newly developing township of Panbula (now called Pambula). The Frawleys eventually moved on, and by around 1845 they were residing in a new growing township...

> "The Walkers made Panbula and Kameruka their head stations. The Panbula station of the Imlays had no buildings other than four stockmens huts so the Walkers built 'Oaklands' in 1842, a single storey residence of four big rooms and made of convict brick. The bricks were made on the property and the timber pit-sawn half a mile to the north. The Walkers also built many other solid structures including boiling-down works for tallow, a store managed by Mr. Bell and the Governor Fitzroy Hotel."

> "Oaklands was surrounded with English gardens, trees and orchards. An enormous oak tree with a girth of more than seven metres stands in front of the house today! William Walker Sr. also kept an extensive aviary of English birds, which were released into

this area and contribute to our broad exotic bird population.

Panbula 'News Weekly', 27th Sept 1995 [24]

In 1845, a census of Aborigines revealed a total of 158 blacks living in the 'Biggah' area, some of who were employed as stockmen, sheep-washers and farm labourers. By December 1848, the "Bermondsey" disembarked immigrants at Eden in Twofold Bay, to work at 'Kameruka' or 'Tarraganda'. Then in March of 1855, another ship called the "Caesar" brought German emigrants directly from Hamburg to Twofold Bay, who also took up positions at 'Kameruka,' and many descendants of these families remain landowners today.

May 1851 saw a disastrous flood sweep many families down the Bega River, with 17 souls dying and being buried at 'Corridgeree' near Tarraganda. The government surveyor Samuel Parkinson had just laid out a township at North Bega, on the site of the present Bega Cheese Factory, but was forced by the flooding to move to higher ground on the southern side of the river where a new town was founded. In 1852 the Walker brothers sold out to the Twofold Bay Pastoral Association. The first town allotments were surveyed in February 1854 and sold at Eden in August of that year. Eden was the only port for communication and transport in the Monaro District, until the port of Merimbula was opened by the proprietors of Kameruka in 1855.

The Frawley family endured the harsh isolation of Warraguberra Station, far from the settled communities of Coolangatta and Wollongong, for two full years, where life on the far South Coast proved to be unforgiving with rugged terrain, relentless weather, and total dependence on the landholders, William Walker & Co. But hardship breeds resolve, and by the summer of 1844, the Frawleys had seized an opportunity, leaving the remote station for the budding township of Pambula. Here, determined to establish a home and a future for themselves, they would carve out a new life, one built on their own terms.

References

1. Death from Exposure (The Teetotaller & General Newspaper, 26 March 1842, p.1)
2. Wikipedia - 'Benjamin Boyd.' [https://en.wikipedia.org/wiki/Benjamin_Boyd]. Retrieved 12th January 2020.
3. Parbery, D.G. (1992). Fabric Of A Family, op.cit.
4. Arrival of Ben Boyd in the "Wanderer" (The Australasian, 20 July 1842, p.2)
5. 'Shipping Intelligence.' Sydney Morning Herald, 1st January to 10th August, 1842.
6. Higgins, J. (1982). Pambula's Colonial Days: A short history of the period 1797-1901. The Merimbula – Imlay Historical Society.
7. NSW Dept of BDM .(1842). Birth & Baptism for Ellen Frawley, 2nd Sept 1842 at Warigubera, #1772/1842 (V18421772 62).
8. Cornell, J. B. (1994). Most Obedient Servants on the Monaro and Far South Coast. Cheltenham, NSW.
9. NSW Dept of BDM. (1843). Birth & Baptism for James Frawley, #1773/1843 (V18431773 62).
10. NSW Dept of BDM .(1842). Birth & Baptism for Ellen Frawley, op. cit.
11. Monaghan, Gerard. (1985). 'Vision For A Valley': Catholic People In The Bega Valley 1829-1985: A History. Self-published.
12. "Recollections of the early days of Moruya." Journal of the Royal Australian Historical Society, 8 (Supplement)(1923), pp. 375-376.
13. Parsons, Vivienne (1967). 'William Walker (1787–1854)', op. cit.
14. Parsons, Vivienne (1967). 'William Walker (1787–1854)', Australian Dictionary of Biography, National Centre of Biography, Australian National University, https://adb.anu.edu.au/biography/walker-william-2767/text3931, published first in hardcopy 1967, accessed online 26 January 2023.
15. Sydney Gazette, 25 Sept. 1823.
16. Crew, B.H. (1963). The History of the Walker and Archer families (M.A. thesis, Australian National University), pp.24-26.
17. Wentworth, W.C. (1819). "A Statistical, Historical and Political Description of the Colony of New South Wales".
18. John Leslie: "From Stockyards to Streets (The Story of the Founding of Coonamble) (1955). Jack Stephens (ed.) ''Coonamble'' (1955). Anny Lists - Great Britain and Ireland, 1785-1835; 27 July, 1808; 16 Feb. 1814; 25 Dec. 1818.
19. Leslie: op. cit. Report of the Select Committee· on Secondary Punishments. P.P. 1831, VII, 276. Evidence of James Walker pp.56-63.
20. N.S.W. Government Gazette, 24 Oct. 1832 p.356.
21. Ibid.
22. Parbery, D.G. (1992). Fabric Of A Family, op. cit.
23. Parbery, D.G. (1992). Fabric Of A Family, op. cit.
24. 'Oaklands House.' Panbula 'News Weekly', Historical Feature, 27 September 1995.

12

PIONEERS OF PAMBULA

John Frawley's journey from convict to free settler was one marked by resilience, adaptability, and an unwavering determination to provide for his family. Transported to Australia as a government-assigned servant, he endured seven years of servitude before transitioning into employment with some of the most influential pastoralists of the region, first with the Imlay brothers and later with the Walker Brothers at Warragaburra. Though never self-employed, Frawley's skills as a labourer ensured he remained a valued worker in an era when manpower was scarce and industrious hands were in high demand.

His years of toil in isolated and often unforgiving conditions were a testament to his endurance. For two years, Frawley and his family lived in the wilderness, a period that tested their resourcefulness and fortitude. Yet, the harsh realities of remote life also underscored the necessity of community. When the opportunity arose to move into the developing township of Pambula, the family embraced the change. The shift from isolation to settlement life brought them into closer contact with others, allowing them to engage socially, build friendships, and integrate into the growing community.

For John Frawley, Pambula offered more than just a place to live, it provided a sense of belonging, a reprieve from solitude, and the prospect of a more stable future for his young family. While he struggled to own land or business, his contributions as a hardworking labourer played a small yet significant role in the economic and social fabric of the region. This chapter explores the life of John Frawley and his family, tracing their struggles, triumphs, and the legacy they left in the evolving landscape of colonial Australia.

Oaklands Manor House

Majestic oak trees, some planted in the mid-19th century and others naturally sprouting from fallen acorns, stand as enduring sentinels of the estate's history. It is from these very trees that the property derives its name of "Oaklands". Today, it remains one of the oldest working properties on the far south coast, with a legacy dating back to the first permanent European settlement in the Pambula district.

The estate's history is deeply intertwined with the pioneering Imlay brothers, Peter, George, and Alexander, who were drawn to the region by the whaling opportunities of nearby Twofold Bay. They quickly expanded their interests, establishing vast pastoral holdings that stretched beyond what is now the Victorian border, north to Bega and Cobargo, and west to the mountain escarpment. Following the enactment of Governor Bourke's 'Crown Lands Occupation Act' in 1836, they secured licenses covering extensive areas of the far south coast, including a 17-square-mile property known as 'Pampoolah' or 'Pamboola'.[1]

By the 1830s, the Imlays had consolidated land spanning from Broulee to south of Twofold Bay and westward into the mountains.

They established cattle runs along the fertile Pambula River flats, making their head station on its banks. By 1833, the brothers were actively developing the rich alluvial soil, grazing cattle for beef production, engaging in dairying for butter and cheese, breeding sheep, and cultivating crops such as potatoes and turnips, essential supplies for the survival of the Australian colonies.

By 1835, the Imlays had initiated trade with Hobart, Port Arthur in Van Diemen's Land, South Australia, and New Zealand, a network that flourished into the 1840s. A description from 1839 details their Panbula Station as spanning 17 square miles, with four slab huts, a stockyard, and 150 acres under wheat and barley cultivation. The station was home to ten residents, with Peter Imlay overseeing operations. The nearest settlement lay 12 miles away.[2]

The Imlays were among the first to export local produce internationally, dispatching the schooner "St. Heliers" to London in 1843. Its cargo included tallow, salted meats, beef, neatsfoot oil, wattle bark extract, and mutton hams. However, by the late 1830s, the unforgiving forces of nature took their toll. A devastating drought, followed by bushfires in 1840, wreaked havoc on their holdings. While Governor Gipps was moving toward granting squatters greater security of tenure, the relief came too late for the Imlays. Unable to recover from their losses before the onset of the colony's first major economic depression, they were forced to cede their Pambula property and most of their other assets to creditors William Walker & Co.

With the Imlays gone, William Walker & Co. emerged as the largest landholders in the Twofold Bay district. In 1844, the original 160-acre freehold "Portion Five" of the Panbula estate was formally granted to William Walker, with additional parcels acquired by various family members over the years. James Walker, William's elder brother, managed the Panbula property, while his son, William Benjamin Walker, focused on securing Kameruka.

In response to the slump in meat prices, the Walkers established a boiling-down works at Panbula in 1847, rendering livestock into tallow, bones, hides, and other valuable by-products, which proved more profitable than selling live animals. Around the same time, James Walker constructed a homestead at Panbula, while the Governor Fitzroy Hotel, licensed to Charles Robertson, opened its doors. The hotel's namesake, Governor Sir Charles Fitzroy (1796-1858), was at least an acquaintance of the Walkers and had visited their Kameruka Estate.

Following the Colonial Government's establishment of a public education system in 1848, James Walker provided a slab hut on his Panbula property for use as a school in 1849. He also played a role in securing two and a half acres within the township for a permanent school building. The Walker estate in Pambula also featured a blacksmith's shop and a general store operated by Charles William Bell.

James and Louisa Walker, along with their three children, remained at Panbula until William Benjamin Walker returned to England to join William Walker & Co.'s head office. At that point, the family shifted their focus to Kameruka. Arthur Manning leased the Panbula property until Edward Walker arrived in April 1853 to finalize its sale to the Twofold Bay Pastoral Association, marking the end of an era for the Walkers in Pambula.

Establishment of Pambula

Today's town of Pambula is a small, but historic town on the far South Coast, and is located 456 km south of Sydney via the Princes Highway and 525 km via the Hume Motorway, through Canberra and Cooma. Prior to the arrival of Europeans the land was inhabited by the Dyirringany and Thaua Aborigines, with 3,000 year old middens in the area. The Princes Highway passes through the middle of Pambula and makes the town, with its cafes and shops, a convenient stopping point for people wanting to break their journey north or south. The town spreads across the Pambula River Valley and has a sweet, unspoiled charm, with its principal attraction being the tranquil, but picturesque Pambula Beach.

The Pambula area was first visited by survivors of the wreck of the "Sydney Cove" in 1797, and a year later by navigator and explorer George Bass, who journeyed south from Sydney in a 28 foot open whaleboat, expanding Cook's observations with more detailed chart of the east coast of New South Wales. Taking shelter in an inlet during a gale, Bass travelled up the Pambula River noting the beauty of the spot in his diary. Bass recorded the beauty of the location in his log book:

> "...were it not for the extreme shallowness of this bar this little harbour would be a complete harbour for small craft....the upper part of this place is a kind of lagoon, or at least a flat, but the lower part downwards as far as the bar is one of the prettiest harbours.... every small bite has its little sandy beach and every turning its trim, rocky point....I have named this place Barmouth Creek."
>
> *George Bass, 18th February 1798* [3]

Bass was describing the 'Jigama River', known today as the Pambula River, with 'pambula' or 'panboola', probably being named by the Thaua speaking clan of the Yuin nation, to mean 'twin waters.' The region was popular amongst the Aborigines for thousands of years due to an abundance of oysters, shellfish and the seasonal 'bardi' grub. Disease and a clash of white and Aboriginal cultures led to social disintegration and a rapid depopulation of the natives, with only a few Aborigines resident in Pambula by 1848.

The early squatters and pioneers were attracted to the area by land, and when they managed to obtain it, their axes rang out as the trees were felled and the timber was shaped for the primitive slab and bark huts. The village quickly developed to serve the early settlers in the locality and Mary Ann Frawley was one of them...

> "At first it meant that cooking was done out in the open, with water carried up from the creek. Dimly, against this rugged backdrop, we see women struggling to make a home in this hostile environment. Women were called upon to face the larger dangers of drought, bushfire and flood, and were forced to hide their fears of childbirth, accident, illness and molestation."
>
> *Jule Higgins* [4]

The town of Pambula was first charted in 1843, when assistant surveyor Thomas Scott Townsend surveyed the land on the river flats. Following his work, F. McCabe drew up the first full town survey in

1847, but there were some unforeseen difficulties...

> "Lack of foresight resulted in the township of Pambula being laid out on the southern side of the flood prone flats, and the Governor Fitzroy Hotel was washed away... along with it's 'splendid cedar fittings'. In 1851 the Sydney Morning Herald reported severe floods, stating... "the township of Pambula became a lake. The whole of the tenants of the frail Australian huts, who could do so, had to seek safety in the two substantial taverns in the town." This flood nearly wiped out the same settlement, which was ultimately re-sited to higher ground on the present site of Pambula town centre. The Anglican (1855) and Catholic (1851) 'slab' churches were reconsecrated in solid stone on their present sites in 1866 and 1867 respectively. The town cemetery was also moved due to the flooding and at least 53 graves had to be exhumed from the Pambula Bridge site. After a census showed that 62% of the population under 21 could neither read nor write, Mr. James Walker supplied a newly repaired hut as a temporary school and Mr. Grearly started teaching on July 23rd 1849, with 37 pupils. It was the seventh school established in NSW, only nine months after the first school. By the following year a four room brick and shingle building had been erected and attendance had risen to a high of 51 pupils. Three quarters of Pambula's settlers were free at a time when 65% of the colony were convicts or had convict origins."
>
> *Jule Higgins [5]*

In 1844 retired naval officer Lt. John Lloyd RN, was granted 300 acres upon which he built 'The Grange'. He employed two local men to help build his substantial homestead and may also have had two convicts assigned to assist with construction.

Born in Ireland, John Lloyd entered into a career in the Royal Navy at just 12 years of age and was by all reports in attendance at the Battle of Trafalgar in 1805.

Much later he moved to Panbula about 1840 becoming one of the original pioneers of that town, and proceeded to build one of the most beautiful homes, a striking two storey Georgian and Edwardian stone residence known as 'The Grange,' which has been a local landmark for almost 170 years and is now one of the oldest buildings in the district.

After securing 302 acres for his Grange Farm in January 1844, Lloyd added further land in 1856, his property at one point embracing the land between the pristine Pambula and Yowaka Rivers. His appointment as a magistrate of the town of Pambula was announced in May of 1848.[6] His eldest son Arthur Lloyd Esq., married Elizabeth Lucy Lloyd at Durdham Down, Clifton in January of 1859, at which time he was still in residence at Pambula. John Lloyd Esq, R.N. died on the 15th December 1868, late of Pambula in the 86th year of his age.[7]

In 1845 a road was completed between Eden and the Monaro Plains, which exactly passed through the small, but developing village of Pambula. Around this time the Governor Fitzroy Hotel was built by the Walker Brothers.

By the late 1840s, opportunities in the Pambula District picked up considerably with a marked increase in available work being advertised by the Walkers and other land holders. This brought on a corresponding increase in the number of ships servicing the area, with many calling directly at Pambula. Being open to the sea the shallow river was an issue, but they use small boats to offload passengers and supplies.

In 1848, 'persons' were given an opportunity to object to the large holdings of the squatters, but few could challenge such powerful men?

> Colonial Secretary's Office, Sydney, September 27. – His Excellency the Governor [Sir Charles A. Fitzroy] directs it to be notified, for the information of all persons interested, that in pursuance of her Majesty's Order in Council, of the 9th March, 1847, the under mentioned persons have demanded leases of the several runs of Crown Land, particularised in connexion with their respective names.
>
> Persons, who object to any of these claims, either wholly or in part, should lodge caveats at this office within two months - from the present date, specifying the lands to which their objections extend, and the grounds on which their objections are based.
>
> It is to be distinctly understood that the Government does not pledge itself to the issue of a lease in any case until due enquiry has been made into the validity of the claim, and whether or not it may be necessary to reserve any portion of the land claimed, for any of the public purposes contemplated in the Order in Council.
>
> By His Excellency's Command
E. Deas Thomson.[8]

A detailed and in depth history of Pambula's colonial days has been written by Jule Higgins (1982), which covers the exploration and origins of the region.[9]

The Frawley Family

The question at this point is whether our ancestor John Frawley, remained in the employ of the Walker's, or were the Frawley's enticed into Panbula Station for some other purpose? Perhaps John Frawley was hired by the Walkers or John Lloyd as a labourer to assist in the construction of their manor houses? In terms of accommodation, there wasn't too much on offer in Panbula at that time, and most residential structures were simple 'bark slab' huts.

> "In Panbula during the twenty years from 1842 there appears to have been an extensive use of home-made bricks. Except for one residence, The Grange, all homesteads and public buildings were erected with brick construction, tending to create a definite brick era. Good clay deposits were close at hand and the lime needed for the mortar was derived from ground-up oyster shells, enormous deposits of these having accumulated due to the aboriginals partiality for oysters over many hundreds of years. This type of construction could also have resulted from an influx of tradesmen from Boydtown around 1847. The 'Grange' was constructed of imported stone and was erected under the supervision of Lt. John Lloyd after he purchased the land in 1843. He was given a grant of land by the Government on his retirement from naval service, in which he had fought alongside Lord Horatio Nelson at the Battle of Trafalgar on the 21st of October 1805."
>
> J. Shannon [10]

The first buildings to be erected on the Panbula flats were simple stockman's slab huts located on the Imlay brothers land. Despite the survey by Thomas Townsend, who toured the area in 1842, no indications of buildings occur on his map of 1847, and no homestead is evident.

If John Frawley did move to Panbula to work in and around the Walkers new 'Oaklands Manor House', the experience gained might explain why he later went on to become a builder/labourer of sorts, as he could have learnt many of the required skills while working on the Oaklands property.

> "A large homestead built of handmade bricks was that of Oaklands in Panbula which was on 160 acres bought by the Walkers in 1844. The date of the homestead's actual erection is not known, but correspondence between the Walker and Archer families in 1847 stated that James Walker's wife was 'thrilled as it [the house] was nearly ready for occupation."
>
> J. Shannon [11]

Regardless of the reasons for their move, sometime before December 1844 when their fourth child Stephen Frawley was born,[12] the Frawley family had already moved from 'Warragaburra' into the developing hamlet of Pambula, bequeathing them the honour of being amongst the very first residents, and pioneers of that early New South Wales town.

Bonded by the mutual difficulties experienced by these intrepid pioneers, it didn't take long for the Frawleys to establish friendships. As the Roman Catholic priests made such infrequent visits to the south coast at this time, the settlers often conducted their own religious ceremonies when they had the opportunity, and a number of baptisms were held on the 11th May 1846, when John and Mary Frawley became godparents at the baptism of Elizabeth, the daughter of their new friends Edward and Elizabeth Kennedy at Pambula.

In March of 1848 the young Frawley family was increased considerably by the birth of their twins Letitia and Patrick Frawley again at Pambula.[13] Although unsure as to the exact address of the Frawleys in Panbula, their last child Thomas Frawley was also born there in June of 1849.[14]

In 1849 too, there was a severe financial crash in the colony, which greatly affected the south coast region. The Boydtown venture failed and Ben Boyd sailed off into the Pacific in his yacht "Wanderer", and disappeared on the island of Guadalcanal. Peter Imlay handed what was left of his Bega Estates in the hands of tenants and resettled in Wanganui, New Zealand. The financial crash also rendered the Walker's cattle trade uneconomic and by 1850 they were faced with the prospect of selling out their holdings for only £20,000. Even though the discovery of gold and the resulting influx of migrants soon created a boom market for cattle and other agricultural products in the colonies, by 1851 the Walkers had decided to sell off their pastoral interests.

Following the failure of Ben Boyd's venture in 1849 and the sale of Walker's holdings, the Twofold Bay Pastoral Association was established with James Manning as manager. The business was based at 'Kameruka' as the main station, with 'Warragaburra' as one of several outstations.[15] Whether John Frawley had any further association with the Imlay's or the Walker Brothers after he left 'Warragaburra' is unknown, but by then the Frawleys were well and truly established in the growing township of Pambula.

By 1856 the newly sited township was prospering with five licensed hotels. The foundation stone for the Pambula Court House was thereafter laid in 1860, but Pambula wasn't officially proclaimed as a town until 1885.

St Peter's Catholic Church, Pambula

Being of Irish descent, the Frawleys were quite involved in the local Catholic community, and a public meeting was convened on the 7th August 1854, where John Frawley became the secretary of a committee of seven residents... "for the purpose of gathering subscriptions for buying a piece of land, for the the erection of a Roman Catholic Chapel."[16]

Over the years, the Frawleys had often donated toward the erection of a Catholic Church in Pambula,[17] with St. Peters Catholic Church eventually being completed in 1867/68. John and Mary Ann had both been active in collecting money for the building of this church, so we can safely assume that they were regular worshippers. The original St. Peter's Church was smaller than the 1868 church, and had a shingled roof. On completion of the latter in July 1868, both Mary and John Frawley were published in the Bega Gazette along with a list of other parishioners to acknowledge their donations.

ST. PETER'S CHURCH, PAMBULA

Mrs. J. Schaback, Mrs. Bickelmire, and Mrs. Frawly, for glazing one window of the church - £3,13,0. Collected by Mr. Behl, Mr Frawly, and Mr. McPhee, for altar - £12.

Bega Gazette, 18th July 1868

In 1853 an interesting letter to the editor of the newspaper 'Empire', described the township and geography of Pambula:

'PANBULA AND ITS NEIGHBOURS'

Panbula lies about 30 miles east of the magnificent tableland district of Monaro, wherein it is estimated with very much confidence that gold exists in great abundance of which the enterport is Panbula. It consists of a plain, or flat, in extent resembling an ordinary rural parish in England, and comprising an extensive government reserve (central), with a contiguous tract of nine acres for a future industrial school, an acre for the national school, an acre of burial ground, a horse-shoe shaped lagoon, which yields fresh water supplies in the dry seasons, several 'streets', 100 links wide... and many five acre allotments, one of which was purchased at 16 pounds an acre. A considerable slope of pleasing aspect under cultivation occupies the open space southwest of the plain, and here are several freehold homesteads. Obliquely across the plain, in a cleared recess of the bush on rising ground, is situated the township, close to which is a supply of good water as inexhaustable as is that of the lagoon half a mile distant. Of the half-dozen brick built houses (the residences of Messrs Walker and Bell, Mr. Bell's store-overseer, the school house and two public houses), one of the last named is, for neatness of style and humble elegance of finish throughout, an ornament to the bush [ie. Oaklands Manor House]. The parish numbers a population of forty to fifty families of Irish, Scot, English, coloured, American and German, and all are too prosperous to know poverty any longer, or feel the fear of it. They form a spirited and stirring community and perhaps worse neighbours might be found in a search for better, taking them on average.

Panbula News Weekly, 29th Sept 1853 [18]

Another letter at this time, sent by an unknown pioneer that arrived in Pambula in June of 1853, was addressed to Henry Pelham-Clinton (1811-1864), 5th Duke of Newcastle, who was at that time the minister for Foreign Affairs in London. It was apparently the privilege of the author to know and be known by the Duke, so by way of a complaint he proceeded to lament that all the district land was held in the possession of either Peter Imlay or the Twofold Bay Pastoral Association, and called for the opening up of reasonably priced blocks of land. Adding weight to the request, he attached the names of occupiers of land, who he regarded to be pioneers of the Parish of Pambula.[19] This letter may actually have had some effect as 'blocks for sale' were opened up in Pambula in 1856, two of which were selected by John Frawley. Apparently William Shea was at that time the anonymous author's tenant and the signatures were obtained by John Whelan, the poundkeeper.[20]

On the 15th of October 1854, John Frawley is recorded as sponsoring the baptism of both James Dunn and Mary Ann Collins in separate ceremonies conducted by Father William Xavier Johnson at Pambula.

But discontent was foaming across the colony at this time and just six weeks later, between 22 to 60 diggers, many of them Irish, were killed by troopers at the 'Eureka Stockade' on the 3rd December 1854.

The rebellion was instigated by gold miners at Ballarat, Victoria, who under their new fashioned flag called the 'Southern Cross' revolted against the colonial authorities.[21]

In December 1855 and on the 19th November 1856, we find John Frawley, a concerned citizen of the new town, acting as secretary for town meetings petitioning the government "to cause a direct line of road from Monaro to Pambula, and devise expenditure for the repair of roads and construction of bridges," at which both John Frawley and Syms Covington were the proposers of motions.[22,23]

Syms Covington (1816-1861),[24] was a well known resident and the Post Master of Pambula, and sailed as a fidler and cabin boy on Charles Darwin's voyages of natural discovery on board "HMS Beagle". Part way through the voyage, Covington became Darwin's assistant, preserving, labelling and packing hundreds of specimens, many new to science, and he was appointed as his personal servant in 1833, continuing in Darwin's service after the voyage until 1839.

Originally named Simon Covington, he was born in Bedford, Bedfordshire, England, the youngest child of Simon Covington V, and Elizabeth Brown. After Covington's trip on the "Beagle", he then emigrated to Australia and settled as the postmaster at Pambula, marrying Eliza Twyford. The Covington house is still standing in the main street of Pambula and is now used as a restaurant.

Thus, by the mid-19th century, John Frawley had firmly established himself as a pioneer of Pambula. His contributions to the town's development, perhaps even to the construction of the historic 'Oaklands Manor House' and Lt. John Lloyd's 'Grange Manor', were significant. His children followed in his footsteps, supporting the construction of St. Peter's Catholic Church, while John himself played a key role in shaping the region's infrastructure as secretary of the roads committee. He successfully applied for a conditional land purchase in the township and was a strong proponent of good education, helping to lead the effort to establish a school for the growing community.

But while John was building a future in Pambula, he was not the only Frawley making a fresh start in Australia. In the next chapter, we turn our attention to another branch of the family, his Frawley cousins, who began arriving in Victoria from about 1854. Their journey was one of determination, hope, and an enduring family bond, one strong enough to span continents. As they sought to reconnect with John, they proved that, despite the vast distance, the Frawley family remained united.

References

1. Bega Shire Hidden Heritage - 101 Objects Revealed - 'Oaklands' Oak Trees, Pambula', [https://hiddenheritage.com.au/heritage-object/?object_id=82].
2. Lambie, John (1839). Commissioner for Lands. (Extract from. Higgins, J. (1982). Pambula's Colonial Days: A short history of the period 1797-1901. The Merimbula – Imlay Historical Society).
3. Bayley, W.A. (1942). History of Bega. op. cit., p.10.
4. Higgins, J. (1982). Pambula's Colonial Days: A short history of the period 1797-1901. The Merimbula – Imlay Historical Society.
5. Ibid.
6. Lt. John Lloyd, R.N. - Magistrate (Sydney Chronicle, 6 May 1848, p.3).
7. Death of Ret. Lt. John Lloyd, R.N. (SMH, 16 December 1868, p.1).
8. Claims To Leases Of Crown Land Beyond The Settled Districts - Maneroo District (SMH, 6 October 1848 & 7 October 1848, p.8).
9. Higgins, J. (1982). Pambula's Colonial Days, op.cit.
10. Shannon, J. (1969). Buildings of Pambula, Twofold Bay. Unpublished Thesis.
11. Ibid.
12. NSW Dept. of BDM. (1843). Birth Certificate for Stephen Frawley, 1844 at Panbula, 1168/1844 (V18441168 63).
13. NSW Dept. of BDM, Birth Certificates for Letitia & Patrick Frawley (twins), 1848 at Panbula, 1415/1848 (V18481415 65).
14. NSW Dept. of BDM, Birth Certificate for Thomas Frawley at Panbula, 1849 at Panbula, 1519/1849 (V18491519 66).
15. Bayley, W.A. (1942). History of Bega, op. cit., p.20.
16. John Frawley - 'Secretary of Committee to Purchase Land for RC Church.' The People's Advocate & NSW Vindicator', 21 August 1854, p.15.
17. John Frawley - RC Church Subscriptions. Freeman's Journal, 12 May 1855, p.10.
18. Panbula News Weekly, 'Signed R. B.' 29th September, 1853. (Reprinted in News Weekly).
19. The 'Foundation of Bega' (The Bega Standard & Candelo, Merimbula, Pambula, Eden, Wolumla and General Advertiser (11th November 1876, p.2).
20. John Frawley, purchaser in 1856 from Index to Deeds - Pambula Town Purchases (NSW, Land Records, 1811-1870).
21. National Museum of Australia. 'Eureka Stockade' [https://www.nma.gov.au/defining-moments/resources/eureka-stockade]. Retrieved 10th June 2021.
22. John Frawley - Petition for Line of Road (Empire, 13 December 1856, p.3).
23. Pambula Meeting - Illawarra Mercury, 1856.
24. Wikipedia - "Syms Covington" [https://en.wikipedia.org/wiki/Syms_Covington].

13

THE FRAWLEYS OF BUNGAREE

The story of the Frawley family is not confined to a single path or destination. While John Frawley remained central to our branch of the family's journey, his brother Patrick and wife Susan Cody took their own bold steps toward a future far from their home in Doora, County Clare. Unlike some emigrants who ventured into the unknown with little connection to those who had gone before, Patrick and Susan's family seem to have been well aware of John's whereabouts. Over a period of several years, from 1854 to 1858, they made the life-altering decision to leave Ireland, undertaking a staggered migration to Australia.[1]

Among their children, Richard Frawley's journey stands out. He did not simply arrive in Australia, but he put down roots. Settling in Pambula, New South Wales, alongside our John Frawley, Richard married and had a son there, ensuring that this branch of the Frawley name would be carried forward in a new land. His presence in Pambula raises intriguing questions: Did he join John Frawley or another relative already established there? Was his path shaped by family letters, guidance, or the pull of opportunity?

However, Richard's time in Pambula was not permanent. Like many Irish migrants drawn by the promise of fortune and new prospects, he later moved away, eventually settling in Ballarat, Victoria. It was there, in 1864, that his life came to an early end. His story, though brief, reflects the restless movement and determination of his family, always seeking, always adapting to the changing landscapes of their adopted country.

This chapter explores the lives of Patrick and Susan's descendants, tracing their migration, settlement, and the impact they had on the communities they joined. Their story, like so many Irish emigrants of the 19th century, is one of resilience, ambition, and the enduring strength of family ties that spanned oceans.

Irish Origins of Patrick Frawley

Evidence reveals that John Frawley had a brother, Patrick Frawley a tenant farmer who lived in the townland of 'Ballyvonnavavn', near Doora, County Clare, Ireland.

Patrick John Frawley was born around 1790 in Doora and Kilraghtis, County Clare, Ireland. In 1821, he married Susan Cody, the daughter of Dennis and Margaret Cody, in County Clare. The 1826 tithe list records that Patrick owned seven and a half acres of land and was required to pay a tithe for the upkeep of the Protestant clergy.

Susan was born in 1796 at 'Jasper's Pound' near Quin, County Clare, Ireland. She emigrated to Australia in May 1858 aboard the "Parsee", accompanied by her daughter Bridget Catherine, and son Patrick. Susan passed away from chronic bronchitis on 19 December 1864 at Warrenheip, Victoria, aged 68. She was buried on 22 December 1864 in the Old Ballarat Cemetery, where she rests alongside her sons Richard and Michael, and Michael's wife, Bridget. Susan was of Roman Catholic faith.

At the commencement of the Irish Famine in 1845, Patrick would have been at least 45 years old. By 1855, land records list Susan as a widow, indicating Patrick had died sometime between 1840 and 1855, and well before Susan's 1858 emigration. The cause of his death remains unknown, perhaps due to famine, accident, or political turmoil.

In 1992, a search conducted by the Clare Heritage Centre at Corofin provided baptismal records for five of the seven children, Patrick, Michael, Richard, Eliza, and Sarah, but failed to locate records for Bridget Catherine and John. These records confirm that the Frawleys were baptized in what is now known as the Parish of Doora, Barfield, County Clare. Unfortunately, Catholic church records before 1864 were often incomplete, leaving many gaps in historical documentation.

Life in Doora and the Famine's Impact

The Frawleys lived in a one-room, earthen-floored cottage in Doora. The structure had a single window and door, additional windows were taxed at the time, making light and ventilation a luxury. Susan and her seven children endured incredibly harsh conditions. It is unknown whether they owned animals or how they survived during the famine. The family's survival suggests they either had enough food or received aid from relatives.

The famine devastated County Clare, with more than 150,000 people perishing or emigrating. Some of the Frawleys may have emigrated as a direct result of these hardships. In 1992, a visit to the remains of Susan's cottage revealed that it had stood until 1997 before being replaced by a modern home.

The Frawley Family's Journey to Australia (1854-1858)

Between 1854 and 1858, the Frawleys left Ireland for Australia aboard three different ships:

In 1854, the "Rodney", a ship of London; Alex Maclean, Master and burthen weight of 877 tons, sailed from the port of London, arriving on the 15th March 1854, at Sydney, New South Wales with

250 adults and 87 children - Government Immigrants. These included Michael Frawley, and his sister Sarah, who arrived in Sydney on March 15, 1854, as assisted immigrants.[2]

In 1855, the "Chowringhee", a ship of Belfast; D. Ferguson, Master and burthen weight of 893 tons, sailed from the port of London, and arrived on the 26th November, 1855, at Sydney, New South Wales with 235 adults and 49 children - Government Immigrants. These included, Anne Frawley (c.1807-1872), who brought with her five of her family members: Patrick, Richard, John, and Bridget, the wife of Michael Frawley, who arrived the year earlier, and another younger Michael (II) Frawley.[3]

In, the "Parsee", a ship of London; Edwin E. Thomas, Master and burthen weight of 1,050 tons, sailed from the port of London, via Southampton, and arrived on the 14th May 1858, at Melbourne (Hobsons Bay) with 437 passengers - Government Immigrants. These included the mother, Susan Frawley (nee Cody), who arrived with her daughter Bridget Catherine, and son Patrick, in Melbourne on May 14, 1858.[4]

The reasons for choosing Australia over the United States remain speculative. However, the presence of relatives, specifically some of Susan's Cody family, who had settled in Warrenheip, Victoria, likely influenced their decision. Additionally, the Frawleys arrived as assisted immigrants, meaning they were likely to have been financially sponsored by relatives or other community networks in Victoria.

Establishing a New Life in Leigh Creek/Bungaree

Upon arrival, the Frawleys settled in Leigh Creek and Bungaree, near Ballarat. This area, part of the Parish of Warrenheip, was rich in Irish Catholic immigrant communities. The Frawleys quickly integrated, purchasing land and raising families. It remains unclear how they funded their passage and land acquisitions, but support from the Cody family or an inheritance from Susan's father, Dennis Cody, may have played a role.

The Eureka Stockade, a defining moment in Australian history, occurred on November 30, 1854, amidst the emigration of the branch of the Frawley family. Though it is unknown whether they were directly involved, the rebellion marked a period of great social and economic upheaval in the gold-mining regions of Victoria.

The Death & Legacy of Susan Frawley

Susan Frawley (nee Cody) passed away in 1864 at the age of 68. For over 126 years, she lay in an unmarked grave in the Old Ballarat Cemetery until 1991, when family members, including Monica Burke (nee Frawley), raised funds to erect a headstone. Her grave, located in Section E1, Row 12, Grave 14, also holds her sons Michael and Richard, and Michael's wife Bridget (nee McMahon).

The McMahon sisters, who married Michael and John Frawley, were also from County Clare. It is possible the families knew each other in Ireland before emigrating to Australia.

The Frawley name remains prominent in various parts of the world, particularly in Ireland, in Boston in the United States, and Australia. Many Irish Frawleys trace their lineage to famine emigrants, while in Ireland, the name has a particular concentration around Kilrush, County Clare.

In an effort to trace the family's roots, every Frawley listed in the Irish telephone directory was contacted in 1992. Out of more than 200 letters, we received 13 responses and maintained regular correspondence with eight individuals. Many had become successful in various trades, including farming, hospitality, and transportation. Several family members also joined religious orders.

The Quest for Answers

Despite extensive research, including four trips to Ireland between 1992 and 1999, the exact details of Patrick Frawley's birth, marriage, and death remain elusive. Extensive searches in churches, cemeteries, and records have yielded little concrete evidence. Some theories suggest

Patrick may have died of natural causes or political violence, as Ireland experienced significant upheaval from the 1798 Irish Rebellion through the mid-1800s.

Future family historians may uncover more through additional research in 'Ballyvonnavavn' and surrounding areas. Questions remain about the family's journey, did they depart from Cork or travel to London before boarding their ships? How did they finance their emigration? Did they receive financial help from the Cody family?

The Frawley family's journey from Ireland to Australia was one of hardship, resilience, and determination. Their story, like that of many Irish emigrants, is interwoven with the broader history of famine, migration, and settlement. While many questions remain unanswered, their legacy continues through generations who seek to preserve and honor their history.

The Next Generation

In the quiet countryside of County Clare, Ireland, in the early 19th century, Patrick John Frawley and Susan Cody raised a large family. Life in Ireland was harsh, and as the years passed, their children sought opportunities beyond the rolling green hills of home. The seven children of Patrick John Frawley and Susan Cody, all Roman Catholics were:[5]

1. Patrick Frawley (1822-1901)

Patrick the eldest, was born in 1822 in co. Clare and christened two years later on 23 January 1824. With Bridget and Patrick Frawley as his sponsors, his future seemed promising. A farmer by trade, he never married. When the call of a new land beckoned, he set sail for Australia in 1858 aboard the "Parsee", accompanied by his mother, Susan, and sister, Bridget. Patrick lived with his brother Michael until his death in Warrenheip, Victoria, on 10 October 1901, aged 78. He was laid to rest in the New Cemetery, Ballarat on the 12 October 1901.

2. Bridget Catherine Frawley (1826-1914)

Bridget born in 1826 in County Clare, Ireland, was a devoted daughter and sister. She, too, arrived in Australia aboard the "Parsee" on 24 May 1858. She later married Matthew Jenkin, a bookmaker from Cornwall, England, in 1866. Together, they had a son, Patrick James Jenkins. Bridget lived a long life, passing away in Ballarat, Victoria, in 1914 at the age of 86.

3. Michael Frawley (1829–1883)

Michael was born in 1829 in County Clare, Ireland, shared his brother Patrick's pioneering spirit. He was baptised on the 27 January 1829 in Doora and Kilraghtis, County Clare. He and his sister Sarah braved the long journey aboard the "Rodney", arriving in Australia on 15 March 1854. A hardworking farmer and labourer, Michael married Bridget (1833–1882), daughter of James McMahon and Anne Hillard at St Mary's in Geelong on 11 September 1855 . They had several children, including Patrick, James, Elizabeth Ann, and Susan, who later married John O'Donohue. Their daughter Bridget wed Francis Kavanagh in 1902, but tragedy struck when she passed away the following year. Michael himself died on the 25 January 1883 in Ballarat, Victoria, aged 55, just a year after losing his wife, and was buried on the 28 January 1883 in the Old Ballarat Cemetery. They produced ten children.

4. Richard Frawley (1831–1864)

Richard was born in 1831 in Doora, County Clare, Ireland and christened on 13th February that year. In 1858, he married Catherine Penderghast, in Pambula, New South Wales, confirming that there was commincation between the Frawley cousins. But sadly, their happiness was short-lived as their infant son, named John, after our John Frawley of Pambula, passed away the same year. Richard was an agricultural labourer, but his own life ended abruptly in 1864, when he died on the 10 June 1864 in Ballarat, Victoria, at the age of 33, and was buried

13 June 1864 in Ballarat General Cemetery. Catherine later remarried William Wexted in 1875, but Richard's memory lived on in the land he had sought for a better future. They had one child, John Frawley (1858–1858).

5. Sarah Frawley (1836–1897)

Sarah was born in 1836 in County Clare, Ireland and baptised on 12 June 1836, shared her brother Michael's adventurous nature. They made the voyage aboard the "Rodney" together on 15 March 1854. Four years later, on 28 April 1859, she married Maurice Bruton (1836–1917). Their family grew over the years, with children like Susan "Suze," Francis "Jack," and Patrick Henry bringing both joy and responsibility. Their daughter Catherine "Kate" Bruton later became a WWI nurse and was awarded the Royal Red Cross for her service. Sarah's life came to an end on St Patricks Day, 17 March 1897 in North Melbourne, aged 60, and she was buried in the Melbourne General Cemetery on the 19 March 1897. They produced ten children.

6. Eliza Frawley (1839–1927)

Eliza entered the world in 1839 in Quin, County Clare, and was baptised on 23 August 1839. As a young woman, she journeyed to Australia, where she found work as a servant. On 25 February 1865, in the small township of Happy Valley, she married Patrick McCormack (1830/1840–1909). Together, they raised a family, welcoming children Mary Susan Rose, Richard Joseph, twins Elizabeth Ellen and Patrick Michael, Alexander John, and Hugh Henry. Eliza worked as a servant and lived a long and full life, passing away on 11 August 1927 in South Melbourne, Victoria, at the age of 88, and buried on 12 August 1927. They produced six children.

7. John Frawley (1840–?)

John the youngest of the siblings, was born in 1840 in County Clare. On 20 April 1865, he married Catherine McMahon (1840–1872) at St

Patrick's Cathedral in Ballarat. They had three children: Susan Mary, Sarah Jane, and Patrick, the last of whom died in infancy. Catherine's own life was cut short in 1872, and little Patrick's remains were later moved to rest beside her. They produced three children.

The Frawley family's story is one of resilience, sacrifice, and new beginnings. From the shores of Ireland to the goldfields and farmlands of Victoria, their legacy endures, carried forward by the generations that followed.

Danny Frawley

Another descendant to achieve recognition, but in a totally different field is Danny Frawley, son of Brian and Shirley Frawley, of Bungaree. He has made his mark on the football field, beginning his playing days with local club Bungaree in the Central Highlands Football League before graduating to East Ballarat in the Ballarat Football League.

Danny was later recruited by St Kilda and went on to play 240 games with the Saints. He was captain from 1987 to 1995 for a total of 173 games, becoming the longest-serving St Kilda captain. He won the St Kilda best and fairest award in 1988. He played 11 state games for Victoria, was named in the All Australian team in 1988 and was vice-captain of the All Australian team in 1990.

After he finished playing in 1995, he accepted a coaching role with Collingwood Football Club for four years before being appointed senior coach of the Richmond Football Club. He has just completed his first year in that position.

Special Thanks

Family history is an ongoing journey, and the Frawley reunion booklet represented an important step in that process. As time goes on, new information will undoubtedly come to light. While some omissions, discrepancies, or inaccuracies may exist, we hope they are minimal. This booklet should be seen as a foundation for a more comprehensive publication in the future.

Compiling details about people and events from 150 years ago, especially in a distant country where record-keeping was not as meticulous as today, is no small feat. We owe a great debt of gratitude to Ivan Frawley for his thorough investigative work and to Trish Lette for her exceptional family history research skills. We encourage other family members to visit Ireland, our ancestral homeland, to deepen their appreciation of our heritage. Such a trip may even uncover missing pieces of our family history puzzle. At the very least, visitors will experience Ireland's warm hospitality and see historic sites significant to our family, such as the location of Susan's cottage in Doora, which stood until 1997.

The year 2004, brought the 150th anniversary of the arrival of Michael Frawley and his sister Eliza in the Bungaree district. This milestone presents a fitting opportunity to hold another family gathering and perhaps publish a more extensive family history book. We welcome all comments and suggestions to help make that possible.

This booklet is the result of many people's efforts, and we sincerely thank everyone who contributed. A special acknowledgment goes to Patricia Lette, who has dedicated countless hours over many years to this project. Her unwavering commitment has been instrumental in both the reunion celebrations and the creation of this booklet. Another invaluable contributor is Ivan Frawley, who is passionate about passing family history on to future generations. He has traveled to Ireland four times, tirelessly researching and uncovering our family's past.

We also extend our gratitude to Monica Burke, whose remarkable memory has been invaluable in preserving details of our ancestors. She recalls names, burial sites, causes of death, marriages, and family connections, insights that many of us wish we had at our fingertips.

The organizing committee has shown tremendous enthusiasm in bringing this event to life, and we are grateful to everyone who played a role, whether in recording family history, planning the reunion, or producing this booklet. Many individuals have worked tirelessly behind the scenes to make this gathering a reality, and we hope their dedication is recognized and appreciated.

One person who deserves special mention is Patricia Lette of Cooma, New South Wales. Trish is the great-great-granddaughter of Maurice Bruton and Sarah Frawley (daughter of Susan and Patrick), who married on April 28, 1859. Sarah passed away on St. Patrick's Day in 1897 at the age of 60, while Maurice lived until 1917, reaching the age of 81. Trish, a true "computer wiz," has spent years reaching out to countless descendants, investing not only her time but also her own resources in phone calls, faxes, postage, and stationery. We also extend our appreciation to her family for their patience and support throughout her research journey.

We hope this booklet offers valuable insights into our family history and that this reunion is both memorable and meaningful for all. Thank you to everyone who has contributed in ways big and small, your efforts ensure that our family's legacy will be preserved for generations to come.[6]

And so, Susan Frawley (née Cody) left behind the rolling green fields of Doora, County Clare, in Ireland, for the uncertain promise of a new world. Widowed and determined, she gathered her children and embarked on the long, perilous voyage by sailing ship to Australia in the mid-1850s. From there, they pressed onward to Leigh Creek and Bungaree in Victoria, where hardship gave way to opportunity. In this fresh land, her family took root, her children thrived, and the generations that followed would multiply, forging a new legacy far from the famine-stricken soil of Ireland.

But while Susan and her children found prosperity, not all of the Frawley family's journey in Australia was smooth. Hundreds of miles away, another chapter of the Frawley family story was unfolding, one marked by struggle, conflict, and the relentless weight of the law. Back in Pambula, John Frawley, the ex-convict was about to face a battle of a very different kind.

References

1. Frawley, Ray (2000). "From Clare to Bungaree", For the occasion of the reunion of descendants of Patrick Frawley and Susan Cody, 7-8 October 2000 at Ballarta & Bungaree.
2. State Records Authority of New South Wales: Shipping Master's Office; Passengers Arriving 1855 - 1922; NRS13278,[90] reel 399. Transcribed by Joyce Pickup, 2004.
3. State Records Authority of New South Wales: Shipping Master's Office; Passengers Arriving 1855 - 1922; NRS 13278, [X93] Reel 402. Transcribed by Tricia Miller, 2003.
4. "Shipping Intelligence" (The Argus [Melbourne], Sat 15 May 1858, Page 4).
5. Frawley, Ray (2000). "From Clare to Bungaree", For the occasion of the reunion of descendants of Patrick Frawley and Susan Cody, 7-8 October 2000 at Ballarta & Bungaree.
6. For more information - contact Ray Frawley (Author) at RMBE 325 Killarney Road, Warrenheip ,Victoria, 3352 Phone (03)5334 7389.

14

PROPERTY & PROSECUTIONS

By 1856, John Frawley was a man of standing in the thriving town of Pambula. A respected figure in the community, he had his hands in many of the town's most vital affairs. As secretary for the roads committee, he helped shape the infrastructure that would connect Pambula to the wider world. He lent his voice to the appeal for the release of land, ensuring the town had room to grow. He reached into his own pocket to support the construction of St Peters Roman Catholic Church and worked tirelessly to improve local education. With property now to his name, it seemed that Frawley's future was set on a steady and prosperous course.

But fortunes, like the tides that lapped at the shores of Pambula Beach, have a way of turning. What began as minor civil disputes soon escalated into a series of legal battles that would test Frawley's resilience and reshape his fate. As accusations mounted and claims against him grew, the man who had helped build the town found himself at risk of losing everything. By the time criminal charges entered the fray, it was clear, John Frawley's run of good luck had come to a sudden and dramatic halt.

Having survived transportation, a seven year sentence as a convict with hard labour, the trials of bush living at 'Warragaburra', hostile aboriginals and floods, one might think John Frawley and his young family had seen the worst that life could throw at them. But no, his life now took a downward spiral as he became entangled in one court case after another. This is the story of how a man who had once stood among Pambula's most valued citizens found himself entangled in the unforgiving grip of the law.

Court Matters I - Frawley v Hayes

By 1855 John Frawley became entangled in court proceedings at the Police Office in Eden on the 9th of January. In partnership with William Shea, he was a co-defendant in a claim lodged over their workmanship in the building of a cottage for Mr. John Hayes. The cottage was in Monaro St, Pambula.

> **BEFORE JUDGE MANNING AND MOWLE**
>
> James McMann (policeman) stated he'd inspected the hut erected for John Hayes, Panbula and found the shingles not properly laid or closed, as claimed by Hayes. Builders John Frawley and William Shea were summonsing Hayes for payment. Hayes stated he wanted his hut "to be as good as the one Mr Covington had built". Blacksmith Davis and Wm McNevin gave evidence that the shingles were bad. Case dismissed with costs three pounds.
>
> *Eden Bench Books, 9th January 1855* [1]

It seems that John Hayes wasn't satisfied with the quality of the shingling so withheld part payment. It would appear in those days that court cases were a regular happening, and many records of the proceedings have survived. In this case, Mr. Hayes insisted that "he wanted his house to be as good as Mr. Covingtons."

A full transcript of the court proceedings between John Frawley, William Shea and Mr. Hayes has been preserved. Mr. Hayes argument and witnesses were obviously convincing and accepted by the judges, the end result being that not only did Frawley and Shea lose the case, but they had to pay £3 in costs! Unfortunately, Mr. Hayes' house has not survived the test of time, the absence of which today adds weight to his argument, that it had not been built anywhere near as good as Covington's house.

In 1856 New South Wales received responsible government when a number of land grants were offered to assist with settlement of the rural areas. Taking advantage of these 'selections', John Frawley applied for and was granted land in the township of Panbula on the corner of Toalla and Quondola Streets, on the 10th of September 1856.[2] John Frawley later sold this land to innkeeper, John Behl in 1872 for just £10,[3] which has since become recognised as 'Toad Hall'.

Despite the scrutiny, it appears that John's choice to reside in Panbula was sound, as a letter published in the Illawarra Mercury of 1856 described the growing township at that time:

> '...a very pretty, flourishing township...there are four or five public houses, as many more stores, a Crown Land Commissioner's office, a Church of England place of worship, two or more schools, about three dozen well erected weatherboard houses together with as many rough huts.'
>
> *Illawarra Mercury, 1856* [4]

Court Matters II - Martin v Frawley

On the 3rd of March 1857 John Frawley was granted a slaughtering licence by the Eden Bench of Magistrates. Unfortunately, by August of 1857, and perhaps caused by his new enterprise, he was back in the local court, this time for stealing and branding a calf, on charges brought by Constable John Marshall Walker of Eden.[5] The court proceedings for this incident, John Martin (plaintiff) against John Frawley (defendant), have also survived. Fortunately, the charges in this trial against John Frawley were dismissed by the magistrate.

Family Reunion

While John Frawley had got himself out of trouble in 1857, on the charge of cow stealing, one of the key witnesses against him was Catherine Penderghast,[6] who, later that same year, went on to marry a member of the Frawley family in Panbula.⁷

This Richard Frawley was John's first cousin from Ireland. He had arrived in Sydney as an assisted immigrant aboard the "Chowringhee" on November 16, 1855, at the age of 22. Travelling with his aunt, Anne Frawley (48), as well as his siblings: Patrick (27), Bridget (25), John (17), and Michael (12).⁸ This Anne Frawley was therefore likely to have been an aunt of John Frawley. According to the "Chowringhee"'s passenger records, Anne Frawley was born around 1807 in Quin, County Clare, while Richard and the rest of the family were born and baptized in Doora, just east of Ennis, County Clare, Ireland.⁹ These locations, Ennis, Doora, and Quin, are situated just 35 kilometers northwest of John and Mary Frawley's hometown of Limerick.

Tragically, the newborn son of Richard and Catherine Frawley passed away at just 17 days old on December 20, 1858, in Panbula. The child had been given the name John Frawley, after his cousin, who then was regrettably recorded as a witness at the infant's burial.¹⁰ By 1859, both John and Richard Frawley were still residing in Panbula and were listed on the Eden District Electoral Roll:

> 1859 EDEN DISTRICT - ELECTORAL ROLL
> #232 John Frawley (Panbula)
> #233 Richard Frawley (Panbula)

A year or so later, Richard Frawley followed the footsteps of his own siblings and trekked south to Leigh Creek and Bungaree in Victoria, where he tragically passed away just a few years later, at just 30 years of age.¹¹ For many years, little was known about the Victorian branch of the Frawley family. However, in 2023, a chance encounter with another Frawley family member unexpectedly revealed new connections between Richard's descendants and our Frawley ancestors of Pambula.

Somewhat surprisingly, the tables were turned on John Frawley soon afterwards when he received a taste of his own medicine, as he apparently had his own horse stolen by a local Aborigine, named Wyman:

14 - Property & Prosecutions

COURT OF PETTY SESSIONS
Moruya - 21st October 1858

Wyman an aboriginal native, appeared, charged with stealing a horse, the property of John FRAWLEY of Panbula in the police district of Eden. John McAllister chief constable of Broulee, stated that he had received a letter from Mr Walker, chief constable of Eden, directing him to apprehend Wyman and forward him to Eden. He was remanded to the Bench of Magistrates at Panbula on the above charge.

Illawarra Mercury, 1st November 1858 [12]

Court Matters III - Ponsonby v Frawley

In early 1860, John Frawley ran into more difficulty with proceedings in the Eden District Court, this time with a plasterer by the name of Mr. Ponsonby. By November, on-going proceedings from this tragic case had a devastating effect on the Frawley family, when not only their house, but all their household furniture were scheduled to be auctioned off.

John and Mary Frawley, their children, friends and neighbours would have witnessed the dreadful sight of their hard earned and valuable possessions being carried off by the Sheriff and his officers. However, by December of that year, John Frawley was back in court against Mr. Ponsonby, and this time the tables were turned with the magistrate ordering Mr Ponsonby to repay the full £148.0.7d. in addition to the costs, but by then, Ponsonby had dissappeared, so whether or not John Frawley and family actually received those monies is another matter.

Pambula National School

The origins of the Pambula School are interesting, as the Frawley children likely all enroled and attended as pupils during this period. Certainly John Jr. (9), Ellen (8), James (6) and Stephen Frawley (5) would have been eligible to attend, when the school opened its doors in November of 1849, which at that time had an enrolment of 20 boys and 17 girls.

> "Following the National Education Act of 1848, Pambula became the seventh public school in the colony and by 1999 was the fourth oldest still in operation. A temporary teacher, Mr. J. Grealy, took charge of the new school supplied with books worth £2,1-. Two and a half acres

197

in Section 4 of the township was claimed by Messrs Walker, Jones and Bell for a permanent school. Construction of the brick and shingle school commenced in November 1849. Mr. Grearly remained in charge of the school until the first permanent teacher, Henry Fowler, arrived to take over. Attendance at the school rapidly increased however, as the local industry was predominantly agricultural and pastoral, but spring and summer brought a marked decrease with children required to help with the planting and harvesting."

Angela George [13]

But there were a number of potential issues, and top of the list was that the school had been built on Pambula Flat, and was therefore vulnerable to flooding. The following description of the devastation inflicted by the flood of 1860 meant that the location of the school had to be re-assessed:

"The school building is sometimes surrounded by floods to a height of three feet. The organization is defective. The children are neither punctual nor regular. Much noise and disorder. The walls are dirty and damp. None but the ordinary subjects are taught, and of those, the smallest quantity possible. The few children present are deficient in acquirements." In 1860... "the National School at Panbula was full in the stream, the doors were burst open and a quantity of mud, sand and timber occupied the place of the teacher for several days. It is a wonder that the Board of Commissioners do not see to this matter as I fear very much that the teacher and the building will make a moonlight flit."

Angela George [14]

By 1861, in excess of 30 scholars were recorded on the school roll with an average daily attendance of just 19. The school situation eventually became so bad that something had to be done and after much agitation on the part of the community and local education authorities, the new public school was relocated to its present site on higher ground, and opened in April of 1869.[15]

The Floods of 1851 & 1860

The old village of Panbula including the first school and churches had all been erected on the flats near the Pambula River, which was planned in 1843 by surveyor Thomas Scott Townsend. But following a gale in early May of 1851, heavy rains commenced and continued almost unabated until the 15th, when drainage from the surrounding hills poured down onto the flat carrying away houses, haystacks and anything else in its path. In several cases families were inundated and compelled to take to their roofs. The settlers living on the flats at Boydtown, Eden, Pambula and Bega all experienced the devastating flood, with some 17 lives being lost.[16] In Pambula, the residents subsequently had to move the entire village to higher ground.

Another more devastating inundation struck in 1860 when John Frawley made the news after he and his son John Jr., assisted in the rescue of the Shea family during the most severe moments of that Pambula flood. This was the same William Shea with whom he had been in partnership when building the house for Mr. Hayes, so they were obviously close friends. The report of the courageous rescue was published in the form of a well composed letter to the editor by an unknown author, written on the 27th July 1860 at Pambula.[17]

Kiandra Gold Rush

In November of 1859, gold was discovered by mountain cattlemen, the Pollock brothers, and by March 1860, some 10,000 miners and storekeepers had raced to the scene. Initial returns were very good, and a 9kg nugget was discovered in river deposits under what became known as 'New Chum Hill'. Kiandra post office opened on 1 June 1860,[18] and it is estimated that the area at its peak accommodated around 15,000 people, served by 25 stores, 13 bakers, 16 butchers, 14 pubs, several banks and four blacksmiths.[19] Nevertheless, by 1861, the Sydney Morning Herald was reporting a "mass exodus" as the easy pickings had been exhausted.[20] Pambula benefitted from being one of the closest towns to the diggings.

> As travelling was slow, many public houses for nourishment and beverages sprang up in the area, many served the miners trying their luck on the extensive local goldfields around Pambula. It is estimated there were more than 20 hotels during the late 1880's in the districts from Eden to Merimbula, today only five remain. The Royal Hotel in Pambula (now known as the Royal Willows Hotel) was built in 1864 and the Commercial Hotel built in 1878 are the last two operating hotels in Pambula today.
>
> *A.T. Shakespeare* [21]

Not being involved in some way or another with the rush to the gold fields would have been hard to avoid, but whether John Frawley tried his luck is unknown. In Pambula, we know that John Frawley had cleared himself of legal difficulties levelled at him by the plasterer known as Ponsonby.

During this difficult time, John Frawley still involved himself in local issues and volunteered his time as committee chairman to publicly thank Dr Richard Bligh, for his work as the town medical practitioner, upon his departure for Sydney on 12th November 1859.

> **TO RICHARD BLIGH, ESQ, PAMBULA**
>
> Dear Sir, We, the undersigned inhabitants of the district of Twofold Bay, knowing that it is your intention to remove from hence to Paddington, in Sydney, wish to convey to you our expression of very sincere regret for the loss we shall individually and collectively sustain by your removal from amongst us after your sojourn here for five years. During your residence amongst us we have become attached to you by your asiduous and kind attention to the sick, by your urbanity of manner, and by your excellent and christian like conduct in your private life. You may rest assured that you will always be most kindly remembered by us, and that you will ever have our best wishes for your own and your family's happiness and prosperity."
>
> *We remain, dear Sir, yours very sincerely,*
> *John Frawley, Mrs Frawley, John Frawley Jr, & Ellen Frawley (amongst other residents)*
> *The Sydney Morning Herald, Saturday 12 Nov 1859* [22]

By July of 1860, John Frawley had acquired two more Crown Land allotments in the names of his son John Frawley Jr. and daughter Ellen Frawley, in the village of Wyndham:

> **CROWN LANDS SALE AT PANBULA**
>
> The following allotments of land were sold on Thursday 19th inst., and are situated in the township of Wyndham, about 25 miles from Eden. A list of lots, prices, and names of purchasers are given below:-
> Town Lots At Wyndham - Lot 53. - John Frawley Jr., 7s. & – Ellen Frawley, 4s.
>
> *Twofold Bay & Maneroo Telegraph, July 1860* [23]

He also expressed support for Mr. Daniel Egan on 7th December 1860, who was then a candidate for local member of Parliament:

> **To Daniel Egan, Esq.**
>
> Sir, - We the undersigned, electors of Panbula and its adjoining Vicinity, having taken particular notice of your late parliamentary career, it is with pleasure we saw you record your vote on the Government side of the Land Bill. We earnestly request that you allow yourself to be nominated for this electorate, and we pledge ourselves to secure your return to the utmost of our power.

> Dear Sir, we tender you our most respectful thanks for your late parliamentary career.
>
> *John Frawley, Chairman*
> *Twofold Bay & Maneroo Telegraph, 7th Dec 1860* [24]

As 1860 drew to a close, the proceedings from the Ponsonby case brought devastating consequences upon the Frawley family, with the Sheriff openly removing their property and all their belongings from their home. How the family got through this dreadful incident can only be imagined. Despite the litigation, his convict past and the mounting setbacks, it would appear that John Frawley still remained a respected member of the local community. Although he had appeared before magistrates for a number of matters, he remained supportive of the community he lived amongst, and lent his support at a public meeting to request a second doctor for the town from the relevant authorities, in 1860.[25]

Interestingly, Daniel Egan eventually won the election. Despite being an emancipist and a defendant in court proceedings on a number of occasions, John Frawley was nevertheless included on a list of all persons within the District of Eden who by nature of his land holdings was now eligible to serve as a juror on court sessions.

LIST OF ALL PERSONS WITHIN THE DISTRICT OF EDEN LIABLE TO SERVE ON SESSIONS FOR 1860
John Frawley, Settler from Panbula; Nature of qualification to serve on sessions – 'Real and personal estate'.

By the dawn of the 1860s, John Frawley had carved out a name for himself in the growing township of Pambula, becoming a man of action, flexibility, and ambition. He had fought to improve local education, championed the need for a doctor, and stood as an advocate for his fellow townsfolk, whether through letters of gratitude or direct acts of heroism in the devastating flood of 1860. His influence stretched from civic affairs to political circles, supporting Daniel Egan's election and even serving as a juror in Eden's Petty Sessions. Yet, for all his accomplishments, shadows loomed over his reputation.

Accusations of shoddy workmanship, unpaid debts, and even an allegation of cattle theft, though it was dismissed, marked a turbulent period between 1856 and 1860. Despite his efforts to establish himself as a respected builder and community leader, legal troubles and financial struggles continued to haunt him.

But if these years had been difficult, they were nothing compared to what lay ahead. John Frawley's fortunes were about to take a catastrophic turn. Stripped of the fragile respectability he had worked so hard to build, he would soon find himself once again a prisoner, bound by the chains of his past.

References

1. John Frawley Sr. - Eden Bench Books, 9th January, 1855.
2. John Frawley - Land Grants Panbula, 1856. NSW Land Titles Office. (1856). .
3. John Frawley - Index to Deeds, Town Purchases, 1856. NSW Index to Registers of land Purchases, 1811-1870.
4. Pambula - Illawarra Mercury, 1856.
5. John Frawley - Indicted for Cow Stealing (Sydney Morning Herald, 28 September 1857, p.5).
6. Eden Bench Books, Court proceedings for John Martin v John Frawley, at Eden Courthouse, Aug & Sept 1857.
7. NSW Dept. of BDM. (1858). Marriage of Richard Frawley & Catherine Pendergast, 1858 at Panbula, #1714/1858.
8. NSW State Archives & Records. (1855). Frawleys on the "Chowringhee." Assisted Immigrants Index 1839-1896 (Reel 2137, [4/4792]; Reel 2469, [4/4946]).
9. Richard Frawley - Baptised at Doora, Ennis, County Clare on 13th Feb 1832 with parents Pat Fraly & Johana [sic. Susan] Cody ("Ireland, Catholic Parish Registers, 1740-1900", database, FamilySearch).
10. NSW Dept. of BDM. (1858). Birth Certificate [#6890], and Death Certificate [#3448] for John Frawley.
11. Victorian Dept. of BDM. (1864). Richard Frawley (son of Patrick & Susan Frawley) - Death Certificate [#2808/1864].
12. John Frawley - Plaintiff re Stolen Horse (Illawarra Mercury, 1 November 1858, p.2).
13. George, Angela (1999). From Bark Hut To Brick Veneer: 150 Years of Education at Pambula Public School. Pambula Public School.
14. Panbula News Weekly, 'Signed R. B.' 29th September, 1853. (Reprinted in News Weekly).
15. Ibid.
16. Storm & Flood - Loss of Seventeen Lives (The Maitland Mercury & Hunter River General Advertiser, 31 May 1851, p.3).
17. John Frawley and son - rescuers during the 1860 Panbula Flood (Twofold Bay & Maneroo Telegraph, 27th July 1860).
18. Brown, Alan G. & Campbell, Hugh M. (1963). New South Wales Numeral Cancellations Victoria: The Royal Philatelic Society of Victoria, Australia, and London: Robson Lowe Ltd.
19. Wikipedia - 'Kiandra, NSW.' [https://en.wikipedia.org/wiki/Kiandra,_New_South_Wales]. Retrieved 15th May 2021.
20. Traveller. 'Guide to Kiandra in NSW.' [https://www.traveller.com.au/kiandra--places-to-see-6df6] Retrieved 17 December 2017.
21. Shakespeare, A.T. (1958). The Kiandra Gold Rush and its impact on surrounding districts. Canberra & District Historical Society, Canberra.
22. Richard Bligh - Farewell (The Sydney Morning Herald, Saturday 12 Nov 1859).
23. John Frawley Jr. - Twofold Bay Land Sale at Wyndham (Twofold Bay & Maneroo Telegraph, 31 July 1860).
24. John Frawley, supporting Daniel Egan (Twofold Bay & Maneroo Telegraph, 7th December 1860).
25. John Frawley at Medical Practitioner at Panbula (The Observor, 30th November 1860).

15

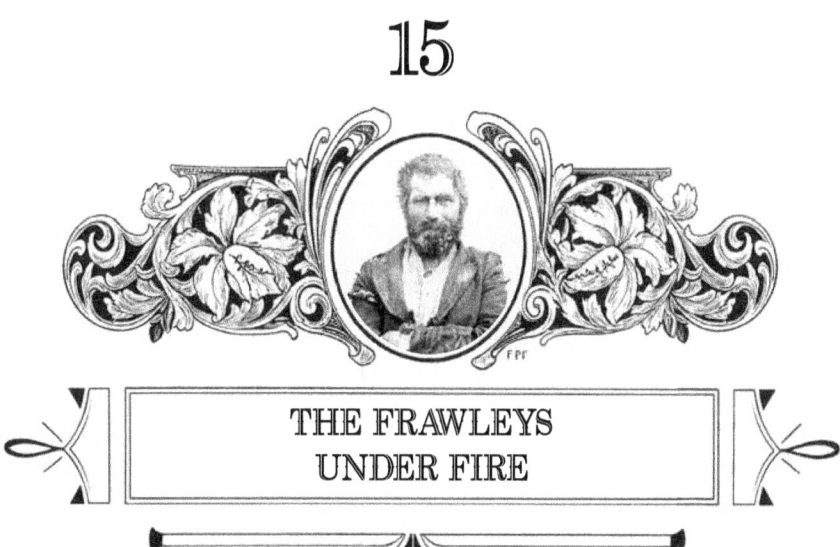

THE FRAWLEYS UNDER FIRE

After enduring the brutal 14,500 mile journey of transportation, serving seven years of hard labour as a convict, and battling the harsh realities of life in the wilderness, which included the dangers of the untamed bush, hostility from Aboriginal groups, and devastating floods, one might assume that John Frawley and his young family had overcome the worst that life could throw at them. But just as the spectre of a sustainable existence seemed within reach, temptation led him astray. What he thought was easy money would soon drag him into the depths of despair, and setting the stage for his next downfall.

Pambula Post Office

In 1861 John Frawley added his name to a list of supporters for Robert Beck, who was at that time the incoming postmaster for Pambula.

POST MASTER GENERAL, SYDNEY
Panbula, August 19th 1861

Sir, We the undersigned inhabitants of the township of Panbula, beg to express our entire confidence in Mr. Robert Beck Senior as a fit and proper person, to discharge the duties of Post Master in this place, and also that he is perfectly solvent, having no interest in the business of his son.

We are sir, your obedient servants
Signed - John Frawley (amongst another 19 residents) [1]

Desperate Times

But not all was well within the Frawley household as various members of the family came under closer scrutiny, as events were about to play out in 1862 and 1863. At a time when the Civil War was raging in the American States, members of the Frawley family were unfortunately engaged in their own battles, and began to fall like nine pins as they were at first suspected, then gradually rounded up by the local authorities.

First to come under suspicion was John Frawley Jr (21), Letitia Frawley (14) and their mother Mary Frawley (49), who were all three charged with 'intent to defraud' on the 15th October 1862. The case concerned a promissory note and bank note to the value of just one pound. The names of the people involved were Joseph Twyford, constable; Isaac Chapple, farmer; Adam Ballantyne, constable; Margery Cameron wife of Duncan Cameron, storekeeper; Llewellyn Heaven, innkeeper; and Ely Heaven.[2]

One month later, John Frawley, then aged about 46, who since receiving his 'Certificate of Freedom' in 1840, had otherwise been a responsible and respected member of the Pambula community, was charged with cattle stealing on the 17th November 1862.[3] This was followed soonafter by his son James Frawley (aged 19) being charged with stealing a horse owned by Frank Boller at 'Tantawangalo', on the 15th December 1862.[4] James went into custody at Eden, but was released on bail:

BAIL RECEIPT
25th April 1863

James Frawley in Custody on committal to take his seat at the next Court of General Quarter Sessions of the

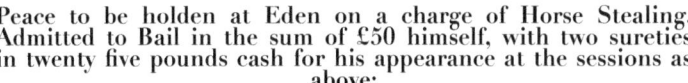

> Peace to be holden at Eden on a charge of Horse Stealing. Admitted to Bail in the sum of £50 himself, with two sureties in twenty five pounds cash for his appearance at the sessions as above:
> Stephen Collier - £25
> Daniel (Purther) - £25
>
> *P.J. Murray (P.W.)*
> *Taken and acknowledged this 25th day of April 1863.*

The trials for all five members of the Frawley family came up for hearing on the same day at the Eden Court House, on Friday 24th April 1863, which was apparently followed with great interest by all the townsfolk of Pambula. In the first case, despite the mother and daughter, Mary and Letitia Frawley being discharged, John Frawley Jr. was found guilty of 'intent to defraud' and sentenced to 12 months imprisonment with hard labour at Parramatta Gaol.[5] In the next case against James Frawley, proceedings were postponed and he remained free on bail, apparently avoiding a gaol sentence due to lack of evidence.[6]

Back In Chains

However, the father John Frawley wasn't so lucky and the proceedings in his case resulted in him being found guilty of 'stealing and branding of a cow' that was owned by James Manning of the Twofold Bay Pastoral Association, from 'Kameruka Station'. John was sentenced by Judge Dowling to five years 'hard labour on the roads or other public works of the colony.'[7] Adding insult to injury, John lost another case that very same day against a Mr. Harte in the amount of £15, incredibly because his incarceration disabled his ability to appear in court as the plaintiff... how very unfair?[8]

It must have been an extraordinary sight as both John Frawley and his son John Frawley Jr. were placed in irons and led out of the prisoner dock at Eden Court House that day. From Eden the two felons were loaded aboard a coastal steamer, from whence they were transported to Sydney and initially admitted to Darlinghurst Gaol.[9] John Sr. couldn't have helped but recall his first appearance in chains in Sydney, when he was temporarily housed in Hyde Park Barracks on Macquarie Street, some 30 years previously.

Hard Labour

In 1865, being sentenced to 'hard labour' meant being forced to perform physically demanding, repetitive, and often pointless tasks in prison, usually involving machinery like treadmills, crank machines, or breaking rocks, with the primary goal of punishment through exhaustion and discomfort, often under harsh conditions with poor sanitation and limited food. Essentially, it was a brutal form of forced labour designed to deter future criminal activity.

Common jobs included 'treadmill walking' where prisoners would continuously climb a large wheel, 'picking oakum', separating strands of old rope, or breaking stones with a hammer, all requiring constant physical exertion with little productive output. Prison regimes were typically very strict, with harsh punishments for not meeting work quotas, including solitary confinement or reduced rations. Prisons at this time were typically overcrowded and unsanitary, with inadequate ventilation and poor quality food, contributing to the overall hardship of the sentence. The monotony and lack of purpose in hard labour could have a significant psychological impact on prisoners, leading to depression and feelings of hopelessness, although this experience led John Frawley to became a 'shoemaker.'

After serving his time, John Frawley Jr. was released from Parramatta Gaol in April of 1864.[10] But in that very same month his younger brother Stephen Frawley aged 20, was charged with stealing a horse, the property of John Carpenter, although luckily, this case seems not to have been pursued.[11] On the 1st of May 1865, the Frauley [sic. Frawley] name again came up in the District Court at Pambula. Firstly as a defendent against a Mr. Wheeler for a breach of contract, and again on the same day as a defendant against Mr. Page, the storekeeper at Merimbula, for the balance of a store account. Unfortunately, both cases were lost and had to be paid, presumably with costs.

PANBULA COURT OF REQUESTS
Monday May 1st, 1865

Wheeler v Frauley for £5 breach of contract. Verdict for plaintiff.
Page v Frauley for £4,13,7 - 1/2 store account. Verdict for plaintiff.

Bega Gazette, 6th May 1865 [12]

But that wasn't the end of it as two more Frawley boys, Stephen again and Patrick were charged in September of 1866, the latter being brought up on trial and convicted of 'horse stealing' on the 31st January 1867. Patrick Frawley was sentenced by Judge Heffernan to 'five years on the roads',[13] and sent initially to Darlinghurst Gaol, but he was transferred in June 1867 to Parramatta Gaol.[14]

Patrick may have even crossed paths with his father as by that time, John Frawley had been transferred from Cockatoo Island as an 'invalid' to Parramatta Gaol on the 9th August 1866.[15] Likely due to his invalidity and good behaviour, John Frawley was released from Parramatta during the month of June 1867, having served four years and three months of his five year term.[16,17] He had been initially sent to Darlinghurst Gaol in 1863, then transferred to Parramatta Gaol, but it seems the majority of his incarceration was spent at Cockatoo Island Gaol, in Sydney Harbour, where he was described as a 'shoemaker' of 'good' character.[18]

Cockatoo Island Gaol

Before the arrival of Europeans, Cockatoo Island was used by the indigenous Australians of Sydney's coastal region, but laid largely undisturbed until 1839 when Governer Gipps chose it for the site of a new penal establishment to alleviate overcrowding on Norfolk Island. Convicts were put to work initially quarrying stone for various projects around the colony. They also built stone prison barracks, a military guardhouse, granary silos, official residences and commenced work in 1847 on the Fitzroy Dock, which took ten years to complete. By 1842, the rock-cut silos on the island stored approximately 140 tonnes of grain for the colony's grain supply, all now part of the island's heritage.

Escape from Cockatoo Island was rare, not least because few prisoners could swim. Supposedly shark-infested waters around the island also tested the resolve of those bent on escape. The prisoner's accommodation was appalling. Living conditions on Cockatoo Island were barely satisfactory, even by the standards of the day. The convict-built barracks were soon overcrowded. Congestion and its attendant ills became a perennial feature of the prison and a constant spur to critics. At times, 500 convicts were crammed at night into the inadequate barracks. A police inspector once described convicts squeezed up against the bars of the prison in an attempt to breathe. With "double tiers of double sleeping berths," prisoners were crammed in "coffin-like apertures" and locked up for 12 hours at night with the stench of the "night tubs" (buckets for excrement).

The convicts themselves provided all the services required to run the penal establishment's infrastructure. In addition to labouring, quarrying and conducting various trades such as bricklaying and carpentry, convicts were gatemen, overseers, messengers, servants, gardeners, hospital attendants, cooks and constables.

In 1869 the prison was closed and the prisoners transferred to Darlinghurst Gaol, which marked the close of the island's convict period. However, the complex was soon put to another use as an industrial school for girls and reformatory. In 1888, the girls moved to Parramatta and the old penal settlement reverted to a gaol for a time to ease the crowded conditions at Darlinghurst Gaol. When the prison finally closed in 1908, it marked the end of an era.

At the end of his term, John Frawley boarded a coastal steamer for the trip down the coast back to Eden, before travelling overland to be reunified with his family at Pambula. But the law wasn't finished with the Frawley's just yet as John Frawley Jr. and his brother-in-law Robert Little, were fined £10 each for 'illegally riding horses'. Despite being a minor crime, neither of them could afford the fine, and had no option other than to accept imprisonment with hard labour, for three months at Darlinghurst Gaol.[19]

Incredibly, the only members of the entire Frawley family, not to have been charged with an offense (that we know of), was the eldest daughter Ellen, who by the mid 1860s had gravitated to Sydney and the youngest brother Thomas.

Rejoining the Pambula Community

Despite his ordeal, but having rejoined his neighbourhood, John Frawley's community-minded spirit came to the fore once again in late 1867 as he signed his name to a petition requesting that the local Post Office be moved into the main township of Pambula.

> TO THE HONORABLE
> THE POST MASTER GENERAL, SYDNEY
> Received 23rd December 1867
>
> Sir, we the undersigned residents in and about Panbula, beg to bring under your notice, the great inconvenience arising from the Post office not being in Panbula, it being at present one mile distant from the Township and across a creek which some months in the year is unfordable, and the bulk of the inhabitants numbering about two hundred, also the Court House, Police Offices, Churches etc. are in the Township, there only being a few straggling houses, numbering between forty and fifty inhabitants near the present P.O.
>
> We also beg to bring under your notice that the former Post Master, Mr. Robert Beck, lived in the Township and on his leaving Panbula, there was no other eligible person living in Panbula at the time to keep it. Since then there are additions to our population, one of whom is a Mr. George King, a storekeeper, who we would beg to recommend to your favourable considerations, as a fit and proper person to keep the Post Office in Panbula. We also beg to say that the above arrangements will not interfere with the duties of the Mail Carrier. Trustful this our humble petition will meet with your approval and we beg to ascribe ourselves.
>
> Yours Gladly
> John Frawley (Settler), Panbula (amongst 44 other petitioners) [20]

A follow up letter was written by the Panbula residents on the 27th February 1868 again urging the Post Master General in Sydney to re-locate the Pambula Post Office to the main township as a matter of urgency. They also recommended Mr. Charles H. Baddeley Esq. J.P., as being available to take charge. A further 43 residents signed their names to this second petition with John Frawley amongst them.

Next, John Frawley was twice imprisoned locally in 1869, probably in Pambula or Eden, first for an assault against John Egan, and secondly for "brutally hammering" his wife, although his prison stays this time around, were just a day or two.

John Frawley most likely returned to work as a labourer, but by 1869 was back in court as a witness in a perjury trial, an outcome of which may have given him an idea for the future.[21] John Frawley also contributed funds to the 'Irish State Prisoners' (Fenians) upon their release in July 1869,²² and in searching for work wherever he could get it, he applied for a 'Timber License', which was approved in early January of 1870.²³

In Trouble Again

With monotonous consistency, John Frawley once again fell into trouble with the authorities when he was this time, charged with forgery. The case was in relation to the collection of a petition at Pambula, involving Father P. Slattery, the Catholic priest at that time. If proven, a conviction would confirm John Frawley's guilt in signing the parish priests name, and the names of others to a petition nominating himself for postmaster!

He was remanded by the magistrate, but permitted to post bail in the substantial amount of £300 by himself, or with two sureties of £150 each, and was committed for trial at the next Quarter Sessions to be held at Bega. The correspondence is set out below:

> Informing that petition forwarded to him for report is a forgery naming Jn. Frawley Sr. for Postmaster
>
> *Stamped Feb 3rd 1870, P.O. at Panbula*
>
> Sir, I beg to acknowledge receipt of a petition signed by residents of Panbula – also a letter signed 'P.Slattery'. I suspected the whole to be a forgery and handed the papers over to the Police, which resulted in Frawley being committed to take his trial for forgery.
>
> *I remain your most obt. serv.*
> *J.H. Bennett, P.M., Panbula*
>
> POST OFFICE RECEIPT
> To the Postmaster at Panbula
>
> The Registered Paper No. 521 relative to having the P.O. at Panbula & naming J. Frawley for P.M. sent to you on the 14th January last has not been returned to this office – I request you will send it back without delay.
>
> *S.H. Lambton, Secretary, General Post Office* ²⁴
>
> Police Panbula 11th August, 1870
>
> Memo, The document referred to is in hands of Crown Law Officers for purpose of Prosecuters.
>
> *David McKee, The Postmaster Yowaka – Panbula* ²⁵

This issue might seem petty to most, but in fact the charge was a blatant case of forgery (although non-fiscal), in which John Frawley was most fortunate to be found not guilty by the jury and discharged at the Bega Quarter Sessions on the 8th March 1870.[26] In June 1870, John Frawley was back in court, this time as a 'key witness' at the Supreme Court in Sydney over an action for 'slander' between Charles H. Baddeley and John H. Bennett, both residents of Pambula and magistrates of the Monaro District.[27]

By the late-1860's the Frawley children were mostly young adults and the two daughters Ellen and Letitia had by this time, moved to Sydney, where on the 3rd of August 1869, aged 27, Ellen married James Mahony O'Sullivan at St. Mary's Cathedral in Sydney, according to the rights of the Roman Catholic Church.[28] No wedding can be found for Letitia, but she produced two children in quick succession named Patrick who died, and Charlotte E. Frawley,[29,30] although no further information can be found for the latter.

In October 1871 four letters for John Frawley of Pambula, were returned from the country to the Sydney GPO.[31] Then in 1872, John Frawley sold his vacant land on the corner of Toalla and Quondola Streets in Pambula to a Mr. John Behl, who had previously accused Frawley of forgery, and who soon built a two storey building on the site, which became known as the iconic 'Toad Hall'. This building is now a craft shop and residence. The land can be found at the roundabout, opposite the Commercial Hotel, which was also owned by John Behl.

> "John Frawley (settler) and called "the elder" was granted land on September 10th 1856 and later sold it to John Behl (innkeeper) in 1872 for ten pounds."
>
> *Bernie Cornell*

By August 1872 and into 1873, a John Frawley was reported as healing occular defects in Tumut. The town was 313km away from Pambula, which likely seems implausible without other verification to substantiate if this was the same John Frawley.[32] Two years later, both John Frawley now aged 60, and John Frawley Jr. aged 34, were listed on the rolls of the Eden Electoral District for 1875. John Frawley Jr. was also listed in the Post Office Directory as residing at 'Three-Mile

Water Hole' near Wolumla from 1875 to 1877.³³

1875 EDEN DISTRICT ELECTORAL ROLL
Eden - #274, John Frawley (Panbula/Res.)
Bega - #283, John Frawley (Wolumla/Res.)

Despite their frequent run-ins with the law, the Frawley family have nevertheless been recognised as amongst the earliest of pioneers not only of Pambula, but also of Bega.³⁴

John Frawley's second incarceration, this time for rebranding and cattle stealing, saw him endure harsh sentences in Darlinghurst, Cockatoo Island, and Parramatta Gaols. Meanwhile, his family's petty crimes, like obtaining money under false pretenses, only reinforced their reputation as troublemakers. When John and his sons eventually returned to Pambula, they tried to rebuild their lives, but the community was unwilling to forget. The Frawleys were ostracised, their presence a lingering reminder of a past that respectable settlers wanted to leave behind.

Like all emancipists, the Frawleys struggled to overcome the convict stain, a burden made heavier by their Irish heritage in a colony still dominated by the English. Though religious freedom was technically upheld, Catholics remained objects of suspicion and scorn, and the Frawleys' long history of legal troubles only cemented their low standing. In Pambula, they were fighting a losing battle.

The need for a fresh start was undeniable, and all it took was a small push. That nudge came from their son, James Frawley. After more than three decades of hard work, amongst neighbours who never fully accepted them, the family saw an opportunity. With little more than determination, they sold up what meagre possessions they had and set their sights on a new home, a place where their past could not follow.

References

1. John Frawley, on the petition list for a postmaster at Panbula (Twofold Bay & Maneroo Telegraph, 19th August 1861).
2. NSW Criminal Court Records. (1862). Letitia, Mary & John Frawley Jr., in Register of Criminal Cases Tried at Eden, NSW 1862-1869.
3. Ibid.
4. NSW Criminal Court Records. (1862). James Frawley in Register of Criminal Cases Tried at Eden, NSW 1862-1869.
5. NSW Criminal Court Records. (1862). Letitia, Mary & John Frawley Jr, op.cit.
6. NSW Criminal Court Records. (1862). James Frawley, op. cit.
7. John Frawley Sr. - convicted of cattle stealing and sent to prison for five years 'hard labour' (SMH, 29th Apr 1863, p.5).
8. John Frawley Sr. - plaintiff v Harte at Eden Court (Sydney Morning Herald, 29th April 1863, p.5).
9. NSW State Archives & Records. (1863). John Frawley Sr. & John Frawley Jr. in the Darlinghurst Gaol Entrance Book, 27th April 1863.
10. John Frawley Jr. - released from Parramatta Gaol (NSW Police Gazette, April 1864).
11. Stephen Frawley - charged with Horse Stealing (NSW Police Gazette, April 1864).
12. Frauley [sic.] in Pambula Court of Requests (Bega Gazette, 6th May 1865).
13. NSW State Archives & Records. (1867). Patrick Frawley, in Return of Prisoners Tried At Eden (Different Circuit Courts & Quarter Sessions, January 1867).
14. NSW State Archives & Records. (1867). Patrick Frawley, in Admission Book, Parramatta Gaol, NSW Gaol Description & Entrance Books, Parramatta, 1863-1873.
15. NSW State Archives & Records. (1866). John Frawley Sr., in Return of Prisoners, Cockatoo Island Prison, 9th August 1866.
16. John Frawley, Released from H.M. Goal Parramatta, NSW Police Gazette & Weekly Record of Crime, 12 June 1867, p.191.
17. Ibid.
18. NSW State Archives & Records. (1866). John Frawley Sr.,op. cit.
19. John Frawley Jr & Robert Little (brother-in-law), Imprisoned for Three Months in Darlinghurst Gaol, NSW Police Gazette & Weekly Record of Crime, 9 Oct 1867, p.297.
20. John Frawley Sr., in Post Office petition (Twofold Bay & Maneroo Telegraph, 23rd December 1867).
21. John Frawley - witness in Perjury Trial (Sydney Mail, 6th March 1869, p.14).
22. John Frawley - donations to the Irish Prisoner Relief Fund (Freeman's Journal, 7th Aug 1869, p.10).
23. John Frawley,- Timber License (NSW Govt Gazette, 11 Jan 1870, p.29).
24. Lambton, S.H., Secretary, General Post Office, Sydney, 29th July,1870.
25. McKee, David. (1870). [Regisse] & 'Frawley Forgery,' The Post Master Yowaka, Panbula, 11th August 1870.
26. John Frawley - charged with 'Forging & Uttering' (NSW Returns of Criminal Cases Heard at Bega Quarter Sessions, 1870).
27. John Frawley Sr. - witness in a Slander Trial at the Supreme Court of NSW (Sydney Morning Herald, 1 June 1870, p.2).
28. NSW Dept. of BDM. (1869). Marriage Certificate for Ellen Frawley & James Mahony O'Sullivan, 3rd August 1869 at Sydney, #757/1869.
29. NSW Dept. of BDM.(1869). Death Certificate for Patrick Frawley, #5776/1868.
30. NSW Dept. of BDM.(1869). Birth Certificate for Charlotte E. Frawley, #2676/1869.
31. John Frawley - Pambula - 'List of Letters Returned From The Country, and Now Lying At The GPO, Sydney (NSW Govt Gazette, 3rd October 1871).
32. John Frawley - providing occular treatments (The Gundagai & Tumut, Adelong & Murrumbidgee District Advertiser, 3rd August 1872, p.2).
33. John Frawley Jr,. - resident at Three Mile Water Hole, nr. Wolumla, Post Office Directory, 1875-77.
34. John Frawley - the Foundation of Bega (The Bega Standard & Candelo, Merimbula, Pambula, Eden, Wolumla and General Advertiser, 11 Nov 1876, p.2).

16

FINAL DAYS IN QUEENSLAND

A new beginning was not just a desire, it was a necessity. All the Frawleys needed was a spark to set their plans in motion, and that spark came from their son, James Frawley. After more than thirty years of toil in a place where they were always outsiders, the family finally saw a way forward. With little more than sheer grit, they gathered what they could, left the rest behind, and set out in search of a place where their history wouldn't cast a shadow over their future.

It was around the year 1876 that the entire Frawley family moved themselves and their possessions from Pambula to Toowoomba in Queensland, a rapidly advancing new community 150km inland from Brisbane. In the years ahead they would move around southeast Queensland, chasing opportunities wherever they could find them. But their journey would be anything but easy, hardship seemed to follow them, testing their resilience at every turn.

The History of Toowoomba

Toowoomba's history can be traced back to 1816 when English botanist and explorer Allan Cunningham, arrived in Australia from Brazil where he had been collecting botanical specimens for Sir Joseph Banks. In June 1827, Cunningham was rewarded for his many explorations when he discovered four million acres (16,000 km²) of rich farming and grazing land bordered on the east by the Great Dividing Range and situated 100 miles (160 km) west of the settlement of Moreton Bay, which later became Brisbane. Cunningham named his find the 'Darling Downs' after Ralph Darling (later Sir Ralph), who was then governor of New South Wales.[1]

However, it was not until 13 years later when George and Patrick Leslie established 'Toolburra Station' some 56 miles (90km) south-west of Toowoomba that the first settlers began arriving on the Downs. Other settlers quickly followed and a few tradesmen and businessmen also settled and established a township of bark-slab shops called 'The Springs', which was soon renamed Drayton.

Towards the end of the 1840s Drayton had grown to the point where it had its own newspaper shop, general store, trading post and the Royal Bull's Head Inn, which was built by William Horton (<1817-1864) and still stands today. Although he was not the first man to live there, Horton is regarded as the real founder of Toowoomba. Early in 1849 Horton sent two of his men, William Gurney and William Shuttlewood, to cut away reeds in a marshy swampland area a few miles away that nobody from Drayton ever visited. When Gurney and Shuttlewood arrived they were surprised to find a pitched tent among the reeds. The tent's owner was bush worker Josiah Dent who was the first man to live in 'The Swamp'. This extraordinary news was the main talking point in Drayton for weeks and people became interested in developing the swamp as useful farming land.[2,3]

Plans were drawn up for 12 to 20 acre (49,000 to 81,000m²) farms, which in the hope of building up the town and attracting more people to the area, which was later drained to become the foundation for the establishment of Toowoomba. Two years later people began purchasing the land and the new farm holdings attracted buyers from Drayton. The year 1851 saw the establishment of a National School at Drayton, which later became Drayton State School. On the 29th August 1852 the town's only churchman, the Rev. Benjamin Glennie who had lived in Drayton since 1848, christened two children at 'Alford'. It was the first Church of England service held in Toowoomba and the first day the word 'Toowoomba' was written on a public document. How the name Toowoomba was derived is still a point of debate with several theories, including:[4]

- that it was derived from the Aboriginal word for swamp which is 'tawampa' as the Aborigines had no "s" in their vocabulary.
- that the aboriginal interpretation for reeds in the swamp 'woomba woomba' was used as the original source.
- that the word Toowoomba was taken from the aboriginal term for a native melon 'toowom or choowoom' which grew plentifully in the township.

Drovers and wagon masters gradually spread the news of the new settlement at Toowoomba and by 1858 the town was growing rapidly with three hotels, a number of stores, and a population of 700. Land selling at £4 an acre (£988/km²) in 1850, was now £150 an acre (£37,000/km²).

On the 30th June 1860 a petition of 100 names was sent to the governor requesting that Toowoomba be declared a municipality. Governor Sir George Ferguson Bowen (1821-1899) granted their wish and a new municipality was proclaimed on the 24th November 1860. The first town council election took place on the 4th January 1861 and William Henry Groom (1833-1901), who had led the townspeople in their petition for recognition, polled the most votes. On the 12th August 1862, Alderman Groom was elected to State Parliament as the member for Drayton and Toowoomba. Telegraphic communication was also opened between Toowoomba and Brisbane in August 1862, and Toowoomba Gaol had opened by 1864, which later became a woman's reformatory and laundry (1883-4), before closing in 1900. The first State School in the town was Toowoomba South State School, which opened in 1865. By April of 1867 a railway line had been built and Toowoomba's rail link with Ipswich and Brisbane was opened.

In 1870 Alderman Spiro replaced William Henry Groom as Mayor. By 1873 Council was granted control of the swamp area and offered a prize of £100 for the best method of draining it. The Toowoomba Gas and Coke Company was floated in 1875 and the Council pledged to erect street lamps to assist with the establishment of the fledgling company. Due to its financial situation Council leased part of the swamp to town brickmakers and also approved construction of the Toowoomba Grammar School, with the school's foundation stone also being laid that year.[5]

First founded as a village in 1849, Toowoomba officially became a town in 1858, a municipality in 1860, and was declared a city in 1904. Situated in southeastern Queensland, on the Great Dividing Range, the town quickly became the principal inland city in the state. Its role as a rail and road junction, a tourist resort, a service centre for the large livestock, grain and dairying businesses in the Darling Downs, and a site of the Perseverence Creek Water Supply Scheme, ensured its future. The city was well planned with many parks and has become an educational centre. The city's industries today include engineering works, railroad shops, and food processing. On the 10th January 2011, severe flash flooding caused by heavy rains engulfed Toowoomba, devastating the city and leaving dozens dead or missing.[6]

The Frawleys Move To Toowoomba

Following his being charged and imprisoned for horse stealing in 1863, John and Mary Ann's son James Frawley, must have thought it best to remove himself from Pambula and district. He likely investigated several potential options, but by 1863 he found himself in the developing township of Toowoomba on the Darling Downs in Queensland, where he was successful in winning a tender for the 'construction of a foot bridge' in November 1863.[7] By 1873 James had gained a firm foothold in the growing district and going from strength to strength, he had secured 120 acres of Crown Land at Meringandan.⁸

Besides riding on the good fortune of their son James Frawley, who was gaining an influential footing in the Darling Downs, the Frawley family's relocation to Toowoomba likely came about from a combination of factors. John Frawley's legal problems had weighed heavily upon him, possible ostracising of the family by Pambula residents, and rumour mongering within a small rural community would all have contributed to their decision to move on.

Whatever their reasons, by 1876 John and Mary Ann Frawley accompanied by their son John Jr, his wife Sarah and their children, had sold up most of their Pambula and Wolumla holdings and moved to Toowoomba in Queensland to join up with their son and brother James Frawley.

The quickest route to Toowoomba at that time was by coastal steamship through Sydney and Brisbane, which was best undertaken initially from either Eden or Tathra to Sydney, where regular shipping services had commenced from the latter in 1862. The Tathra Wharf, built on turpentine supports and set into solid rock, was recently restored by the National Trust, and local residents, and is the only remaining coastal steamer wharf in New South Wales.⁹

After arriving in Sydney, the Frawley's would not have stayed long before re-embarking on another coastal steamer for Brisbane. Once on the dock in Brisbane, their best option for travelling to Toowoomba was by the relatively new rail line. Toowoomba Railway Station with just one platform and a passing loop had opened in 1867, but in due course it became the junction for the Western, Main and Southern Queensland lines.¹⁰

The Frawleys first house was in Herries Street, the main street of Toowoomba. But sadly, much hope and confidence for their relocation sunk when John Frawley Jr. died from an infection of the lungs on the 9th October 1878, aged just 37 years.¹¹

This devastating and unexpected event placed the entire Frawley family at risk. John and Mary Frawley were both over 60 with limited work capacity. John Frawley Jr. had died with four children under the age of 12, and from all accounts, his wife Sarah wasn't able to cope with either rearing the children or bringing forth an income. In short, John Jr.'s untimely death dealt a catastrophic blow, from which the family found it hard to recover. However, their other son James Frawley seemed to be making a success of himself through land acquisition, and perhaps by becoming a publican with an interest in horse racing.

Examing the electoral rolls for that period reveals that John Frawley resided in the township of Highfields from 1878 to 1884, while his sons James, Patrick and Thomas resided at nearby Meringandan.[12] By this time, their daughter Ellen O'Sullivan had produced a family of her own, adding three sons and two daughters to John and Mary Frawley's growing pride of grandchildren.[13] Ellen and her husband James Mahony O'Sullivan were residing at Dalmorton until 1883, when they moved to Moonee Creek, just north of Coffs Harbour.

The Committment of Mary

John and Mary Frawley would certainly have supported their widowed daughter-in-law Sarah, and their four grandchildren, but as the children grew, the lack of a disciplined father began to affect their upbringing. However, events came to a head in 1880 when the matriarch, Mary Ann Frawley had to be committed to the Benevolent Asylum at Dunwich,[14] after which their daughter-in-law Sarah, became totally unable to cope, and the children had no one to keep them in check. Young Agnes Maude Frawley was the worst affected when at just 14 years old, she turned to associating with larrikins and prostitutes. Following in her grandmothers footsteps, Agnes fell foul of the law, was charged and sent to the Toowoomba Industrial and Reformatory School for Girls in 1887, for seven long years.[15]

The Benevolent Asylum, Dunwich

The Dunwich Asylum opened on 13 May 1865 with the initial transfer of patients from the Benevolent Ward of the Brisbane General

Hospital.[16] The Dunwich Asylum on North Stradbroke Island admitted 21,000 people over its 80 years of operation.[17] From the 1890s to 1946 there were around 1,000 inmates present at any one time with 1,600 in its peak year of 1903. The Asylum had over twenty wards including a distinct women's section and a separate ward for 'Asiatics'. By the 1930s, it included a police station and lock up, visitor centre, public hall, bakery, kitchen, laundry and ancillary service buildings, ward buildings, tent accommodation and recreational facilities. It was only electrified in 1926 with its own power station using oil generators. It also had its own dairy herd and piggery.

Inmates were predominately old, though not exclusively. People could be assigned to the asylum by a hospital, by police order or by their families. It seems that many inebriate men were confined by their spouses. Inmates came from across Queensland with a very detailed process of getting them by boat and/or rail from the north and the west to the Yungaba Immigration Depot at Kangaroo Point, and then by boat to Dunwich.

Six times as many men as women were inmates. The backgrounds were mainly rural and urban workers with, in the nineteenth century, a considerable number of people who had been transported to the Australian colonies as convicts. There was however, a sprinkling of middle class people fallen on hard times or drink. One was John Filhelly, Deputy Leader of the ALP under Theodore and one of the founders of the Queensland Rugby League, who is listed in the Australian Dictionary of Biography. Another was Johnny Cassim, who was of Indian origin and transported as a convict from Mauritius to become a hotelier and respected citizen of Cleveland.

The Asylum was always inadequately staffed and funded. In current (2013) values Queensland Government funding was $1,900 per person/per year in 1900 and $2,900 in 1932. In the twentieth century, inmates who received a Commonwealth old age pension paid part of this to the Asylum. The operating principle was that able-bodied inmates were meant to perform work and staff the Asylum. Unfortunately, apart from some of the inebriates, age prevented most inmates from doing a full day's labour. In addition, many complained as the Brisbane Courier of 1874 reported 'These old gentlemen at Dunwich do not as a rule approve of being asked to work. They meet every request to do with the categorical retort... "Why should I work ! If so be I could work, why be I sent here?"

From the 1880s to the 1920s there were rarely more than 20 official staff to 900 or 1,000 inmates. The Asylum needed cheap and permanent labour, which they found from the 'Quandamooka' Aboriginal people of the island who lived at One Mile outside Dunwich, and who did what Goodall says was "heavy and unpleasant work" from the 1870s. By the 1920s up to 30 aboriginal men were in the 'outside gang', which included the dairy and piggery. Some aboriginal men were in trade, skilled and semi-skilled jobs including carpentry and operating the power station. Around 15 aboriginal women were employed as cooks, nursing assistants and domestics including in the houses of the senior staff of the Asylum. The aboriginal workers formed a substantial part of the total work force for the Asylum, at times over half, right up to its closure in 1946. Aboriginal workers were originally paid in rations, but from the 1920s onwards took action to be paid wages.

Those who supported the creation of the first early 19th century public and private hospitals recognized that one important mission would be the care and treatment of those with severe symptoms of mental illnesses. Like most physically sick men and women, such individuals remained with their families and received treatment in their homes. Their communities showed significant tolerance for what they saw as strange thoughts and behaviors. But some such individuals seemed too violent or disruptive to remain at home or in their communities.

But the opening decades of the 19th century brought to Australia new European ideas about the care and treatment of the mentally ill. These ideas, soon to be called "moral treatment," promised a cure for mental illnesses to those who sought treatment in a very new kind of institution, an "asylum." The moral treatment of the insane was built on the assumption that those suffering from mental illness could find their way to recovery and an eventual cure if treated kindly and in ways that appealed to the parts of their minds that remained rational. It repudiated the use of harsh restraints and long periods of isolation that had been used to manage the most destructive behaviors of mentally ill individuals. It depended instead on specially constructed hospitals that provided quiet, secluded, and peaceful country settings; opportunities for meaningful work and recreation; a system of privileges and rewards for rational behaviors; and gentler kinds of restraints used for shorter periods.

By the 1890s, however, these institutions were all under siege. Economic considerations played a substantial role with local governments avoiding the costs of caring for the elderly residents in almshouses or public hospitals by redefining what was then termed "senility" as a psychiatric problem and sending these men and women to state-supported anylums. Unsurprisingly, the numbers of patients in the asylums grew exponentially, well beyond the capacity and willingness of government.

Deaths of John & Mary Ann Frawley

Throughout this period, Mary Ann was doggedly hanging onto life at the Dunwich Benevolent Asylum, which was established under the Benevolent Asylum Wards Act of 1861 to provide accommodation and care to poor people unable to care for themselves due to illness or infirmity.

As an inmate at Dunwich, the matriarch of the family Mary Ann Frawley, experienced oppressive institutional conditions, which in most circumstances would normally have hastened her end, but she somehow doggedly clung to life for a further nine years, before succumbing to the inevitability of senile decay on the 7th November 1889.[18]

But Mary Ann Frawley's death inevitably occurred at the age of 79, at the Benevolent Asylum on the 7th November 1889, and we hope that some of the Frawley family were in attendance at the burial of their dear mother.[19] Those who died in the asylum were generally buried in the Dunwich Cemetery, unless families made other arrangements. In the 80 years spanning 1867-1947, 8,426 former inmates of the Dunwich Benevolent Asylum were buried in the Dunwich Cemetery.

Interestingly, her death certificate stated that she had lost four boys and two girls. John Jr most certainly died in 1878, and its possible that Patrick, who changed his name to Marr, might also have been thought to be deceased, but when and where the other two deceased males and two deceased females came and went is unclear. John Frawley was arrested and charged again in 1892, but was apparently exonnerated... offense unknown.[20]

John Frawley's Second Marriage

Without his wife, John Frawley moved to Maryland Station near Tenterfield,[21] where he may have been present at the 'Tenterfield Oration' a speech in favour of federation, delivered by Sir Henry Parkes (1815-1896), Premier of New South Wales, at the Tenterfield School of Arts in Tenterfield, New South Wales, on 24 October 1889.[22]

For reasons that are unclear, John Frawley then moved south from Toowoomba to Stanthorpe and the area called Maryland in NSW, by the 1890s. John outlived his dear and long suffering wife by a further 12 years, and by the time of his own death at 84 years of age, he was still working as a miner.[23] He even found the energy to take on a new partner, some 30 years younger and remarried on the 27th February 1894 to a widow by the name of Rose Emily Curtis (1845-1923), the daughter of Samuel Colstone and Eliza Goodeve.[24] By that time, all of John's grandchildren had come of age and so he moved away to a small and quieter community called Maryland, close to Stanthorpe in southeast Queensland, which was on the New South Wales border. These were the days before pensions and so despite his advanced age, in order to survive and support his new wife, John Frawley continued to work wherever he could, so the intrepid old soul turned to 'tin mining'.

John Frawley was even elected 'Trustee of the Common' at

Maryland,[25] and while he survived into the 20th century, his inevitable death came at the age of 84, on the 25th of January 1901, a labourer until the very end. He was buried in an unmarked grave at the bush cemetery at Maryland.[26] His second wife, Rose Emily Frawley (nee Curtis), being much younger, survived until the 15th December 1923, and was buried at Toowong Cemetery in Brisbane aged 78, without any additions to John Frawley's issue.

The lives of John and Mary Frawley were defined by adversity, resilience, and an unyielding determination to carve out a better life, which speaks to the strength of the human spirit. Despite their turbulent pasts, their journey from convicted criminals to respected pioneers of the Australian frontier exemplifies the capacity to rebuild and thrive in the face of overwhelming odds. In the end, their story was continued through the lives of their descendants, those who would carry the weight of their legacy forward.

In the final chapter of this book, we turn our attention to the next generation: the children of John and Mary Ann Frawley. What became of them? How did the struggles and triumphs of their parents shape their own lives, and what imprint did they leave on the communities they helped build? Join us as we explore the lives of the Frawley descendants, revealing the remarkable continuities and changes in the family's journey, and the legacy of two pioneering souls who, against all odds, helped shape the history of a young nation.

References

1. T. M. Perry, 'Cunningham, Allan (1791–1839)', Australian Dictionary of Biography, National Centre of Biography, Australian National University, [https://adb.anu.edu.au/biography/cunningham-allan-1941/text2323], published first in hardcopy 1966, accessed online 1 February 2023.
2. Hall, Thomas, 1845-1928. (1920). The early history of Warwick district and pioneers of the Darling Downs / Thomas Hall. [Toowoomba? : s.n [http://nla.gov.au/nla]. obj-37325731.
3. Hall, Thomas, 1845-1928. (1920). The early history of Warwick district and pioneers of the Darling Downs / Thomas Hall. [Toowoomba? : s.n [http://nla.gov.au/nla]. obj-37325731.
4. Wikipedia - "Toowoomba" [https://en.wikipedia.org/wiki/Toowoomba.
5. Kids Kiddle - Toowoomba [https://kids.kiddle.co/History_of_Toowoomba,_Queensland].
6. Brittanica - Toowoomba [https://www.britanica.com/place/Toowoomba].
7. James Frawley - Payment for Construction of Foot-Bridge (The Toowoomba Chronicle & Queensland Advertiser, 12 Nov 1863, p.2.
8. James Frawley - Land Selections at Darling Downs North (The Brisbane Courier, 14 March 1873, p.3).
9. James Frawley - Land Selections at Darling Downs North (The Brisbane Courier, 14 March 1873, p.3).
10. Wikipedia - 'Tathra Wharf.' [https://en.wikipedia.org/wiki/Tathra_Wharf]. Retrieved 13th June 2021.
11. Queensland Dept of BDM. (1878). Death Certificate for John Frawley Jr., 9th October 1878 at Herries St, Toowoomba, #878/C/896.
12. John Frawley - Carrier at Meringandan (Queensland PO Directory, 1894, p.483).
13. NSW Dept of BDM. (1909). Death Certificate for Ellen O'Sullivan, 4th August 1909 at Newcastle, #10250/1909.
14. Queensland State Archives. (1880). 'Mary Frawley, Admission Paper to the Benevolent Asylum, Dunwich', 21st October 1880.
15. Agnes Frawley - Neglected (The Telegraph [Brisbane], 10 May 1887, p.5).
16. Wikipedia. 'Benevolent Asylum, Dunwich,' op. cit.
17. Wikipedia. 'Benevolent Asylum, Dunwich.' [https://en.wikipedia.org/wiki/Dunwich_Benevolent_Asylum]. Retrieved 13th June 2021.
18. Queensland Dept of BDM. (1889). Death Certificate for Mary Frawley (nee McGarry) at Dunwich Benevolent Asylum, 1889/3633-1695.
19. Queensland Dept of BDM. (1889). Death Certificate for Mary Frawley (nee McGarry), op. cit.
20. Queensland Govt. (1892). John Frawley - Arrested Toowoomba, 12 July 1892 (in Index to Prisoners Tried, Toowoomba, 1864-1903, #3/104859/PRI4/1).
21. NSW State Archives & Records. (1891). John Frawley of Maryland, Tenderfield, in 1891 Census, New South Wales." Mitchell Library, Sydney.
22. Henry Parkes Tenterfield Oration 1889". Friends of Sir Henry Parkes School of Arts. Archived from the original on 17 May 2014. Retrieved 23 October 2018.
23. NSW Dept of BDM. (1901). Death Certificate for John Frawley, 25 January 1901 at Maryland, NSW, #03256/1901.
24. Queensland Dept of BDM. (1894). Marriage Certificate for John Frawley & Rose Emily Curtis, 27th February 1894, #1894/C/1672.
25. NSW Dept of Mines & Agriculture. (1895). John Frawley, Trustee of Maryland Common.
26. NSW Dept of BDM. (1901). Death Certificate for John Frawley, op. cit.

17

DESCENDANTS OF JOHN & MARY ANN FRAWLEY

As we reach the final chapter, our journey turns to the next generation, the children of John and Mary Ann Frawley. What paths did they carve for themselves? How did the trials and triumphs of their parents shape their futures? And what mark did they leave on the communities they helped to build? In these pages, we uncover the stories of the Frawley descendants, tracing the threads of resilience, ambition, and change that wove their family's legacy into the fabric of a young nation. What is known of John and Mary Ann Frawley's children is as follows:

1. John Frawley Jr. (1841-1878)

Their first born, John Frawley Jr. arrived on the 7th May 1841 at Alexander Berry's Coolangatta homestead, and was baptised by the Rev. John Rigney at Wollongong on the 19th May 1841, with Martin

Grealis and Bridget Leary as the sponsors.[1] But it appears he may have also been baptised a second time on the 18th March 1844 at 'Warragaburra Station' on the far South Coast of New South Wales, this time by the Rev. Michael Kavanagh with Fenton Brien and Bridget McNamara as the sponsors.[2]

After likely attending the school at Pambula from its opening in 1850,[3] John Frawley Jr. later began a relationship with Sarah Maud Little (1850-1911) although, no record can be found of their marriage in the New South Wales Births, Deaths & Marriages Index. Regardless, they soonafter began a family with the birth of their son William Frawley on the 23rd May 1865, who was registered as being born in Wolumla, but was unnamed in the official records.[4] Next was Anna Gilmour Frawley who was born at Wolumla on the 12th July 1867, but was also unnamed in the official registers.[5]

In October of 1862, John Frawley Jr, along with his mother Mary Ann Frawley and sister, Letitia Frawley were charged with intent to defraud, which concerned a promissory note and bank note to the value of one pound. The writing in this case is difficult to understand, and translation of these court proceedings has not been undertaken. However, although the mother and daughter, Mary Ann and Letitia Frawley were discharged, John Frawley Jr. was convicted and sentenced to Parramatta Gaol for 12 months.[6] Later in 1867, John Frawley Jr. was listed in the National Directory of NSW as residing at Wolumla.[7] However, October 1867 saw John Frawley Jr. once again charged by the local police. This time for illegally riding a horse with his brother-in-law Robert Little, which was the property of one Archibald Spence.[8] Frawley and Little were fined £10, but had to serve three months in Darlinghurst Gaol for default of payment, being released on 23rd December, 1867.[9]

Another son arrived in 1869 to John Jr and Sarah, who was again unnamed in the register,[10] and another unnamed child came along in 1870, both of who died in infancy.[11] This was followed by a second daughter named Agnes Maude Frawley in 1872.[12] Another son arrived in 1874 in Charles Frawley. These children were all born at Wolumla, just 16km north-west of Pambula, although seemingly without official registration as no baptismal records have been found to date. By March of 1872 John Frawley Jr. was in the news again as a defendant at the District Court in Bega, up against a Mr. James, for an unknown matter.

> **BEGA DISTRICT COURT - JAMES V FRAWLEY**
> Mr. Rawlinson drew his Honor's attention to the unavoidable absence of Mr. James and the case was allowed to stand over.
> *Bega Gazette, 19th March 1872*

John Frawley Jr. was listed in the NSW Post Office Directories of 1872 and 1875-77 as residing at 'Three-Mile Water Hole' near Wolumla.[13,14] By 1876, he was listed on a petition of 'Free Selectors' for the foundation of the township of Bega,[15] and in 1879, John Jr. was listed in the NSW Government Gazette as having 'favor deeds' with the government.[16]

Despite being officially registered as residing at 'Three-Mile Water Hole' near Wolumla, by 1876 John Jr., and his family had moved to Toowoomba in Queensland as it was there that he died on the 9th October 1878 at his residence in Herries St, Toowoomba.[17] His unexpected death wrought devastation upon the Frawley family at that time, although some of his descendants still likely reside in the Toowoomba area. John Frawley Jr. was buried in the Drayton and Toowoomba Cemetery.[18] The following pages contain memorials from Australian Service Records, for descendants of John Jr. and Sarah Frawley, who enlisted in the Australian forces.

2. Ellen Frawley (1842-1909)

John and Mary Ann Frawley likely arrived at Twofold Bay about six weeks prior to the birth of their second child Ellen Frawley, which occurred at 'Warragaburra Station' on the 2nd of September 1842.[19] John Frawley was then employed on that remote property by the Imlays as a shepherd or labourer. Consequently, Ellen Frawley is believed to have been one of the first, if not the very first white child born on the far South Coast, with her baptism taking place on the 18th March 1844 at 'Warragaburra'.[20] She would almost certainly have attended the public school at Pambula, which opened in 1850.[21]

Her husband James Mahony O'Sullivan arrived in Melbourne, from Rathmore, Co. Kerry, Ireland aboard the "Ocean Chief", which docked in Port Phillip Bay on the 25th February 1859.[22,23] He was a gold miner, and married firstly at the goldfields town of Donnellys Creek in Victoria's Gippsland region,[24] to a countrywoman from County Kerry, who sadly died of typhus during the first year of their marriage.[25]

While this was happening, Ellen Frawley left Pambula and drifted to Sydney before meeting and later marrying James Mahony O'Sullivan on 3rd August 1869 at St Mary's Cathedral in Sydney.[26] Ellen didn't list an occupation on her marriage papers and was a spinster at the time of her wedding. Shortly after their wedding, the O'Sullivans departed Sydney for the Fish River gold diggings near Oberon, where their first son Humphrey Joseph O'Sullivan (1871-1905) was born on the 5th May 1871.[27]

After toiling for 18 months with little success, they travelled back to Sydney and boarded a coaster paddlesteamer for the town of Grafton on the Clarence River. The O'Sullivans initially set themselves up at Villiers St, Grafton, where their second son, James Alexander O'Sullivan was born on the 22nd August 1872.[28] However, they didn't remain in Grafton long, as James likely brought his wife and two infant sons out to his next mining venture. The family next travelled overland to Dalmorton, a new gold town, perhaps via Pinkerton's Coaches, which had commenced a weekly service from Grafton to the goldfields in July of 1872.

Gold was discovered in the greater Dalmorton area in the 1860's by a Cunglebung Station leaseholder. Thereafter, gold was worked sporadically on the tributaries of the Mann and Boyd Rivers until the main 'rush' was precipitated in early 1871 by the discovery of a gold bearing quartz reef called 'Union Reef' at Quartz Pot Creek, located south of Dalmorton. This piqued the interest of prospectors and lead to the rapid discovery of over 50 workable reefs in the greater Dalmorton area. By March of the same year the rush to the Boyd River and Dalmorton had begun and as per any new gold discovery, prospectors flocked there from all over the country.[29]

In Dalmorton, James O'Sullivan would have quickly converted their tent accommodation into a slab hut dwelling, having gained valuable experience from his mining days in Victoria. After solving their housing problems the next hurdle facing the early miners was obtaining food, which they initially had to bring with them, but it wasn't long before a store opened. The O'Sullivans remained in Dalmorton from 1872 until 1883, and produced more children including John Washington O'Sullivan (1877-1947),[30] Ellen Theresa O'Sullivan (1880>1932),[31] and Blanche Zenobia O'Sullivan (1882-1942),[32] amongst three others that died in infancy. But the population of Dalmorton inevitably began to decline, and settlers like James Mahony O'Sullivan realised that the township wasn't really growing. Added to that was the difficulty of bringing up a family amidst the poor health, behaviour and vices of the mostly single miners in the community.

James was obviously in touch with regional developments and he likely heard of a new community opening up on the coast, 50 miles to the south east of Grafton. With the Dalmorton School closing, and the village in decline, James and Ellen O'Sullivan thought it best to move on, which in benefitting their family, still allowed James to travel back and forward to his gold leases in Dalmorton. So they piled up their belongings and moved the whole family, likely by horse and cart to Sapphire Beach at Moonee Creek, situated just north of todays Coffs Harbour where they arrived as pioneers of that region well before Christmas of 1883.[33]

Together they produced 12 children, although only five lived to adulthood.[34] The extent to which Ellen kept in contact with her parents and wayward siblings in both Pambula and Toowoomba is unclear, but her life events and descendants are recorded in more detail in the book "The Path That Few Travel" *(see Volume 4 of the Rockwell Genealogies).* James Mahony O'Sullivan died in 1891 and Ellen O'Sullivan survived until the 4th August 1909, aged 67 and is buried in Sandgate Cemetery at Newcastle, NSW.[35] The following pages contain memorials from Australian Service Records, for descendants of Ellen and James O'Sullivan, who enlisted in the Australian forces.

3. James Frawley (1843<1901)

James Frawley was born on the 14th November 1843 and baptised on the 18th March 1844 by Father Michael Kavanagh at 'Warragaburra' homestead on the far South Coast of New South Wales.[36] He was the third child of John and Mary Ann Frawley, and would have attended the public school at Pambula, which opened in 1850.[37] But like his father and older brother, he became entangled with the local authorities as a youth.

In late 1862, at age 19, James Frawley was charged with stealing a horse from Frank Boller at Tantawangalo, and found himself placed in custody at Eden Police Station on the 15th December 1862.[38] He was summonsed by the Eden District Court to defend the allegations, with a trial date set down for the 24th April 1863, but was bailed for £50.

BAIL RECEIPT - 25TH APRIL 1863

James Frawley in custody on committal to take his seat at the next Court of General Quarter Sessions of the Peace to be holden at Eden on a charge of Horse Stealing.

Admitted to Bail in the sum of £50 himself, with two sureties in twenty five pounds cash for his appearance at the sessions as above: Stephen Collier (£25/0/0); Daniel [Purther] (£25/0/0). Taken and acknowledged this 25th day of April 1863.

P. J. Murray, Clerk, Eden Court

Unfortunately, the outcome of this case is unknown, as it appears that the chief evidence in the case viz, the horse, could not be found, therefore the charge was likely dropped, with James narrowly avoiding a gaol sentence. After this close call, what happened to James Frawley next is uncertain, but he likely sought to avoid such events in the future and left Pambula.

In attempting to put space between himself and the long arm of the law, James travelled to Queensland, where a contractor of that same name appears in Toowoomba on the 12th November 1863, receiving payment for the construction of a foot-bridge.[39] As John and Mary Ann Frawley, together with their son John Frawley Jr., his wife Sarah and their five children William (11), Anna (9), Agnes (4), Charles (2) and Eden (1), all relocated to Toowoomba about 1876, there had to be a reason why they chose that town? Compelling the entire family to relocate north was likely the good fortune of James Frawley, who was likely the trailblazer for his parents and his older brother's family.

To avoid further scandal in Pambula, James Frawley likely journeyed north, about the same time that his father and brother were imprisoned in Darlinghurst Gaol in 1863. About that time, a James Frawley does appear in a number of newspapers in South East Queensland from late 1863, especially in the Toowoomba and Meringandan Districts. For example, a James Frawley obtained good acreage as a selector at Meringandan in 1873, and a James Frawley even established a hotel at Meringandan, although it later burnt down in 1900. Could this have been the same James Frawley?

The Queensland Post Office Directory for 1894 listed a number of Frawley's including three brothers named James, Patrick and Thomas, all farmers, while a John Frawley was conducting a 'carrying' business at Meringandan in Queensland. But muddying the trail somewhat is the presence of two other Frawley's also living in the Toowoomba area at that time. A James Frawley 'selector' at Withcott, and a Thomas Frawley 'farmer', at Cawdor. Were these people the same family from Pambula, or another Frawley family? Somewhat confusingly, it seems that there was indeed, another James Frawley residing in Toowoomba at this very same time, which has confounded the research, and made it difficult to follow.

At the death of John Frawley (Sr.) in 1901, his death certificate stated that he was survived by two daughters who were Ellen and Letitia, but only two of his five sons, who could only have been

Stephen and Patrick. While the death indexes have been unsuccessfully searched for James Frawley in New South Wales, Queensland and Victoria, it seems certain that he died sometime before 1901. No other information is known about any possible issue or his death, although possible marriages for a James Frawley held in Queensland Dept of Births, Deaths and Marriages were:

    1865 to Ellen Murphy (#C78)
    1876 to Ellen Hegarty (#C206)
    1883 to Ann Doran (#C1756)

Unfortunately, without a verified marriage or descendants the trail for James Frawley goes cold at this point, but these leads may at some future stage assist further research and help untangle this branch.

4. Stephen Frawley (1844-1930)

Stephen Frawley was born on 26th December 1844 and baptised by Father Michael Kavanagh on the 11th May 1846 at the family residence in Pambula.[40] He was the fourth child of John and Mary Ann Frawley, and would have attended the public school at Pambula, which opened in 1850.[41] Like his two older brothers, Stephen Frawley also fell foul of the law and was charged with horse stealing in April 1864 (aged 19) and again in 1866, although fortunately for him, no convictions were seemingly recorded in either case.[42,43]

Stephen moved to Queensland and may have worked as a carrier for a time. From 1912, as the last surviving member of his family, was listed on electoral rolls as residing at Rubyvale, west of Emerald in Queensland. The name Rubyvale was derived from a ruby weighing 5 to 6 pennyweights (0.27 to 0.33oz; 7.8 to 9.3g) found near the town by miner William Dunn in the early 1900s. Dunn was very proud of the ruby and did not sell it, but showed it to people he trusted, although after his death the ruby could not be found. Stephen apparently never married, preferring a remote and isolated existence over marital domesticity. Living relatively close to one another, Stephen likely maintained contact with his brother Patrick in Townsville, but no other information is known about a marriage or issue for Stephen Frawley, who lived the longest of all his siblings before dying on the 14th July 1930, aged 86. He was buried at 'Norman Gardens' in the North Rockhampton Cemetery.[44]

5. Patrick Frawley/Marr (1848-1926)

The fifth surviving child of John and Mary Ann Frawley was Patrick Frawley, born on St Patricks Day, the 17th March 1848 and baptised with his twin sister Letitia, by Father Michael Kavanagh on the 8th September 1848, at the family residence in Pambula.[45] Along with his brothers and sisters, he attended the public school at Pambula, which opened in 1850.[46]

Patrick grew up in Panbula, and like his father and three older brothers John Jr, James and Stephen, Patrick also became a rebel, and as a young man was a well known figure in the eyes of the local police. He initially tried his hand as a prospector at what was then known as the 'Gulf Diggings' at Deep Creek in the vicinity of Mount Dromedary, just to the west of Tilba Tilba, New South Wales. But unfortunately for Patrick, while unsuccessful at finding gold, while there he inadvertently became a witness to a shooting and robbery.

In the 1800s horses were of course the primary mode of transport in the colony, and were comparable back then to the motor vehicles of today. Although horse stealing was a serious crime, it proved to be a popular pastime amongst the Frawley boys as they were all, save young Thomas, charged with that offence at some time or other, and this also included Patrick Frawley.

Incarceration

The police eventually caught up with Patrick on the 20th October 1866 when he was arrested and charged with horse stealing.[47] He appeared before the bench at Eden Court House on the 21st January 1867, where he was found guilty and sentenced to five years hard labour on the roads.[48] At just 19 years old Patrick was removed from Eden by coastal steamer and admitted to Darlinghurst Gaol.[49]

DARLINGHURST GAOL
Description & Entrance Books
Record for Patrick Frawley[50]

Name:	Patrick Frawley
Birth Year:	Abt 1848
Age:	19
Arrival Date:	1865
Vessel Arrive In:	Born In Colony
Date Of:	1867
Goal:	Darlinghurst
Goal Location:	Darlinghurst, NSW
Record Type:	Description Book

HORSE AND CATTLE

The mare No. 15 in this week's list, the property of Thomas Jones, is supposed to have been taken to Bega or Panbula by Stephen and Patrick Frawley. The former is about 25 years of age 5 feet 9 inches high, dark complexion, round features, black hair, worn native fashion, black goatee, no wiskers; the other is about 20 years of age, 5 feet 5 1/2 inches high, dark complexion, round features, good looking, no warrant issued.

NSW Police Gazette, 5 Sep 1866

Witness Against Bushrangers

It was while in Darlinghurst Goal that Patrick Frawley testified as a witness to a robbery that had occurred the year before. He stated that he was present on the 9th April 1866, at Deep Creek when bushranger Thomas Clarke, together with his uncles Patrick and Thomas Connell and four other criminals, William and Joseph Berriman, Bill Scott and William Fletcher, robbed a Chinaman, who was on the way to the bank from the 'Gulf gold diggings'.[51] They took all of the Chinaman's savings, with several others being held up including a small boy, and they called upon Mr. John Emmott, the storekeeper from Moruya to surrender. But Emmott wasn't about to lose his £100 and a parcel of gold dust, so he put spurs to his horse and galloped away.

Both Thomas Clarke and Patrick Connell fired at Emmott with their revolvers with one of the shots wounding him in the thigh, and the other killing his mount from under him. After relieving Emmott of his valuables, he and the other prisoners who had already been bailed up were marched off in the direction of Mrs. Groves store. Because of his wound Emmott could not walk quickly so the bushrangers pistol-whipped him over the head and left the poor man lying semi-conscious and helpless on the road.[52]

Patrick Frawley's testimony may have reduced his sentence as after a few months at Darlinghurst, he was transferred to Berrima Gaol for a time, before his removal again to Parramatta Gaol, arriving there on the 15th June 1867. In a coincidental twist of fate, Patrick may very well have arrived at Parramatta Gaol just before the release of his father, John Frawley, which occurred that very same month. If so, his father's gaol connections may well have helped Patrick in his new prison environment, where he likely also received visits from his two sisters, Ellen and Letitia.

Unfortunately, no record of Patrick's release from any New South Wales gaol has been found, but his incarceration couldn't have extended beyond 1871. After gaining his freedom, he likely returned to Pambula, where under difficult circumstances he tried at first to blend back into the town. However, lending creedence to the theory that his older brother James Frawley, had already pioneered the move to the Darling Downs District, Patrick later travelled to south-east Queensland, where he made his next recorded appearance.

Daring Escape From Police Custody

It was around this time that Patrick decided to change his surname to 'Marr', and relocate to Queensland, but there was seemingly no change in his behaviour as four years later, he was brought before the Police Magistrate at Roma, Queensland, about 350km west of Toowoomba, on the 20th October 1875, on the charge of cattle rustling![53] A group of prisoners including James Montgomery, Samuel Thompson and Patrick Marr were all brought up on remand, charged with stealing certain cattle, the property of John Town, who deposed the following circumstances:

> BEFORE THE POLICE MAGISTRATE.
> Wednesday October 20.
>
> Mr. Thompson appeared for the prisoner Thompson. I John Town deposed I am a grazier residing at Berarba, in New South Wales. I was at the pound yard yesterday morning, and saw twenty nine head of my cattle there; there are four or five head I can swear positively to without the brands ; I saw the cattle in the middle of July last at Berarba on the Gil Gil; I swear to the balance of those

cattle by the brands, the brand is — over JT over oo -near rump; it is registered in New South Walbs, and belongs to my father and myself; I have never sold any of those, cattle, or authorised any one else to do so ; I missed some of the cattle now here when I was mustering the fat cattle ; I have known prisoner, Montgomery upwards of ten years ; I saw him' last on the Gil Gil at his brothers, whose place joins mine ; he knows our brand well ; it is about 250 miles from here to the Gil Gil.

Western Star and Roma Advertiser , 23 Oct 1875.

The three prisoners were committed to take trial at the next sitting of the Roma District Court. Thompson and Marr were admitted to bail, themselves in £100 each, and two sureties of £50 each respectively, with events being closely followed in the newspapers...

At the hearing Patrick Marr pleaded "Guilty" to a charge of using threatening language to Terence Byrne. He was fined £1, but in default of immediate payment, was sentenced to four weeks imprisonment.

Western Star and Roma Advertiser, 30 Oct 1875.

Roma - 29 February 1876

Patrick Marr, one of the three men on bail charged with cattle stealing in New South Wales, has been again arrested for horse-stealing. March 1. Marr, charged with horse-stealing, has been acquitted. Smith, a witness in the case, has been committed for trial on the same charge, and also for perjury.

The Queenslander, Brisbane, 4 March 1876

Roma - 18 March 1876
(From our Correspondent - March 13).

A STRANGE case of turning the tables occurred at the Police Court on the 1st instant. A man, named Patrick Marr, was arrested for stealing a horse from one Owen Mullavey. Among the principal witnesses against him was a man named William Smith. Several other witnesses deposed that they saw Marr buy the horse from Smith. A receipt was produced in Court by the prisoner Marr, which he said he got from Smith. The receipt was denied by Smith in open Court. The Police Magistrate, to make the matter sure, asked Smith to write a receipt. The two receipts were compared, and found to be in the same handwriting. Marr was accordingly discharged, and Smith was arrested for perjury and horse stealing. He was committed next day for trial, bail allowed, four at £40 each, and himself £80.

The Queenslander, Brisbane, 18 March 1876.

Roma - 6 April 1876

At the District Court sittings, the following cases have been tried: Montgomery and Marr, charged with stealing cattle from New South Wales, were discharged, but again taken into custody to be tried in New South Wales.

The Queenslander, Brisbane, 8 April 1876.

22 April 1876

Patrick Marr, James Montgomery, and Samuel Thompson, charged with cattle-stealing, in New South Wales, were discharged, the Court having no jurisdiction. Marr and Montgomery were at once re-arrested on a warrant from New South Wales. Samuel Thompson, on a second charge of cattle-stealing, was sentenced to eighteen months' hard labor in Brisbane Gaol. I presume he will be sent to New South Wales to take his trial with Marr and Montgomery.

The Queenslander, Brisbane, 22 April 1876.

If Patrick intended to conceal his identity with the change of surname, the ruse obviously failed as he was soon identified as Patrick Frawley! What occurred next was either extraordinarily brave or foolhardy on the part of Patrick. While in police custody, he made a daring but calculated break for freedom, and the newspapers had a field day:

ROMA
(From our own Correspondent).

A man named Frawley, charged with horse-stealing, has been brought here for trial his defence being that he bought the horse in question. Patrick Marr, remanded for horse-stealing to New South Wales, has escaped from the police escort.

The Brisbane Courier, 2 May 1876.

ONE day last week news (says reached town The Western Star) that Patrick Marr, who was remanded from Roma to New South Wales on a charge of cattle stealing, had escaped from Constable Kelly, who was escorting him. Kelly states that about forty miles below St. George, Marr struck him on the head with the handcuffs, the blow completely stunning him. Marr then galloped away on the Government horse he was riding handcuffed as he was, with leg-irons on also and has not since been heard of. As this is the second prisoner that has escaped from this escort in this district within the last few months, it is time some action was taken by the authorities to make such a thing next to impossible. In this case there seems to have been negligence somewhere, as there were two constables together, as well as a black trooper, escorting two prisoners, and surely the one that was unhurt could have secured his prisoner, and started off in pursuit.

Rockhampton Bulletin, 10 May 1876.

On Tuesday last, a man known as Marr, and supposed to be a brother of Patrick Marr, who escaped from Constable Kelly a few days ago, rode into the police yard in this town, and delivered up the horse on which Patrick Marr escaped, with saddle and bridle. As he would not account for the animal being in his possession, he was arrested, brought up before the Bench on Monday last and remanded for the, arrival of Constable Kelly. On being taken to the lock-up he gave the name of Rawley Patrick Marr, who escaped from his escort a few days ago, has not yet been re-arrested, and as he is known to be a good bushman chances of his capture are small.

Western Star and Roma Advertiser, 6 May 1876.

St George - 28 April 1876
(From our own Correspondent)

PATRICK J. MARR, a prisoner on remand from Roma to New South Wales, on a charge of cattle stealing, escaped from the custody of Constable Kelly, on the 18th instant, while en route to his destination. The two prisoners, Marr and Montgomery, left here in charge of Constables Dargin and Kelly; Kelly having charge of the former and Dargin the latter. They stayed at 'Nindy Gully Station' on the Monday night, and started for Kunopia, on the Weir River, on the Tuesday morning. When they had got about twelve miles from Nindygully, they took a bridle track through a scrub, and Marr made some excuse for getting off the horse he was riding. The constable got off also to assist him, as he was handcuffed. When Marr got into the saddle again, Constable Dargin and the black boy, with the other prisoner, were out of sight. Marr called the constable's attention to the fact, and said, "Where are the tracks ?" Kelly leant forward on the saddle and was seized with a fit of coughing; Marr took advantage of the opportunity, and struck him on the back of the neck with his manacled hands, partially stunning him, then pulled the reins of the bridle from him and darted off into the scrub. The constable followed him for some time, but did not succeed in finding him, and returned here 'for assistance'. He started next day with a black tracker, but up to this no tidings of the fugitive have been received.

The Queenslander, Brisbane, 13 May 1876.

We learn that the enquiry into the escape of Patrick Marr has resulted in the dismissal from the force of Constable Kelly, who had the escaped prisoner in charge. The prisoner Montgomery, who was sent from Roma at the same time as Marr, was committed last week to take his trial for cattle-stealing in New South Wales.

Western Star and Roma Advertiser, 20 May 1876.

APPREHENSIONS

Patrick Marr, who escaped from the Queensland Police whilst on escort on remand to Moree, on a charge of stealing 41 head of cattle, the property of John Town, has surrendered himself to the Moree Police Remanded. Patrick Marr charged with stealing cattle the property of John Town, has been discharged by the Moree Branch on his own recognisance in £40 to appear when called upon.

NSW Police Gazette, 1876, p.170.

But it seems that after May 1876 nothing more was printed about this case or the extraordinarily bold escape, and no evidence has been found about any subsequent trials or incarceration. Therefore, we can only assume that Patrick Marr (Frawley) abided by the bond he made with the Moree Police, and lived out the remainder of his life without further incident.

Patrick Frawley Becomes Marr

Perhaps as a result of his time spent in prison, Patrick Frawley now made the conscious decision to keep the name change from Frawley to 'Marr'. The exact reason for choosing the surname of Marr is unclear, but it was likely done to block any association with prior felonious activities.

After his release from prison, Patrick Marr fell in with a woman by the name of Eliza Jane Quigg, by whom he was soon delivered of a son who arrived in 1872 and was named Harold Marr. Eleven more children were to arrive over the next 27 years with all of them being christened under the surname of Marr, which extinguished the Frawley surname from that branch of the family.

At the age of 40, Patrick James Marr became a 'carrier', and after producing seven children, he finally married his long time partner Eliza Jane (1862-1949), daughter of John Quigg and Mary Jane Hamilton, on the 11th February 1888 at the Roman Catholic Church, Eidsvold, in Queensland.[54] His marriage certificate reveals that his age lines up exactly with details on his 1848 certificate of baptism, and his mother was listed correctly as Mary McGarry although, there was no mention of his father, which he likely witheld so as not to divulge his new identity.

> **SMALL DEBTS COURT.**
> **Thursday, 12th December.**
>
> Before the Acting Police Magistrate. - Undefended Cases. In the following undefended cases verdicts were given for the plaintiffs for the amounts claimed with costs :
>
> **P. J. MARR v W. STENHOUSE & CO.**
>
> In this case the plaintiff claimed £5 2s. 6d, as agistment for horses. Mr. R. A. Brumm appeared for the plaintiff, and Mr. J. Patti son for the defendant. A verdict was given for the plaintiff for the 15s. paid into Court, and for the balance a verdict was given for the defendant with £1 1. professional costs and 2s. costs of Court.
>
> *Morning Bulletin, 13 December 1895*

Patrick continued on in his work as a 'carrier' as we hear little more of him until his death on the 24th August 1926 at Townsville Hospital,[55] by which time he had re-located the family to Townsville.

FUNERAL NOTICE

The friends and relatives of the late James Patrick Marr (Oonoonba) are respectfully invited to attend his funeral which will move from the general hospital this (Wednesday) morning at 10.30 o'clock.
F. Heatley And Sons, Ltd, Undertakers.
Telephones: 162 Day, 998 Night

Townsville Daily Bulletin, 25th August 1926

The informant for Patrick's death certificate was his wife Eliza who outlived him by 25 years, eventually dying in Coogee, NSW on the 11th May 1949, aged 87.[56] The following pages contain memorials from Australian Service Records, for descendants of Patrick and Eliza Marr, who enlisted in the Australian forces.

6. Letitia Frawley (1848>1901)

Despite the well documented exploits of Patrick Frawley, one can't say the same of his twin sister Letitia (1848>1901), of whom very little is known. Letitia Frawley was born a twin to Patrick on 17th March 1848 and baptised by Father Michael Kavanagh, on the 8th September 1848 at the Frawley family residence in Pambula.[57] Attending school in Pambula with her twin brother Patrick from 1853 to 1860, we know little of her former years, except that at age 14, she was implicated with her brother John Frawley Jr. in obtaining monies under false pretences in October 1862, but was discharged.[58]

Later moving to Sydney, Letitia Frawley co-habited with a partner for a time whose first name was John, and by him had at least two children, but as they didn't marry her issue were born illegitimately and both given the surname of Frawley.

6.1 Patrick Frawley (1868-1868)[59]
6.2 Charlotte Ellen Frawley (1869-?)[60]

While her son Patrick died as an infant, research has failed to find any further mention of her daughter Charlotte. Letitia appeared as a bridesmaid for her older sister Ellen, at her wedding to James Mahony O'Sullivan in Sydney, in 1869.[61] However, after that no other references to a Letitia Frawley have been found. The marriage and death indexes have been unsuccessfully searched for the unusual christian name of

'Letitia' across New South Wales, Queensland or Victoria from 1869 to 1900. At this stage no other information is known about any marriages, further issue or her death.

7. Thomas Frawley (1849<1901)

Thomas Frawley was the last child of John and Mary Ann Frawley, and was born on 24th June 1849 and baptised by Father Michael Kavanagh on the 18th October 1849 at the Frawley family residence in Pambula.[62] He attended school in Pambula, but little else is known of Thomas, except that he died somewhere between 1889 and 1901, as this fact was stated on his fathers 1901 death certificate. The marriage and death indexes have also been unsuccessfully searched for New South Wales, Queensland and Victoria. Thus at this stage, no further information is known about Thomas Frawley's marriages, issue or death.

Frawley Legacy & Inheritance

With seemingly very little to pass on to beneficiaries, an inheritance issue arose when the estate of John Frawley Jr, who had died 33 years previously, was re-examined in 1911. John Frawley's youngest daughter Eden (or Edith) Frawley, who by then was Mrs Sanders, pressed for her share of two parcels of land, sold for £36, which had been held by her late mother Sarah Frawley, until her death in April 1911. The correspondence states that apparently two daughters and two sons of the marriage were still living and stood to inherit the sum, who were likely to have been Mrs. Anna Gilmour Cuddihy, Charles Frawley and the plaintiff, Mrs. Eden [Edith] Alice Sanders.

The legacy of the Frawleys was memorable, although probably not for the right reasons. Gayle Lloyd, a 3rd great grand-daughter of John and Mary Ann Frawley commented in July of 2020…

> "Ahh… the Frawleys, lots of stories about them… such crooks, but very interesting. One story I recall was when the police came around at Toowoomba, asking if they knew anything about stolen saddles… "Saddles, what saddles?" they exclaimed… then the very next minute, the ceiling collapsed and down came all the saddles."[63]

Summary

John Frawley (c.1816–1901) and his wife Mary Ann McGarry (c.1813–1889) lived lives marked by hardship, resilience, and pioneering spirit. Born in Ireland, both were convicted of petty crimes, John for stealing clothes and Mary Ann for receiving stolen goods. Their punishment was transportation to Australia, where John spent seven long years in servitude under Alexander Berry at Coolangatta homestead, a common fate for many convicts seeking redemption in an unfamiliar land.

In 1840, after completing their sentences, John and Mary Ann married in Wollongong, a fledgling town on the New South Wales South Coast. With great determination, they ventured south to the Monaro District, carving out a life in the untamed wilderness. They found work at Warragaburra Station before joining the earliest settlers of the small coastal hamlet of Pambula. There, they raised a family of seven children and contributed to the growth of their community.

John was a man of strong will and deep involvement in his surroundings, and his unwavering support of the Catholic Church provided a moral anchor throughout his life, reinforcing his commitment to community and family. But his path was not without further trials. Though a respected member of Pambula, he made a costly mistake, convicted of cattle stealing, he was sentenced to five years of hard labour. This second incarceration cast a shadow over the Frawley family, and they faced intense scrutiny and backlash from a judgmental community. Unable to reclaim their place in Pambula, they left behind their hard-earned home and moved north to Toowoomba, Queensland, in search of a fresh start.

Mary Ann's final years were marked by sorrow and struggle. She passed away in 1889 at Dunwich Asylum, a tragic end for a woman who had endured so much. Following her death, John Frawley remarried, choosing a much younger wife. Yet, despite a lifetime of toil, his work never ceased. He laboured until his final days, passing away in 1901, a testament to the endurance that had defined his existence.

Though their lives were fraught with hardship, John and Mary Ann Frawley left behind a lasting legacy. Their children carried their story forward, and their pioneering efforts played a role in shaping the communities they once called home. Their journey, from convicted criminals to pioneers of the Australian frontier, epitomizes the spirit of survival and the unbreakable will to build a better life, even in the face of great adversity.

References

1. John Frawley Jr. - Transcription of Birth on the 7th May & Baptism on the 19th May 1841 at Wollongong (NSW BDM #V121A, 1450).
2. NSW Dept of BDM. (1841). Birth & Baptism Certificate for John Frawley Jr., #1450/1841 (V18411450 121A).
3. Pambula School - in a List of NSW National Schools by August of 1850 (The Maitland Mercury & Hunter River General Advertiser, 7 Aug 1850, p.3).
4. NSW Dept. of BDM. (1865). Birth of a Male Frawley to John & Sarah Frawley, 1865 registered at Eden, #8498/1865.
5. NSW Dept. of BDM. (1867). Birth of a Female Frawley to John & Sarah Frawley, 1865 registered at Eden, #9040/1867.
6. NSW Criminal Court Records. (1862). Letitia, Mary & John Frawley Jr., (in Register of Criminal Cases Tried at Eden, NSW 1862-1869).
7. John Frawley Jr, resident at Three Mile Water Hole, nr. Wolumla, (Post Office Directory, 1875-77).
8. John Frawley Jr & Robert Little (brother-in-law), Imprisoned for Three Months in Darlinghurst Gaol (NSW Police Gazette & Weekly Record of Crime, 9 Oct 1867, p.297).
9. John Frawley Jr., Released from Darlinghurst Gaol (NSW Police Gazette, 4 Dec 1867, p.358).
10. NSW Dept. of BDM. (1869). Birth of a Male Frawley to John & Sarah Frawley, 1869 registered at Eden, #10365/1869.
11. NSW Dept. of BDM. (1872). Birth of Agnes Maude Frawley to John & Sarah Frawley, 1872 registered at Bega, #6915/1872.
12. NSW Dept. of BDM. (1872). Birth for Agnes Maude Frawley to John & Sarah Frawley, 1872 registered at Bega, #6915/1872.
13. John Frawley Jr, resident at Three mile Water Hole, near Wolumla (Post Office Directory, 1872).
14. John Frawley Jr, resident at Three mile Water Hole, nr. Wolumla (Post Office Directory, 1875-77).
15. John Frawley Jr. - 'Free Selectors' for the foundation of the township of Bega (The Bega Standard & Candelo etc, 11th November 1876, p.2).
16. John Frawley Jr. - 'Favor Deeds' (The Bega Standard & Candelo etc, 20 Sept 1879, p.2).
17. Queensland Dept of BDM. (1878). Death Certificate for John Frawley Jr., 9th October 1878 at Herries St, Toowoomba, #878/C/896.
18. Find a Grave - John Frawley - Buried on the 9th October 1878. (https://www.findagrave.com/memorial/199235721/john-frawley: accessed 04 February 2023), memorial page for John Frawley (unknown–9 Oct 1878), Find a Grave Memorial ID 199235721, citing Drayton and Toowoomba Cemetery, Toowoomba, Toowoomba Region, Queensland, Australia; Maintained by F.P.McLoughlin (contributor 48316713).
19. NSW Dept of BDM .(1842). Birth & Baptism for Ellen Frawley, 2nd Sept 1842 at Warigubera, #1772/1842 (V18421772 62).
20. Ibid.
21. Pambula School - in a List of NSW National Schools by August of 1850, op. cit.
22. Jas. O'Sullivan & Corn. Healy, Passengers on the "Ocean Chief." (Australia: Inward, Outward & Coastal Passenger Lists 1826-1972).
23. "Ocean Chief," arrived Melbourne from Liverpool, Geelong Advertiser, 24 February 1859, p.2.
24. Victorian Dept of BDM. (1866). Marriage Certificate for James Mahony O'Sullivan & Margaret Buckley, 9th April 1866 at Donnelly's Creek, Vic., #1508/1866.
25. Victorian Dept of BDM. (1866). Death Certificate for Margaret O'Sullivan, 26 October 1866 at Raspberry Creek, Vic, #12-268/1866.
26. NSW Dept. of BDM.(1869). Marriage Certificate for Ellen Frawley & James O'Sullivan, 3 August 1869 at Sydney, #757/1869.
27. NSW Dept. of BDM. (1871). Birth Certificate for Humphrey Joseph Vincent O'Sullivan, 5 May 1871 at Fish River Creek, NSW, #6704/1871.
28. NSW Dept. of BDM. (1872). Birth Certificate for James Alexander O'Sullivan, 1872 at Grafton, #10684/1872.
29. "The Little River Reefs." (Sydney Mail and New South Wales Advertiser, 13 July 1872. p.2).
30. NSW Dept. of BDM. (1877). Birth Certificate for John Washington O'Sullivan,16th November 1877 at Dalmorton, NSW, #12652/1877.
31. Ellen O'Sullivans Family Bible. "Ellen Theresa O'Sullivan, born 3rd August 1880 at Dalmorton." Rockwell Family Tree on ancestry.com.au.
32. Ellen O'Sullivans Family Bible. Blanche Zenobia O'Sullivan, born 22nd February 1882 at Dalmorton." Rockwell Family Tree on ancestry.com.au.
33. NSW Dept. of BDM. (1884). Birth Certificate for William O'Sullivan, 12th April 1884 at Moonie Creek, NSW, #23815/1884.
34. NSW Dept of BDM. (1909). Death Certificate for Ellen O'Sullivan, 4th August 1909 at Newcastle, #10250/1909.

35. Ibid.
36. NSW Dept. of BDM. (1843). Birth & Baptism for James Frawley, #1773/1843 (V18431773 62).
37. Pambula School - in a List of NSW National Schools by August of 1850, op. cit.
38. James Frawley - Horse Stealing (Sydney Morning Herald, 29th Apr 1863, p.5).
39. James Frawley - Payment for Construction of a Foot-Bridge (The Toowoomba Chronicle & Queensland Advertiser, 12 Nov 1863, p.2).
40. NSW Dept. of BDM. (1843). Birth Certificate for Stephen Frawley, 1844 at Panbula, 1168/1844 (V18441168 63).
41. Pambula School - in a List of NSW National Schools by August of 1850, op. cit.
42. Stephen Frawley - Charged with Horse Stealing (NSW Police Gazette, April 1864).
43. Stephen & Patrick Frawley - Wanted for Horse Stealing (NSW Police Gazette, Sept 1866).
44. Queensland Dept of BDM. (1930). Death Certificate for Stephen Frawley, 14th July 1930, #1930/C/3041.
45. NSW Dept. of BDM. (1848). Birth Certificates for Letitia & Patrick Frawley (twins), 1848 at Panbula, 1415/1848 (V18481415 65).
46. Pambula School - in a List of NSW National Schools by August of 1850, op. cit.
47. Patrick Frawley - Prisoners Tried at Eden Quarter Sessions, 21st Jan.1867.
48. Patrick Frawley - Return of Prisoners (NSW Police Gazette, January 1867).
49. NSW State Archives & Records. (1867). Patrick Frawley - Darlinghurst Gaol Entrance Book.
50. Record for Patrick Frawley - Darlinghurst Gaol Description & Entrance Books, 1867 (New South Wales Police Gazette New South Wales, Australia, Goal).
51. Patrick Frawley - Witness for the Crown (The Empire, 16th February 1867).
52. The Sydney Morning Herald, 12th May 1866.
53. Western Star and Roma Advertiser , 23 Oct 1875.
54. Queensland Dept of BDM. (1888). Marriage Certificate for Patrick Marr & Eliza Jane Quigg, 11th February 1888 at Eidsvold, #1888/C/213.
55. Queensland Dept of BDM. (1926). Death Certificate for James Patrick Marr, 24th August 1926 at Townsville Hospital, #1926/C/3797.
56. Eliza Jane Marr (nee Quigg) - Death Notice (SMH, 12 May 1949, p.18).
57. NSW Dept. of BDM. (1848). Birth Certificates for Letitia & Patrick Frawley (twins), op. cit.
58. Letitia Frawley & John Frawley Jr. - Eden Quarter Sessions List, 24 April 1863.
59. NSW Dept. of BDM. (1868). Death Certificate for Patrick Frawley - son of Letitia Frawley & John Unknown (NSW BDM #5776/1868).
60. NSW Dept. of BDM. (1869). Birth Certificate for Charlotte E. Frawley - dau. of Letitia Frawley (NSW BDM #2676/1869).
61. Letitia Frawley - Witness (NSW Dept. of BDM.(1869). Marriage Certificate for Ellen Frawley & James O'Sullivan, 3 August 1869 at Sydney, #757/1869.
62. NSW Dept. of BDM, Birth Certificate for Thomas Frawley at Panbula, 1849 at Panbula, 1519/1849 (V18491519 66).
63. Gayle Byrne (nee Lloyd), 4th cousin by the name of 'gaggs8,' on Ancestry.com (4 July 2020).

EPILOGUE

This story has drawn from the surviving fragments of record, convict indents, ship musters, parish registers, land grants, and colonial correspondence, woven together to restore two lives that history had almost allowed to vanish. Where possible, dates, names, and documents referenced herein have been cross-checked against the official archives of the New South Wales State Records, the UK National Archives, and the Irish Prison Registers held in Dublin.

In writing the narrative, I have followed the guiding principle that genealogy is not merely the tracing of descent, but the reconstruction of experience. The lives of John Frawley and Mary Ann McGarry illuminate the broader story of Ireland's dispossessed and of those who endured the long voyage from servitude to self-sufficiency. Where the record falls silent, the texture of daily colonial life, drawn from court transcripts, ship surgeons' journals, and contemporary reports, fills the gaps to evoke their world as faithfully as possible.

This book is part biography, part social history, a meditation on exile, endurance, and the transformation of two ordinary souls into unwilling pioneers of the South Coast of New South Wales. It is also a tribute to their descendants, who now inherit not the misfortune of transportation, but the quiet pride of perseverance.

This volume forms part of the Australian Ancestry Series: True Stories of Convicts, Settlers, and Pioneers of Australia, a collection of biographical narratives tracing the real men and women who, through exile, endurance, and determination, helped to shape the foundations of colonial New South Wales and beyond. Each title in the series unites careful genealogical research with vivid storytelling to preserve the legacy of those whose lives bridged two worlds: the old and the new.

Dr Tracy Paul Rockwell
Sydney, Australia

INDEX

Symbols

21st Regiment of Foot 82
40th Regiment of Foot 68

A

Aberdeen, Scotland 143
Aborigines 24, 36, 37, 38, 51, 65, 66, 73, 94, 97, 100, 102, 130, 138, 141, 142, 143, 156, 157, 162, 164, 171, 175, 203, 207, 216, 221
Absolute Pardon 132
Act of Union (1801) 33, 47, 50, 56, 59, 105, 108, 109
Adams
  Thomas, (convict, died on "Java") 82
Adelaide, SA 144
Adventure Bay, TAS 43
Aghalust, County Longford 115
"Alacrity" 121
"Alexander" 23
Allan
  Andrew, (grantee) 73
  David, (grantee) 67, 73
American Revolution 23, 56, 57, 79, 106
Amity Point, QLD 100
Andrew
  Allan, (grantee) 74
Angevin Empire 80
"Anne" 39, 40
Appin, Sthn Tablelands 68, 136
Archer
  Mr, (R.N. officer) 64
Archer family 175
Arklow, County Wicklow 58
"Aron" 165
Arthur
  Lt-Gov. Sir George 144
Aspinall
  Thomas, (settler) 148
"Assistant" 43
Assisted Immigrants 184
"Astrolabe" 25
"Atlantic" 27
Australia Day 25

B

Baddeley
  Charles H., (magistrate) 209, 211

Badgery
  Henry, (squatter) 142
Badgery settlement, Monaro 158
Baker
  William, (mapmaker) 157
Ballantyne
  Adam, (constable, Panbula) 204
Ballarat Football League 189
Ballarat General Cemetery 188
Ballarat, VIC 182, 184, 187
Ballinahinch, County Galway 58
Ballyvonnavavn (townland),
  County Clare 182, 186
Bank of New South Wales 164
Banks
  Sir Joseph, (naturalist) 20, 23, 215
Bankstown, Sydney 28
Bantry Bay, County Cork 58
Barmouth Creek, Pambula 172
Barrack Hill, Illawarra 74
Barrack Point, Illawarra 66
Bartley
  Joseph, (settler) 143, 157
  William, (b.1841) 160
Bass
  Dr George, (explorer) 27, 29, 30, 39, 43, 141, 148, 172
Bass Strait 30, 32, 141
Bateman
  Capt. Nathaniel, (commander) 20
Bateman's Bay, Shoalhaven 20, 26, 38, 160
Bath, England 27
Bathurst
  Henry, 3rd Earl Bathurst, (politician) 157
Battle of Trafalgar 173
Battle of Vinegar Hill (1798) 58, 108
Beaumont, Shoalhaven 63
Beck
  Robert, (postmaster, Pambula) 203, 209
Bedford, England 179
"Bee" 135
Bega Cheese Factory 166
Bega District Court 228
Bega, Monaro 141, 142, 143, 145, 146, 156, 157, 160, 166, 169, 176, 199, 210, 212, 228
Bega Quarter Sessions 211
Bega River, Monaro 143, 146, 159, 166
Bega Valley, Monaro 157, 161

Behl
  John, (innkeeper, Pambula) 177, 195, 211
Belfast, County Antrim 57, 184
Bell
  Charles William, (storekeeper) 165, 171, 178, 198
Bellambi, Illawarra 136
Bellawongarah, Shoalhaven 63
Bendeela, Shoalhaven 66
Bennelong, (Aborigine) 27
Bennet
  John, (survivor of "Sydney Cove") 29
Bennett
  John Henry, (postmaster, Yowaka) 210, 211
Bentinck
  William, (3rd Duke of Portland) 32
Bercury
  Michael, (convict, died on "Java") 82
Berkeley (homestead) 74
Bermagui, Monaro 142
"Bermondsey" 149, 166
Berriman
  Joseph, (bushranger) 235
  William, (bushranger) 235
Berry
  Alexander, (surgeon, explorer & grantee) 68, 74, 75, 87, 89, 90, 92, 93, 94, 95, 96, 97, 98, 99, 100, 102, 124, 127, 129, 131, 137, 140, 160, 226, 243
  David, (manager) 99, 101
  John, (manager) 99, 137
  William, (manager) 99, 137
Berry Estate, see Coolangatta (homestead) 137
Berry (nee Wollstonecraft)
  Elizabeth, wife of Alexander Berry 96
Berry's Canal, Shoalhaven 93
Berry, Shoalhaven 40, 64, 97
Bickelmire
  Mrs, (Pambula pioneer) 177
Biggah (homestead) 146
Bigge
  John, (commissioner) 86, 164
Billy's Islands, Shoalhaven 40
Birbeck
  Capt., (commander) 37
Bishop

Capt. Peter (soldier & explorer) 68
Colin, (owner of Coolangatta) 101
Norma, wife of Colin Bishop 102
Bissett
Capt. James F., (master) 119
Black Head, Shoalhaven 134
"Blanche" 93, 96
Bligh
Dr Richard, (physician, Pambula) 200
Gov. William 42, 44, 63
Blinksell
John, (boat builder) 99
Blowhole, Kiama, Illawarra 30
Blue Mountains, NSW 28, 35
Bly
Thomas, (spearing victim) 38
Boller
Frank, (farmer, Pambula) 204, 231
Bong Bong, Illawarra 67
Boston Grammar School 27
Boston, Massachusetts 185
Botany Bay, Sydney 21, 22, 24, 28, 31, 37, 40
Bourke
Gov. Sir Richard 62, 143, 169
"Boussole" 25
Bowen
Lt. Richard, (commander) 26
Bowen Island, Shoalhaven 27, 63
Boyd
Benjamin, (entrepreneur) 148, 149, 158, 161, 165, 176
Boyd & Company 150
Boyd River, Clarence District 230
Boydtown, Twofold Bay 148, 149, 176, 199
Braidbo, NSW 146
Braidwood, NSW 142, 146, 160, 161
Brandt
Dr., (surgeon) 32
Breadalbane Plains, NSW 144
"Breeze" 147
Brianderry (homestead) 143, 157
Brichago (homestead) 146
Brien
Fenton, (baptism witness) 227
Brierly
Sir Oswald, (artist) 147
Brisbane 100, 214, 215, 216, 217, 218, 224
Gov. Sir Thomas 74, 164
Brisbane General Hospital 219
Brisbane Water Steam Passenger Co 136
British Admiralty 19, 21, 24
British Army 48
British Empire 22
British Government 27, 42, 47, 58, 73, 105
British Home Office 23, 24, 25
British House of Commons 22, 63, 110
British Military 108
British Parliament 109, 110
British Royal Navy 18, 27
Brogo, NSW 142
Brooks
Capt. Richard, (grantee) 67, 73
"Brothers" 159
Broughton Creek, Shoalhaven 40
Broughton's Pass, Illawarra 136

Broulee, Shoalhaven 146, 158, 162, 169
Brown
Andrew, (pastoralist) 164
George, (grantee) 135
Mr, (explorer) 43
Brown's Mountain 43
Brundee (homestead) 74
Bruton
Maurice, husband of Sarah Frawley (Vic) 188, 191
"Buffalo" 39
Bugong Gap, Shoalhaven 66
Bulli, Illawarra 20
Bulli Pass, Illawarra 135
Bundanoon Creek, Sthn Tablelands 66
Bungaree, VIC 184, 189, 191, 196
Bungonia Creek, Sthn Tablelands 66
Burke
Patrick, (settler) 83
Burrier, Shoalhaven 40, 66
Byron
George Gordon, (6th Baron Byron, poet) 55

C

"Caesar" 166
Cahill
W.F., (publisher) 136
Calcutta, India 28, 82, 162
Callala Beach, Shoalhaven 40
Cambell
Yankey, (spearing victim) 37
Cambewarra Lookout 63
Cambewarra Mountain 63
Cambewarra, Shoalhaven 67
Camden, NSW 67
Cameron
Duncan, (storekeeper) 204
Margery, wife of Duncan 204
Campbell
J.F., (colonial secretary) 62, 65
John, (squatter) 142
Robert, (merchant) 162
Campbelltown, NSW 136
Canberra, ACT 160
Cape Howe, Monaro 20, 29
Cape of Good Hope 23, 32, 39, 81, 120
Cape St George, Shoalhaven 20
Cape Town, South Africa 32
Carpenter
John, (Pambula resident) 206
Carthann the Fair, (Eoganachta king) 49
Cash
Martin, (convict) 83
Cassim
Johnny, (convict & hotelier) 220
Castlebar, County Mayo 58
Castle Hill, Sydney 36
Catholic Association (1823) 110
Catholic emancipation 108
Cattle Bay, Monaro 148, 165
Cedar cutters 44, 59, 61, 67, 94, 96, 135
Census of Aborigines (1845) 166
Census of Australia (2011) 48
Census of Convicts (1837) 99
Census of England & Wales

(1891) 52
Census of New South Wales (1828) 84
Census of New South Wales (1841) 136, 137
Central Highlands Football League 189
Certificate of Freedom 99, 132, 204
Chapple
Isaac, (farmer) 204
Charcoal Will, (Aboriginal) 93
"Charles" 135
Chisholm
Capt. Archibald, husband of Caroline 121
Caroline, (humanitarian) 121
"Chowringhee" 184, 196
Churchill
John, (1st Duke of Marlborough) 80
Civil War, American 204
Civil War, England 80
Clare Heritage Centre, Corofin 183
Clarence River 229
Clark
William, (survivor of "Sydney Cove") 29
Clarke
Thomas, (bushranger) 235
Clinton
Mr S., (settler) 148
Clonmel, County Tipperary 116
Clyde River, Shoalhaven 145
Coalcliff, Illawarra 29, 67
Cobargo, Monaro 142, 145, 146, 158, 169
Cody
Dennis, father of Susan Frawley 182, 184
Margaret, mother of Susan Frawley 182
Cody family 184, 186
Coffs Harbour, NSW 219, 230
Collier
Stephen, (bail sponsor) 205, 231
Collingwood Football Club 189
Collins
Capt., (commander) 64
David, (judge advocate) 26
Mary Ann, (Pambula, resident) 178
Colonial Office 143
Colstone
Samuel, father of Rose Emily Curtis 223
Comerong Island, Shoalhaven 94
Commercial Hotel, Pambula 199, 211
Company of Surgeons 27
Conditional Pardon 132
Connell
Patrick, (bushranger) 235
Thomas, (bushranger) 235
Convict Applications to Marry 134
Convicts 17, 22, 23, 24, 25, 27, 32, 40, 44, 48, 51, 53, 64, 66, 68, 73, 75, 78, 79, 80, 81, 82, 83, 84, 95, 96, 98, 99, 100, 102, 105, 111, 119, 120, 121, 123, 127, 129, 131, 133, 134, 135, 138, 144, 164, 207, 220, 243

Index

Coogee, Sydney 241
Cook
  Lt. James, (explorer) 18, 20, 21, 22, 24, 26, 141, 172
"Coolangatta" 96
Coolangatta Creek, Shoalhaven 100
Coolangatta Historic Village Motel 102
Coolangatta (homestead) 67, 74, 75, 77, 87, 89, 92, 95, 97, 101, 102, 124, 126, 129, 131, 133, 134, 137, 138, 140, 156, 160, 166, 226, 243
Coolangatta Mountain, Shoalhaven 40, 89, 93, 96, 97, 99
Coolangatta, QLD 96
Coomondery Swamp, Shoalhaven 96
Cork, County Cork 54, 79, 80, 82, 83, 84, 186
Corofin, County Clare 113
Corridgeree (homestead) 166
County Antrim, Ireland 58
County Clare, Ireland 47, 52, 113, 181, 182, 183, 185, 186, 187
County Cork, Ireland 115
County Donegal, Ireland 55
County Down, Ireland 55
County Kerry, Ireland 49
County Limerick, Ireland 55, 105, 106, 115
County of Argyle, NSW 67, 144
County of Camden, NSW 137
County of Cumberland, NSW 157
County Offaly, Ireland 49
County of Murray, NSW 161
County Tyrone, Ireland 55
County Wexford, Ireland 108
County Wicklow, Ireland 109
Coura, Shoalhaven 67
Covington
  Elizabeth, mother of Syms Covington 179
  Eliza (nee Twyford), wife of Syms Covington 179
  Simon V, father of Syms Covington 179
  Syms 179, 194
Cowper
  Thomas, (squatter) 142
Crawley
  James, (convict, died on "Java") 82
Croft
  John, (pastoralist) 165
Cromwell
  Oliver, (Lord Protector of England) 49, 80
Crooked River, Shoalhaven 134
Crookhaven River, Shoalhaven 93
Crookhaven, Shoalhaven 40
Croom, County Limerick 115
Crown Lands Occupation Act (1836) 169
Cunglebung (homestead) 229
Cunningham
  Allan, (botanist) 147, 215

D

Dalcassian Clan 49
Dalmorton, Clarence District

219, 229
Dapto, Illawarra 73, 136
Darling
  Gov. Sir Ralph 74, 75, 146, 157, 215
Darling Downs District, QLD 215, 217, 218, 236
Darwin
  Charles, (naturalist) 179
Davey
  Lt-Col. Thomas 74
Davis
  John Charles, (blacksmith & witness) 194
Dawes Point, Sydney 163
Deep Creek, Monaro 234, 235
Deighton
  Robert, (military convict) 82
Delagoa Bay, Mozambique 32
Dent
  Josiah, (pioneer) 215
Deptford, England 31
Derwent River, TAS 30
Dharawal Clan 43
"Diamond" 116, 119, 120, 122, 124, 134
Dickson
  Robert, (ships surgeon) 81, 82, 83
Dilba, (Aborigine) 28, 29
"Dolphin" 135
Donnellys Creek, VIC 229
Doora, County Clare 47, 52, 181, 182, 183, 187, 190, 191, 196
Double Creek, Monaro 146
Dowling
  Judge 205
Drayton, QLD 215
Drayton State School 216
Drayton & Toowoomba Cemetery 228
Dr George Mountain, Monaro 147
Driscoll's Inn, Monaro 146
Dry River, Monaro 160
Dublin Castle, Ireland 110
Dublin-Cork Railway 50
Dublin, County Dublin 57, 78, 108, 110, 119
Dublin Penitentiary 119, 120
"Duchess of Northumberland" 121
Dunlop Vale (homestead) 74
Dunn
  James, (Pambula, resident) 178
  Michael, (hutkeeper & spearing victim) 143, 157
  William, (miner) 233
Dunwich Benevolent Asylum 114, 219, 222, 223, 243
Dunwich Cemetery 223
Dyirringany Clan 171

E

Eardley-Wilmot
  Lt-Gov. Sir John 145
East Boyd, Monaro 148
Eden District Court 197, 205, 231, 234
Eden Electoral District 211
Eden, Monaro 142, 143, 146, 147, 148, 153, 156, 169, 174, 197, 199, 201, 204, 205, 208, 218, 234

George, 1st Earl of Auckland 148
Eden Police Station 231
Eden Post Office 211
Edenshead Manor, Fife 162
Egan
  Daniel, (Pambula resident) 200, 201
  John, (Pambula resident) 209
Electoral District of Port Phillip 151
"Eliza" 162
"Elizabeth" 144
Elrington
  Major William S., (soldier & squatter) 142
Elyard
  Dr. William, Sr. 66
  William, Jr. 74
"Emerald Isle" 121
Emmet
  Robert, (Irish revolutionary) 109, 110
  William, (overseer) 67
Emmott
  John, (storekeeper) 235
Enniscorthy, County Clare 108
Ennis, County Clare 47, 52
Eóganachta Dynasty, Munster 49
Eora Clan 24
Escape from Police Custody 236
Eurambene Mountain, Monaro 142
Eureka Stockade (1854) 178, 185
Evans
  George William, (explorer) 39, 41, 63
  Thomas, (spearing victim) 37
Exeter, NSW 66
Exmouth (homestead) 74

F

Fairlie, Ferguson & Co 162
Female Factory, Parramatta 122
Ferguson
  D., (Master) 184
Fife, Scotland 96, 162
Filhelly
  John, (politician) 220
First Fleet 23, 28, 80
Fischer
  Tim, (politician) 131
Fish River, NSW 229
Fitzroy
  Gov. Sir Charles 174
Fitzroy Dock, Cockatoo Island, Sydney 207
Five Islands, Illawarra 44, 65, 67, 68, 73
Fletcher
  William, (bushranger) 235
Flinders
  Lt. Matthew, (explorer) 27, 28, 29, 30, 43, 142, 148
"Fly" 37, 38
Forester Peninsula, TAS 144
Fort Macquarie, Sydney 121
Fowler
  Henry, (teacher, Pambula) 198
Fox
  Charles James, (statesman) 107
  Michael, (military convict) 82
"Francis" 30
Fraser

James, (military convict) 82
Frawley
Agnes Maude, daughter of John Frawley Jr. 46, 219, 227, 232
ancestors 47, 51, 52, 53, 56, 112, 115
Anna Gilmour, daughter of John Frawley Jr. 46, 227, 232, 242
Anne (c.1807-1872), daughter of Michael Frawley 46, 59, 184, 196
Brian & Shirley, parents of Danny Frawley (Vic) 189
Bridget Catherine (Jenkin), daughter of Patrick Frawley Sr. (Vic) 182, 183, 184, 187
Bridget (McMahon), wife of Michael Frawley (Vic) 182, 184, 185, 187, 196
Catherine (McMahon), wife of John Frawley (Vic) 188
Catherine (nee Kenny), wife of John Frawley Sr. 46, 53, 54, 55, 56, 58
Charles, son of John Frawley Jr. 46, 228, 232, 242
Charlotte Ellen, daughter of Letitia Frawley 46, 211, 241
Eden 'Edith' Alice, daughter of John Frawley Jr. 46, 232, 242
Eliza Jane (nee Quigg), wife of Patrick Frawley/Marr 46
Eliza (McCormack), daughter of Patrick Frawley Sr. (Vic) 183, 187, 188, 190
Ellen (O'Sullivan), daughter of John Frawley 46, 137, 158, 159, 160, 161, 165, 197, 200, 208, 211, 219, 228, 229, 232, 236, 241
family in NSW 56, 59, 165, 174, 176, 177, 180, 181, 204, 205, 208, 212, 214, 218, 222, 228, 242
family in Victoria 180, 183, 185, 186
Ivan, (researcher & Vic descendant) 190
James Joseph, (director) 52
James, son of John Frawley 46, 160, 161, 197, 204, 212, 214, 217, 218, 219, 231, 232, 234, 236
John (c.1816-1901) 17, 33, 45, 46, 51, 53, 54, 56, 57, 61, 65, 76, 77, 79, 80, 82, 84, 89, 97, 98, 99, 102, 124, 126, 129, 131, 132, 133, 134, 135, 137, 138, 140, 141, 153, 155, 156, 158, 160, 165, 166, 169, 174, 176, 177, 179, 181, 187, 191, 193, 194, 195, 197, 199, 200, 201, 203, 205, 207, 211, 217, 218, 223, 224, 226, 228, 231, 232, 233, 234, 236, 242, 243
John Jr., son of John Frawley 46, 137, 155, 158, 159, 160, 161, 197, 199, 200, 205, 206, 208, 211, 218, 223, 226, 227, 228, 232, 234, 241, 242

John, son of Patrick Frawley Sr. (Vic) 183, 184, 185, 188, 196
John, son of Richard Frawley (Vic) 196
John Sr., (c.1788-1868), son of Michael Frawley 46, 53, 54, 55, 56, 58, 84
Letitia, daughter of John Frawley (twin) 46, 176, 204, 205, 211, 227, 232, 234, 236, 241
Margaret (nee MacNamara), matriarch 46, 53
Mary Ann (nee McGarry), 1st wife of John Frawley 33, 46, 103, 105, 106, 111, 113, 114, 115, 116, 121, 122, 124, 126, 131, 133, 134, 135, 137, 141, 155, 156, 158, 159, 160, 165, 172, 176, 177, 197, 200, 204, 205, 217, 218, 219, 222, 223, 224, 226, 227, 228, 231, 233, 234, 240, 242, 243
Michael (c.1768-c.1850), patriarch 53
Michael, mystery? (Vic) 184, 196
Michael, son of Patrick Frawley Sr. (Vic) 182, 183, 184, 185, 187, 188, 190
Monica Burke (nee Frawley), (Vic descendant) 185, 190
Patrick Jr., son of Patrick Frawley Sr. (Vic) 182, 183, 184, 186, 196
Patrick, son of John Frawley (twin, see also Patrick Marr) 46, 176, 219, 223, 232, 233, 234, 235, 236
Patrick, son of Letitia Frawley 46, 211, 241
Patrick Sr. (c.1790-1854), son of Michael Frawley 46, 53, 59, 181, 182, 183, 185, 207
Ray, (author & Vic descendant) 53, 192
Richard, son of Patrick Frawley Sr. (Vic) 181, 182, 183, 184, 185, 187, 196
Rose Emily (nee Curtis), 2nd wife of John Frawley 46, 53, 54, 223, 224
Sarah (Bruton), daughter of Patrick Frawley Sr (Vic) 183, 184, 187, 188, 191
Sarah Maud (nee Little), wife of John Frawley Jr. 46, 218, 219, 227, 228, 232, 242
Stephen, son of John Frawley 46, 175, 197, 206, 207, 233, 234, 235
Susan (nee Cody), wife of Patrick Frawley Sr. 46, 53, 181, 182, 183, 184, 185, 186, 190, 191
Thomas, son of John Frawley 46, 176, 208, 219, 232, 242
William Clement, (actor) 52
William, son of John Frawley Jr. 46, 227, 232
Freeman
Charles, (spearing victim) 38
French Revolution (1789) 50, 56, 57, 108
"Friendship" 23

Furneaux Islands, TAS 28, 30

G

Galway, County Galway 54
Garrett
Thomas, (publisher) 136
GenealogyBank 115
General Steam Navigation Company 136
"George" 37
Georges River, Sydney 136
German emigrants 166
Gernon
Luke, (magistrate & author) 49
Gerringong, Shoalhaven 96, 101, 134
Gibraltar 81
Gipps
Gov. Sir George 121, 134, 150, 170, 207
Gippsland, VIC 29
Glennie
Rev. Benjamin, (Anglican minister) 216
Golden Vale, County Limerick 50
Gold rushes/mining 148, 176, 185, 189, 199, 229, 234, 235
Good Dog Mountain, Shoalhaven 63
Goodeve
Eliza, mother of Rose Emily Curtis 223
Goodlet
Robert, (spearing victim) 38
Goodwin
Mr, (passenger) 119
Gordon
Lewes, (settler) 148
Goulburn Plains, Sthn Tablelands 66
Governor Fitzroy Hotel, Pambula 165, 171, 173, 174
Grafton, Clarence District 229
Grant
Lt. James, (explorer) 31, 32
Grealis
Martin, (baptism witness) 137, 226
Grearly
Mr J., (teacher, Pambula) 173, 197
Great Britain 47
Great Dividing Range 215, 217
Greece 22
"Greenock" 144
Greenway
Francis, (convict architect) 85, 121
Greenwell Point, Shoalhaven 74
Groom
William Henry, (mayor) 217
Grose
Major Francis, (soldier & Lt.Gov.) 26, 27
Grossis Creek, Monaro 146
Guadalcanal 176
Gulf Diggings, Monaro 234
Gundary (homestead) 161
Gurney
William, (pioneer) 215

H

"Haldane" 162

Index

Hamburg, Germany 166
Hamilton
   Capt. Guy, (commander) 28
Harte
   Mr, (defendant) 205
Hawkesbury River, Sydney 30, 39
Hawksworth
   Dr John, (editor) 22
Hay
   Alexander Berry, son of Alexander Hay 101
   Alexander, half-brother of Dr John Hay 101
   Dr. John, cousin of Alexander Berry 101
   Elizabeth, 2nd wife of Alexander Berry Hay 101
Hayes
   Capt. John, (commander) 30
   John, (plaintiff) 194
   Mr. 199
Heaven
   Ely 204
   Llewellyn, (innkeeper) 204
Heffernan
   ancestors 113, 114, 116
   Catharine (nee Hennessy), grandmother of Mary Ann McGarry 46, 116
   Christy, (hurler) 114
   John, grandfather of Mary Ann McGarry 46, 116
   Judge 207
   William Daniel, (Australian politician) 114
   William J., (American politician) 114
Heston
   Father, (Catholic priest) 161
Hicks
   Lt. William, (of "HMS Endeavour") 20
Higgs
   Joshua, (convict settler) 158
Highfields, Darling Downs 219
Hirst
   Mr. W., (settler) 148
"HMAT Supply" 25
H.M. Gaol, Berrima 236
H.M. Gaol, Cockatoo Island 207, 212
H.M. Gaol, Darlinghurst 205, 207, 208, 212, 227, 232, 234, 235, 236
H.M. Gaol, Parramatta 205, 206, 207, 212, 227, 236
H.M. Gaol, Toowoomba 216
"HMS Alligator" 147
"HMS Beagle" 179
"HMS Bounty" 42
"HMS Buffalo" 38
"HMS Endeavour" 18, 19, 20
"HMS Hyacinth" 120, 147
"HMS Rattlesnake" 147
"HMS Reliance" 27
Hobart, TAS 30, 42, 144, 145, 147, 165, 170
Hoche
   Gen. Lazare, (French commander) 58
Hoddle's Track, Illawarra 67
Horton
   William, (pioneer & hotelier) 215

Howe
   Adm. Richard, (1st Lord Howe) 20
Hughes
   Robert, (author) 25
Hume
   Hamilton, (explorer) 66, 67, 93, 96
Hunter
   Gov. John 24, 27, 30
Hunter River, NSW 32, 39, 136
Huskisson Hill, Shoalhaven 66
Hyde Park Barracks, Sydney 83, 85, 86, 205

I

Illawarra District, NSW 33, 35, 43, 59, 61, 62, 64, 65, 67, 68, 69, 73, 75, 99, 130, 134, 135, 136, 137, 140
Illawarra Farm (homestead) 74
Illawarra Mercury 136, 195
Illawarra Steam Packet Company 135, 136
Imlay
   Agnes (nee Bron), mother of Imlay Brothers 143
   Alexander, father of Imlay Brothers 143
   Dr Alexander, (surgeon & squatter) 143, 147, 153, 164, 169
   Dr George, (surgeon & squatter) 143, 147, 153, 164, 169
   Dr Peter, (surgeon & squatter) 143, 145, 147, 153, 164, 169, 170, 176, 178
   Jane (nee Maguire), wife of Dr Peter Imlay 147
   Sophia (nee Atkins), wife of Dr Alexander Imlay 147
Imlay Brothers 138, 143, 145, 148, 149, 156, 158, 160, 162, 164, 165, 169, 170, 175, 176, 228
Industrial Revolution 18
"Industry" 159
Insurrection Act, Ireland (1796) 58
International Genealogical Index 53, 115, 116
Ipswich, QLD 217
Irish Famine (1848) 48, 50, 53, 111, 112, 183
Irish House of Commons 107
Irish House of Lords 107
Irish Militia 106
Irish Parliament 105, 106, 108, 109
Irish Protestants 106
Irish Rebellion (1798) 18, 33, 45, 48, 55, 56, 58, 59, 108, 109, 186
Irish Town, Limerick 78
Iron Gangs & Road Parties 84
Isle of Man 119

J

Jamberoo, Shoalhaven 73, 74
Jasper's Pound, Quin, County Clare 182
"Java" 80, 82, 84
Jellat Jellat tribe 157
Jenkin
   Matthew, husband of Bridget

   Catherine Frawley (Vic) 187
Jenkins
   Robert, (grantee) 73
Jerrinja Clan 89
Jersey Milk Company 101
Jervis
   Adm. Sir Richard, (Lord St Vincent) 27
Jervis Bay, Shoalhaven 20, 26, 27, 36, 37, 38, 39, 40, 41, 63, 64, 66, 67, 94, 97
Jigama River (see Pambula River) 172
Johnson
   Father William Xavier, (Catholic priest) 178
Johnston
   George, (grantee) 73
   Lt. Robert, (commander) 68, 93
Johnston's Meadows, Illawarra 67
Jones
   Thomas, (storekeeper, Pambula) 198, 235
Jorgenson
   Jorgen, (explorer) 32

K

Kameruka (homestead) 164, 165, 170, 176, 205
Kangaroo Ground, Shoalhaven 67, 74
Kangaroo Island, SA 38, 142
Kangaroo Point, Brisbane 220
Kangaroo River, Shoalhaven 66
Kangaroo Valley, Shoalhaven 63, 66, 67
Katungal Clan 141
Kavanagh
   Father Michael, (Catholic priest) 160, 161, 227, 231, 233, 234, 241, 242
Kelly
   Maria, (baptism witness) 116
Kembla, Illawarra 73
Kennedy
   Edward, (Pambula resident) 176
   Elizabeth, (Pambula resident) 176
   Elizabeth, (the daughter) 176
Kenney
   James, (playwright) 55
Kenny
   Sister Elizabeth, (nurse) 55
   William, (judge & politician) 55
Kenny ancestors 54, 56
Kent
   Capt. William, (commander) 38, 39, 40, 64
Keogh
   Patrick, (marriage witness) 134
Kiah (homestead) 160
Kiama, Illawarra 30, 75, 133, 134
Kiandra, Monaro 148, 199
Kiandra Post Office 199
Kilkenny, County Kilkenny 54
Killala, County Mayo 58, 108
Kilrush, County Clare 185
King
   Gov. Philip Gidley 36, 38, 39, 41, 63
   Mr George, (storekeeper) 209
   Mrs Anna (nee Coombe), wife of Gov. King 42

King Charles I 112
Kingdom of Thomond, County Clare 49
King George III 109
King Henry II 80
King Henry VIII 114
Kinghorn Point, Shoalhaven 66
King Island, TAS 37
King James II 49, 80
King John 79
King John's Castle, Limerick 49, 155
King's Island, Limerick 48, 78, 114
Kingston Harbour, Dublin 119, 120
Kingswood, Monaro 143
King William of Orange 49
Kirwan
  Elizabeth, wife of James Kirwan 160
  James, (squatter) 148, 160
Kurnell, Sydney 21

L

"Lady Nelson" 31, 32, 41, 63
Lake
  Gen. Gerard, (British commander) 58
Lake Illawarra 28, 43, 67, 74, 136
Lambton
  S.H., (secretary GPO) 210
La Pérouse
  Jean-François de, (explorer) 25
Leary
  Bridget, (baptism witness) 137, 227
Lee River, County Cork 80
Leigh Creek, VIC 184, 191, 196
Leslie
  George, (pioneer settler) 215
  Patrick, (pioneer settler) 215
Lette
  Patricia, (genealogist) 190
Levey
  Solomon, (merchant) 68
Lewis
  William George, (convict) 100
Limerick, County Limerick 17, 48, 49, 51, 53, 54, 56, 58, 76, 77, 79, 103, 106, 111, 112, 113, 114, 115, 116, 118, 119, 122, 124, 126, 196
Limits of Location, NSW (1826) 146, 156
Little
  Robert, brother of Sarah Little 208, 227
Liverpool, Sydney 44, 68, 136
Lloyd
  Arthur, Esq., son of Lt. John Lloyd 173
  Elizabeth Lucy, wife of Arthur Lloyd 173
  Gayle, (descendant of John Frawley Jr.) 242
  Lt. John, (R.N. & magistrate) 173, 179
London, England 98, 121, 144, 162, 164, 170, 183, 186
London Gazette 27
Lookout Point, Eden 148
Lord Lieutenant of Ireland 110,

119
Loughmore, County Limerick 115

M

MacHugh of Leitrim Clan 112
Maclean
  Alex, (master) 183
Macquarie
  Gov. Lachlan 41, 62, 64, 65, 66, 73, 85, 86
  Mrs Elizabeth (nee Campbell), wife of Gov. Macquarie 41
Macquarie's Gift (homestead) 67, 74
Madras, India 82, 121
"Maitland" 135, 136
Manning
  Arthur 171
  A.W., (magistrate) 194
  Edye, (merchant & shipowner) 135, 165
  James A.L., of Kameruka (squatter) 165, 176, 205
  William Montagu, (barrister & politician) 165
Maori 19
Marr
  Annie Ellen 'Thea', daughter of Patrick Frawley/Marr 46
  Eliza Jane (nee Quigg), wife of Patrick Frawley/Marr 46, 241
  Emma Magdalen, daughter of Patrick Frawley/Marr 46
  George Benedick, (descendant of Patrick Frawley/Marr) 46
  Harold, son of Patrick Frawley/Marr 46, 240
  Helen Ada, daughter of Patrick Frawley/Marr 46
  James Livingstone, son of Patrick Frawley/Marr 46
  John 'Jack', son of Patrick Frawley/Marr 46
  Justin Christian, son of Patrick Frawley/Marr 46
  Michael William, son of Patrick Frawley/Marr 46
  Patrick, son of John Frawley (twin, see also Patrick Frawley) 236, 239, 241
  Percival Patrick, son of Patrick Frawley/Marr 46
  Richard Sydney, son of Patrick Frawley/Marr 46
  Stephen Henry 'Tiger', son of Patrick Frawley/Marr 46
Martin
  John, (plaintiff of Yowaka) 195
  William, (surgeon's assistant) 27
Marulan, Sthn Tablelands 66
Maryland, NSW 223
"Matilda"
  #1 (1779-1792) 27
  #2 (c.1805-?) 64
Matra
  James, (sailor & diplomat) 23
McAllister
  John, (constable, Broulee) 197
McCabe
  Mr F., (surveyor) 172
McCormack

Patrick, husband of Eliza Frawley (Vic) 188
McDowell
  William, (ships surgeon) 120
McFarland
  Alfred, (judge) 69, 73
McGarry
  ancestors 111, 114
  Bill, (footballer) 113
  family 106, 115, 116
  Johanna (nee FitzGerald), wife of Michael McGarry 115
  Mary (nee Heffernan), mother of Mary Ann McGarry 46, 115, 116, 118
  Mary, passenger on "Marmion of Liverpool" 112
  Michael, brother of Mary Ann McGarry 115
  Patrick, brother of Mary Ann McGarry 115
  Patrick, father of Mary Ann McGarry 46, 111, 114, 115, 116, 118
  Seán, (politician) 112
McKee
  David, (postmaster, Yowaka) 210
McLaren
  David, (overseer) 144
McMann
  James, (policeman & witness) 194
McNamara
  Bridget, (baptism witness) 227
  John, (settler) 82
  Michael, (settler) 82
  Patrick, (settler) 82
McNiven
  William, (witness) 194
McPhee
  Mr, (Pambula pioneer) 177
McQuiggan
  Hugh, (military convict) 82
Meares
  Rev. Matthew Devenish, (Anglican minister) 124, 126, 133
Meehan
  James, (explorer) 38, 39, 40, 66
  William, (baptism witness) 116
Melbourne General Cemetery 188
Melbourne, VIC 29, 184, 188, 229
Melville
  Mr, (whaler & explorer) 26
Merimbula, Monaro 166, 199
Meringandan, Darling Downs 218, 219, 232
Meryla Pass, Sthn Tablelands 66
Metropole Hotel, Sydney 102
Molle
  George, (grantee) 73
Monaro District, NSW 33, 35, 140, 141, 143, 144, 146, 147, 149, 157, 158, 159, 161, 166, 179, 211, 243
Montagu
  John, (4th Earl Sandwich, statesman) 23
Montgomery
  James, (prisoner) 236
Moonee Creek, NSW 219, 230
Moree Police 239
Moreton Bay, QLD 68, 84, 215
Morris

Index

Dudley, (marriage witness) 134
Mort
   Thomas Sutcliffe, (businessman) 165
Moruya Court House 197
Moruya, Eurobodalla 161, 235
Moruya River, Eurobodalla 162
Moss Vale, Sthn Tablelands 66
Mount Brown, Illawarra 43
Mount Dromedary, Monaro 20, 234
Mount Gambier, VIC 32
Mount Lofty Ranges, SA 144
Mount Pleasant, Illawarra 134
Mowle
   Stewart, (J.P.) 194
Mumbla Range, Monaro 146
Mungret Monastery, Limerick 49
Murramarang, Shoalhaven 20
Murray River, NSW 144
Murrell
   Mr, (spearing victim) 37

N

"Nancy" 36
Napoleonic Wars 18, 48, 50, 56, 106
National Directory of NSW 227
Nelson
   Adm. Lord Horatio 175
New Britain 22
Newcastle, NSW 68
New Cemetery, Ballarat 186
New Chum Hill, Kiandra 199
New England, USA 22
New Holland 19, 32
New Ireland 22
New North Wales 22
New Plymouth, NZ 145
New Ross, County Wexford 58
New Scotland 22
New South Wales Corps 41
New South Wales Legislative Council 151, 157
New South Wales Penal Colony 58, 59, 61, 62, 77, 79, 83, 119
New South Wales Post Office Directory 228
New South Wales Public Education (1848) 171
Newtown (homestead) 144
Newtown-Pery, Limerick 78
New Zealand 19, 68, 101, 145, 164, 170, 176
Nicholls
   Capt., (commander) 44
Nicholson
   Mr., (explorer) 146
Ninety Mile Beach, VIC 29
Nine Years' War 107
"Norfolk" 30
Norfolk Island 63, 84, 207
Normans 49, 52
North Rockhampton Cemetery 234
"Northumberland" 20
Norton
   James, (solicitor) 94
Numbaa (homestead) 74
Numba Clan 94
Numbugga Swamps, Monaro 146

O

Oaklands Manor House, Pambula 165, 169, 175, 178, 179
O'Brien
   Charles, (overseer) 67
   Donal Mor, King of Munster 79
"Ocean Chief" 229
O'Heffernan
   Aeneas, (Bishop of Emly) 114
   William Dall, (gaelic poet) 114
Old Ballarat Cemetery 182, 185, 187
Oonoonba (homestead) 241
O'Sullivan
   Blanche Zenobia, daughter of Ellen Frawley 46, 230
   Ellen Theresa, daughter of Ellen Frawley 46, 230
   Humphrey Joseph, son of Ellen Frawley 46, 229
   James Alexander, son of Ellen Frawley 46, 229
   James Mahony, husband of Ellen Frawley 46, 211, 219, 229, 230, 241
   John Washington, son of Ellen Frawley 46, 230
   Mary Zenobia, daughter of Ellen Frawley 46
   Rupert Clarence, son of Ellen Frawley 46
   William, son of Ellen Frawley 46
   Zenobia, daughter of Ellen Frawley 46
Owneybeg, County Limerick 113
Oxford, England 49

P

Pacific Islanders 100
Paddington, Sydney 200
Page
   Mr, (storekeeper, Merimbula) 206
Pambula Beach 171, 193
Pambula Court House 177
Pambula, Monaro 165, 166, 169, 171, 172, 173, 174, 176, 177, 179, 180, 181, 187, 191, 193, 194, 195, 197, 199, 203, 205, 208, 209, 211, 212, 214, 217, 218, 228, 229, 230, 231, 233, 234, 236, 241, 242, 243
Pambula National School (1849) 171, 197, 198, 227, 229, 231, 233, 234, 241, 242
Pambula Police Office 194
Pambula River 170, 171, 173, 198
Panbula (homestead) 145, 158, 170
Parkes
   Sir Henry, (premier of NSW) 223
Parkinson
   Samuel, (surveyor) 166
Parramatta, Sydney 36, 122, 208
"Parsee" 182, 184, 186
Paterson
   Capt. William, (soldier & Lt.Gov.) 27
"Pedlar" 135
Pelham-Clinton
   Henry, 5th Duke of Newcastle

   (politician) 178
Penal Laws, Ireland 48, 50, 105, 106
Penderghast
   Catherine, wife of Richard Frawley (Vic) 187, 195, 196
Peron
   Francois, (naturalist) 30
Perseverence Creek Water Supply Scheme 217
Perth, Scotland 164
Peterborough (homestead) 67
Petition for clemency, Ireland 119, 122
Pheasant Ground, Illawarra 67
Phillip
   Gov. Arthur 23, 24, 25, 26, 27
Pickersgill
   Richard, (master's mate) 20
Pigeon House Mountain, Shoalhaven 20
Pinkerton's Coaches, Grafton 229
Pitt
   William, the Younger, (Prime Minister) 108
Plymouth, England 19, 149
Point Danger, NSW 100
Point Hicks, VIC 20, 141
Polding
   Bishop John Bede, (Catholic archbishop) 161
Pollock Brothers 199
Polly
   Robert, (died on "Java") 82
Ponsonby
   Mr, (plasterer, Pambula) 197, 200, 201
Port Arthur, TAS 170
Port Hacking, Sydney 28
Port Jackson, Sydney 24, 25, 26, 28, 29, 31, 32, 39, 64, 82, 83, 84, 121, 158
Port Kembla, Illawarra 66, 75
Port Phillip, Melbourne 29, 150, 229
Portsmouth, England 23, 31
Poynings' Law, Ireland (1494) 107
Pratt
   Charles, (1st Earl Camden, statesman) 41
Preservation Island, TAS 28, 141
Prince Albert, of Saxe-Coburg 148
Prospect Hill, Sydney 28
Prostitution 219
Protestant Ascendancy, Ireland 107
"Providence" 43
Pryce
   Rev E.G., (Anglican minister) 160
Ptolemy, (Roman geographer) 49
Further
   Daniel, (bail sponsor) 205, 231

Q

Quandamooka tribe 221
Queanbeyan, Sthn Tablelands 160, 161
Queen Elizabeth I 107
Queen Mary I 107
Queen Mary II 50
Queensland Post Office Directory

232
Queen Victoria 148
Quin, County Clare 182, 188, 196

R

Raine
  Capt. Thomas, (mariner & squatter) 142
Rathmore, County Kerry 229
Red Point, Illawarra 66, 67, 75
Regan
  Catherine, (convict) 120
Relief Act (1778) 106
Ribbon Society, Ireland 110
Richmond Football Club 189
Rigney
  Father John, (Catholic priest) 134, 137, 226
Rio de Janeiro, Brazil 23
Ritchie
  John, (settler & pioneer) 73
River Shannon, Ireland 49, 78, 114
River Thames, England 31
Rixon's Pass, Illawarra 135
Robertson
  Charles, (hotelier) 171
Robinson
  Mr J.P., (settler) 148
Rockites, Ireland 48, 106
Rockwell
  Dr Tracy, (author & descendant of Ellen Frawley) 7
"Rodney" 183, 187, 188
Roma District Court, QLD 237
Roma, QLD 236
Roscommon, County Roscommon 54
Rose
  Mrs Celia, (chronicler) 161
"Roslyn Castle" 144
Ross
  Major Robert, (First Fleet officer) 24
Rowley, (servant) 67
Royal Bull's Head Inn, Drayton 215
Royal National Park, Sydney 43
Royal Red Cross Award 188
Royal Society, London 18, 23
Rubyvale, QLD 233
Rum Rebellion, Sydney 41, 43
Rushworth
  Mr, (commander) 37
Ryan
  Mr. Thomas, (settler) 122

S

Saint Canice 54
Saint Finbar 80
Saint Munchin 49
Saint Patrick 49
Saint Patrick's Cross 109
Sandgate Cemetery, Newcastle 231
Sawyers & Woodcutters 94
"Scarborough" 23
Schank
  Capt. John, (commander & inventor) 31
Schoobert

Mr James, (coal mining pioneer) 136
Schubach
  Mrs, (Pambula pioneer) 177
Scott
  Bill, (bushranger) 235
Seven Hills, Sydney 36
Shadforth
  Thomas, (shipping proprietor) 135
Shea
  William, (Pambula resident) 178, 194
Sheehan
  Daniel, (settler) 83
Shellharbour, Illawarra 66, 74
Shoalhaven District, NSW 33, 35, 38, 39, 59, 61, 64, 89, 93, 94, 95, 97, 99, 101, 103, 124, 131, 133, 134, 135, 138, 140
Shoalhaven Heads 94, 96, 101
Shoalhaven River 31, 40, 43, 44, 66, 68, 89, 92, 93, 96, 99, 102
Shuttlewood
  William, (pioneer) 215
Silver Beach, Kurnell 21
Slattery
  Father P., (Catholic priest) 210
Smith
  B., (convict at Coolangatta) 137
"Snapper" 66, 68
Snug Cove, Eden 142, 147
Society of United Irishmen 108
Solander
  Dr Daniel, (botanist) 20
Solomon Islands 25
"Sophia Jane" 135
Southampton, England 184
South Australia 170
South Australian Company 144
South Coast 229
South Coast, NSW 26, 27, 28, 33, 35, 39, 45, 59, 68, 75, 77, 85, 89, 130, 135, 136, 137, 138, 141, 143, 144, 153, 156, 158, 159, 164, 166, 171, 227, 231, 243
Southern Cross (flag) 179
Southern Highlands, NSW 43
South Sea Islands 43
Spence
  Archibald, (Pambula resident) 227
Spiro
  Henry, (magistrate & mayor) 217
Squatters 59, 61, 142, 147, 150, 159, 172
Standford
  Edward, (military convict) 82
St. Andrew's Cathedral, Sydney 147
Stanley
  Capt. Owen, (commander) 147
Stanthorpe, Darling Downs 53, 54, 223
Steele
  Capt. (master) 99
St. Francis Xaviers Church, Wollongong 135
"St. Heliers" 170
Stingray's Harbour, Botany Bay 21
St. Jago, Cape Verde Islands 31

St. Mary's Cathedral, Limerick 49, 79, 155
St. Mary's Cathedral, Sydney 211, 229
St. Patrick's Cathedral, Ballarat 188
St. Patrick's Catholic Church, Eidsvold 240
St. Patrick's Day 188, 234
St. Peter's Catholic Church, Pambula 179, 193
Sullivan
  John, (settler) 82, 83
"Sydney Cove" 28, 141, 172
Sydney Cove 25, 93
Sydney GPO 211
Sydney Infirmary 144
Sydney, NSW 25, 27, 29, 30, 35, 36, 37, 38, 41, 43, 53, 62, 63, 68, 76, 77, 83, 84, 85, 89, 94, 96, 97, 99, 101, 102, 116, 121, 123, 124, 134, 136, 141, 147, 156, 158, 161, 162, 164, 165, 171, 172, 174, 183, 205, 208, 211, 218
Sydney Opera House 121

T

Table Bay, South Africa 23, 32
Tahiti 19, 147
"Tamar" 100, 135
Tank Stream, Sydney 26
Tantawangalo (homestead) 204, 231
Tapitallee Mountain, Shoalhaven 63
Tarlington
  William Duggan, (explorer & squatter) 142, 161
Tarraganda (homestead) 143, 164, 166
Tasmania 30, 43, 147
Tasman Sea 43
Tathra, Monaro 159, 218
Tathra Wharf, Monaro 218
Tenterfield, NSW 223
Tenterfield Oration 223
Tenterfield School of Arts, NSW 223
Terra Australis 19
Terranora Inlet, QLD 100
Terry
  Samuel, (grantee) 74
Terry's Meadows (homestead) 74
Thaua Clan 171
Thawa tribe 141
The Grange, Pambula 173, 179
The Royal Willows Hotel, Pambula 199
Therry
  Father John Joseph, (Catholic priest) 68
Therry (née Connolly)
  Eliza, wife of John Therry 68
The Springs, Drayton 215
Third Fleet 27
Thomas
  Edwin E., (Master) 184
Thomond Bridge, Limerick 49
Thomondgate, Limerick 49
Thomond Park, Limerick 49

Index

Thompson
  Hugh, (first mate of "Sydney Cove") 29
  Samuel, (prisoner) 236
Three-Mile Water Hole, (homestead) 211, 228
Throsby
  Dr Charles, (surgeon & explorer) 44, 66, 68, 135
Tibbermuir, Scotland 164
Ticket of Leave 132
Tilba Tilba, NSW 234
Timor 43
Tithe Wars, Ireland 110
Toad Hall, Pambula 195, 211
Todd
  Capt. John, (master) 81, 82, 83
"Tom Thumb" 27
"Tom Thumb II" 28
Tom Thumb's Lagoon, Illawarra 28
Tone
  Theobald Wolfe, (Irish revolutionary) 57
Toolburra Station, QLD 215
Toongabbie, Sydney 36
Tooth
  Edwin, (merchant & brewer) 165
  Robert, (merchant & brewer) 165
Toowong Cemetery, Brisbane 224
Toowoomba Council 217
Toowoomba, Darling Downs 214, 215, 216, 217, 218, 228, 230, 232, 236, 243
Toowoomba Gas & Coke Company 217
Toowoomba Grammar School 217
Toowoomba Industrial & Reformatory School for Girls 219
Toowoomba Railway 217, 218
Toowoomba South State School 216
Town
  John, (grazier) 236
Townsend
  Mr T.A., (settler) 148
  Thomas Scott, (surveyor) 148, 172, 175, 198
Townshend
  Thomas, (1st Viscount Sydney, statesman) 23, 25
Townsville Hospital 240
Townsville, QLD 233
Transportation Act (1717) 22
Treaty of Limerick (1691) 49, 50
Treaty Stone, Limerick 50
Trustee of the Common, Maryland 223
Tumut, NSW 211
Tupaia, (Tahitian interpreter) 19, 20
Tweed River, NSW 100
Twofold Bay, Monaro 20, 37, 138, 141, 142, 143, 146, 148, 149, 155, 158, 159, 160, 161, 166, 169, 170, 200, 228
Twofold Bay Pastoral Association 165, 171, 176, 178, 205

Twyford
  Joseph, (constable) 204

U

Ulladulla, Shoalhaven 20
Ulster Province, Ireland 57, 106
Underhill
  Henry, (b.1842) 160
  Thomas & Jane, (settlers) 160
United Irishmen 56, 57
United States 184, 185
Upolu, Samoa 147
Utzon
  Jan, (Danish architect) 121

V

Van Diemen's Land 28, 29, 30, 32, 41, 43, 63, 142, 144, 170
Vanikoro, Solomon Islands 25
"Venus" 37
Vikings 48, 49, 52, 114

W

Wagin, (Aborigine) 94
Waite
  Jack, (convict & explorer) 67
Walker
  Archibald, father of the Walker Brothers 162
  Archibald, nephew of the Walker Brothers 162
  Edward, (banker & pastoralist) 145, 171
  Isabel, 2nd wife of Archibald Walker 162
  James, (banker & pastoralist) 145, 146, 164, 170, 173, 175
  John Marshall, (chief constable, Eden) 195
  Louisa, wife of James Walker 171
  Mr, (constable) 197
  Sydney, (banker & pastoralist) 145
  Thomas, nephew of the Walker Brothers 162
  William, (banker & pastoralist) 146, 162, 164, 165, 170
  William Benjamin 170
Walker Brothers 162, 165, 168, 170, 174, 175, 176, 178, 198
Wallerawang (homestead) 164
Wandella, Monaro 142, 158
"Wanderer" 158, 176
Wanganui, NZ 147, 176
Warragaburra (homestead) 137, 138, 143, 146, 153, 156, 157, 158, 159, 160, 161, 164, 165, 168, 175, 176, 194, 227, 228, 231, 243
Warragamba Dam, Sydney 39
Warragamba River 39
Warrenheip, VIC 182, 184, 186, 192
Waterford, County Waterford 54
Waterford-Limerick Railway 50
Waterloo (homestead) 74
"Waterwitch" 162
Wattamolla, Sydney 29

Weatherhead
  Capt. Matthew, (commander) 27
Wellesley
  Arthur, (Duke of Wellington) 119
  Richard, (1st Marquess Wellesley) 119
Wentworth
  D'Arcy, (surgeon) 67
  William Charles, (explorer & statesman) 164
Western Port, VIC 29
West Indies 43, 81
Westmacott Pass, Illawarra 135
Wexford, County Wexford 57, 108
Wexted
  William, 2nd husband of Catherine Penderghast 188
Whalers & Sealers 41, 59, 61, 142, 143, 144, 145, 148
Wheeler
  Mr, (plaintiff) 206
Whelan
  John, (poundkeeper) 178
Whiteboys, Ireland 48, 56, 106
Wholohan
  Conor, (overseer) 67
Wild
  Joseph, (convict & explorer) 44, 67
Williamites, Ireland 49
Williamite War, Ireland 49, 107
"William Jardine" 119
Williams River, Newcastle 136
"William The Fourth" 136
William Walker & Co 162, 165, 166, 170, 171
Wilson
  Col., (convict superintendant) 122
  Dr Thomas Braidwood, (surgeon & squatter) 142
Wilson's Promontory, VIC 30
Windsor, Sydney 121
Wingecarribee River, Sthn Tablelands 66
Wollongong, Illawarra 29, 43, 64, 69, 74, 75, 123, 124, 127, 131, 133, 134, 135, 137, 140, 166, 226, 243
Wollstonecraft
  Edward, (grantee) 74, 89, 92
Wolumla, Monaro 143, 212, 218, 227, 228
World War I 18
Wright
  William, (settler & pioneer) 73
Wrixon
  Lt. John Nicholas, (soldier) 82
Wyllie
  John, (grantee) 74
Wyman, (Aborigine) 196
Wyndham, Monaro 200

Y

Yager, (Aborigine) 94
Yarranung (homestead) 143
Yarrunga Creek, Sthn Tablelands 66
Yowaka River, Pambula 173
Yuin Clan 141, 172

THE AUTHOR

Dr. Tracy Rockwell began his career as a teacher in both primary and secondary schools before being appointed to the Dept of Human Movement, where he spent 25 years as a lecturer in the Faculty of Education at Sydney University. He later transitioned into a multifaceted career as an author and artist. As an athlete, he was a competitive swimmer, surf lifesaver, rugby player, and a New South Wales representative in water polo. In 2021, he became the Oceanic Indoor Rowing champion for his age group. With a deep interest in history, he published "Water Warriors: Chronicle of Australian Water Polo" in 2009 and was awarded the 'Harry Quittner Medal' for his contributions to the sport. A passionate genealogist, he launched his 'Rockwell Genealogies' series in 2020, adding to the list with this latest publication. Dr. Rockwell's other books and illustrated journals are available through Pegasus Publishing [*pegasus-publishing.square.site*].

TITLE	ISBN	GENRE	FORMAT	PUB.	PAGES
Water Warriors: Chronicle of Australian Water Polo	978-0-646488-61-5	Sports History	Hardback	2009	597
The Complete Guide to Rugby World Cup (2015)	978-0-994201-42-3	Sports History	Ebook	2015	161
Play Water Polo: An Interactive Instructional Sports Guide	978-0-994201-40-9	Sports Development	Ebook *[interactive]*	2016	94
The Unknown Journey, by Joseph Anaman (*Edited & pub by TR*)	978-0-994201-48-5	Autobiography	Ebook	2016	136
The Unknown Journey, by Joseph Anaman (*Edited & pub by TR*)	978-0-994201-49-2	Autobiography	Paperback	2016	136
How to Play Water Polo: The Complete Guide to Mastering the Game	978-0-994201-41-6	Sports Development	Paperback	2018	215
Juega Polo Acuático: Guía Interactiva de Deportes de Instrucción	978-0-994201-43-0	Sports Development	Ebook	2018	96
Love Never Lets You Go: Aphorisms about Love Journal [*illust.*]	978-0-994201-46-1	Sociology	Paperback	2018	216
One Day at a Time: Aphorisms about Life Journal [*illust.*]	978-0-994201-47-8	Sociology	Paperback	2018	218
Journal of Life's Lessons: With Vintage Images and Aphorisms [*illust.*]	978-0-994201-44-7	Sociology	Hardback	2019	218
Who's There? Worlds Funniest A-Z Book of 737 Knock Knock Jokes	978-0-994201-45-4	Childrens-Fiction	Paperback	2019	107
Who's There? Worlds Funniest A-Z Book of 737 Knock Knock Jokes	978-1-925909-28-9	Childrens-Fiction	Ebook	2019	107
Australian Seascapes Journal [*illust.*]	978-1-925909-05-0	Sociology	Paperback	2019	128
Australian Landscapes Journal [*illust.*]	978-1-925909-06-7	Sociology	Paperback	2019	128
The Complete Guide to Rugby World Cup (2019)	978-1-925909-07-4	Sports History	Paperback	2019	198
My Handy Cruise Journal [*illust.*]	978-1-925909-10-4	Sociology	Paperback	2019	130
My Handy Travel Journal [*illust.*]	978-1-925909-11-1	Sociology	Paperback	2019	130
A History of the Ancestors of James Mahoney O'Sullivan and Ellen Frawley	978-1-925909-00-5	History-Genealogy	Paperback	2020	584
Australian Animals: Through the Looking Glass	978-1-925909-01-2	Childrens-Animals	Paperback	2020	68
Bush Dreaming and Other Plays, by Dr Frank Davidson (*Edited & pub by TR*)	978-1-925909-02-9	Literature-Drama	Paperback	2020	212
The Spirit of Bronte: A History of Bronte Amateur Water Polo Club 1943-1975	978-1-925909-03-6	Sports History	Paperback	2020	329
Tracy Rockwell: Catalogue Raisonné 2000-2020	978-1-925909-12-8	Visual Arts	Paperback	2021	342
Mystery at Melon Flats, by Dr Frank Davidson (*Edited & pub by TR*)	978-1-925909-04-3	Literature-Novel	Paperback	2022	192
Mystery at Melon Flats, by Dr Frank Davidson (*Edited & pub by TR*)	978-1-925909-09-8	Literature-Novel	Ebook	2022	192
The Long Road To Grafton: A Genealogy of Thomas Eastman Shoveller	978-1-925909-08-1	History-Genealogy	Paperback	2022	362
Nostalgia for Naremburn: The Ancestors of Robert & Corelli Rockwell	978-1-925909-13-5	History-Genealogy	Paperback	2023	290
Mystery at the Minerva Club, by Dr Frank Davidson (*Edited & pub by TR*)	978-1-925909-15-9	Literature-Novel	Paperback	2024	128
An Olympic Journey & Beyond, by Robert Menzies (*Edited & pub by TR*)	978-1-925909-14-2	Autobiography	Paperback	2024	258
From Prisoners to Pioneers: A Genealogy of John Frawley & Mary McGarry	978-1-925909-19-7	History-Genealogy	Paperback	2025	344
The Royal & Noble Blood: Pedigree & Descent of Tracy Paul Rockwell - Vol I	978-1-925909-16-6	Genealogy	Paperback	2025	500
The Royal & Noble Blood: Pedigree & Descent of Tracy Paul Rockwell - Vol II	978-1-925909-17-3	Genealogy	Paperback	2025	530
The Royal & Noble Blood: Pedigree & Descent of Tracy Paul Rockwell - Vol III	978-1-925909-18-0	Genealogy	Paperback	2025	486
To The Great Southern Land: A Genealogy of Robert Bantin & Mary Barrett	978-1-925909-20-3	History-Genealogy	Paperback	2025	396
Salt, Soil & Second Chances: The Life & Times of John Frawley	978-1-925909-21-0	Colonial History	Paperback	2025	262

www.ingramcontent.com/pod-product-compliance
Lightning Source LLC
Chambersburg PA
CBHW061215070526
44584CB00029B/3850